Bumping the Dock

A Story of God's Grace and an 18-Wheeler

Annette F. Wilcox

En Route Books and Media, LLC
St. Louis, MO

⊕ENROUTE
Make the time

En Route Books and Media, LLC
5705 Rhodes Avenue
St. Louis, MO 63109

Cover credit:
Design by TJ Burdick
Lower cover photo courtesy of Sue Navrkal. [The truck pictured on the cover is one Annette drove many years later, and for a different company than the one that trained her.]
Interior diagrams by Karl R. Frey

Library of Congress Control Number:
2020930929

ISBN-13: 978-1-950108-95-4

"The trucking industry is basically a slave industry with truckers working on the average over 70 hours per week, many of which are not paid while sitting in shippers' parking lots sometimes 8 hours or more after specified load time (a whole working day for average Americans)."

--quoted verbatim from thetruckersreport.com

ADVANCE PRAISE FOR
Bumping the Dock

"Having read the book twice has given me a new perspective I would otherwise never have had. I would say that this book is a MUST READ for new folks looking to drive a truck who have no previous experience with trucks or drivers. It has given me insight into how a 'newbie' sees things and will arm me with the tools I need to be a better mentor and advisor. Thank you, thank you to Annette for writing this. The book is informative and takes you down the road with her in a way that is engaging and educational." **–Idella M. Hansen, 50-year trucker, 2017 Citizen Driver Honoree, Real Women in Trucking, Founding Board Member**

"*Bumping the Dock*, about a middle-aged woman becoming a semi-truck driver, is a rollicking book to read. Why would someone like me who took 4 driving tests before passing in a small car even enjoy such an account? Because, as well as being a humorous story, it is also a Christian parable about courage in lifestyle shifts and an insightful look at relationships between women and men, in this case our heroine and a male truck-driving trainer. With every chapter I felt more courage to think outside the box on my own personal decisions – that with God many impossible things could be possible!" **— Dr. Ronda Chervin, contributor and co-author with Sebastian Mahfood of *Catholic Realism: A Framework for the Refutation of Atheism and the Evangelization of Atheists***

"Annette Wilcox gives Jack Kerouac a run for his money in this story of how God's grace works in the cab of an 18-wheeler on American highways and byways." **– Dr. Sebastian Mahfood, OP, author of *The Narrative Spirituality of Dante's Divine Comedy***

"*Bumping the Dock* is a fascinating, amusing, and deeply personal account of how this highly educated woman ended up behind the wheel of a semi. She brings her insights to the job of the over-the-road trucker, relating her experiences in a world that is all around us but about which most of us know too little. This book brings you along as she learns new skills, visits new places, overcomes challenges both personal and professional, and grows as a person. If you've always wondered what a trucker's life was like, ride beside Annette Wilcox in *Bumping the Dock*. It's a journey you'll never forget." — **Roger Thomas, author of *From Afar, The Last Ugly Person, and The Accidental Marriage*, among others.**

"In *Bumping the Dock, a Story of God's Grace and an 18-Wheeler*, Annette Wilcox details the many difficulties of learning to safely operate the largest vehicle on the highway while demonstrating her courage, tenacity and relentless faith. Her tale is one of overcoming challenges while refusing to bend her character or sacrifice her spirituality to succeed in a male-dominated industry that isn't always welcoming to women or Christians. Best of all, she sets a lofty example by her reliance on her Savior for day-to-day accomplishments, regardless of her own considerable abilities." — **Cliff Abbott, 35-year industry veteran, Special Correspondent to The Trucker newspaper and author of *Chronicles of an American Trucker: Which Way is the Road to Happiness?***

"*Bumping the Dock* will first surprise you — because it's much more than a book about trucking — then delight you. Part travelogue, part diary, this book is also a revelation of Annette's making the best out of a lousy hand. Readers are drawn smoothly and effortlessly into the world of learning to drive a 'big rig' by the author's making them feel as if they're sitting down with an old friend to catch up over a cup of coffee, only to find that in the end they really do admire her spunk and stamina and good judgment all the more."
— **Dcn. Chris Sandner, assistant to Bishop Barron**

DEDICATION

For all the people who, like me, have wondered what life driving a semi is like, and especially for Johnny, who trained me.

A CAVEAT

This is an account written by a "newbie," that is, from the perspective of only three months of experience. I learned all I could in three months but that is pathetically little to those who have driven for years. As someone who really knows hockey will see a lot more during a game than a first-time spectator, I was only gradually learning where to look, which road signs I needed to read and what to look for in pulling into rest areas, or truck stops. I hope that the limitation of a beginner's view is compensated for by a certain freshness. The beginner's eye sometimes sees clearly things that others may have come to take for granted.

NOTE

There is very little fiction in this book. Some names have been changed to protect the guilty and innocent alike.

CONTENTS

INTRODUCTION

"The steadfast love of the Lord never ceases.
His mercies never come to an end.
They are new every morning, new every morning,
Great is Thy faithfulness, O Lord.
Great is Thy faithfulness."

-From a song based on Lamentations 3:22

I am an unlikely person to be a long-haul trucker. People comment that I look more like a librarian or an English teacher than a trucker. And I have been both. Being a trucker really doesn't go with my BA or MA either, much less with the *Phi Beta Kappa* key that lives a shamefaced existence in a keepsake box in my storage unit.

The larger truth is that truckers are a heterogeneous group. We are, as a driving friend once said, a "subculture." What we have in common is only the ability to drive 550 or more miles per day, day after day.

Trucking is physically a little too hard for me. Perhaps for this reason, my life as a trucker has been one of radical dependence on God. I have learned, as St. Thérèse of Lisieux taught, that it's okay to be dependent on God, American independence notwithstanding. "Except ye become as little children ..." [St. Matthew 18:3].

The truck runs by grace and I'm on the road only as long as God wants me to be. The trucking industry is a harsh one. It doesn't take very many mistakes before one is an ex-trucker. And I've had lots of practice in being scared but just doing the thing anyway, after a heartfelt petition for help. Help comes in the doing. I have truly

i

experienced that God's mercies are new every morning and are inexhaustible. He always helps! That's what this story is about.

PROLOGUE

There was blank astonishment in the night dispatcher's voice as she asked, "You can only drive 478 miles in a day?"

I answered the tone of voice: "I'm a beginner, you know."

"Yes, I know," the woman said, but her voice was unrelenting.

"And actually I drove 537 miles today and, yes, that probably is as much as I can drive in a day."

"You'd better talk to Kevin in the morning," was the response.

That ended the conversation. I got off the phone, tears in my eyes, wondering how many miles they expected from a driver. Even 478 miles seemed like a lot to me.

I asked myself, as I often had, what a 53-year old woman with a master's degree was doing driving a semi. True, I had always loved driving. When I was four years old, I announced to my parents that I wanted to learn to drive, only to be told I'd have to wait until I was 16 before that could happen. I had waited through every one of those twelve years, always wishing I could drive.

In my twenties, I had sometimes thought of becoming a trucker, if only because truck drivers travel constantly. I loved traveling. I liked shifting gears, and I had heard that semis had a lot of gears. But then marriage and children intervened, so I dropped the idea of being a trucker for three decades, while I raised four children, was divorced, earned a BA in Economics, then an MA in TESOL (Teaching English to Speakers of Other Languages), thinking and hoping that these degrees would make it possible to get a good job.

I taught English in Hungary for a year, taking the three children still young enough to be at home to Budapest with me. When we came back to the States I found a part-time job at the local library while the twins, my youngest children, went to high school.

Prologue

Jobs were harder and harder to find as I neared 50. I wasn't politically correct enough and was far too religious. Both were disqualifications for advancement to full-time employment at the library. I badly needed a full-time job though, once the twins started college. I went to Africa to teach English for a year, a wonderful year, but since coming back had been completely unable to find a full-time job that offered benefits, one that would allow me to make enough money to rent an apartment and live independently.

Then I lost the hearing in my left ear. This happened one morning in Steubenville, Ohio. I was standing in a motel room with my son when all of a sudden I felt dizzy and my left ear blocked up, or so I thought. What had happened was what is called a "circulatory accident." The capillary carrying blood to my eighth cranial nerve got blocked for a few minutes. During those minutes the nerve died and with it any possibility of ever hearing out of my left ear again.

Once I understood what had happened, and this was weeks later after four different doctors and an MRI, I found myself in the position of having to accept it as God's will for me somehow.

Losing my hearing had several ramifications. It put an abrupt end to playing the violin or cello. It also made me unwilling to walk into a classroom. For one thing, I could no longer pick out voices from a noisy environment. For another, I couldn't tell the direction that noises came from, two ears being necessary to pinpoint the origin of a noise, just as two eyes are necessary for depth perception.

Even apart from the hearing problem, I had the wrong kind of degree. Although I had an MA, I wasn't certified to teach, which pretty much left me in the world of adjunct instructors, part time, at community colleges.

These were familiar thoughts. I walked into the truck stop's restroom and studied my face in the mirror, seeing myself only in patches — some gray hair, wrinkles, no makeup. I never learned to use makeup somehow. Seeing myself in a mirror always pained me. I turned away from the sight of my dumpy, middle-aged body and big hips.

I walked back out to the truck and climbed in, cherishing its familiarity. The one unchanging thing in the world these days was the inside of my truck. I had arranged it to be as nearly as possible like my trainer Johnny's truck. I had it all to myself, though, and could spread out a little. Living in a truck was like living in a walk-in closet, or a camping trailer. The amount of space was roughly equivalent. It was well organized, and my few possessions were stowed in the various cubby holes, compartments and drawers.

I lay down on my bed, still upset about the conversation with the night dispatcher. Well, Kevin, my regular dispatcher, would help me figure it out in the morning. He was the "beginner's dispatcher," a personable young man of 25 or 26 with the nicest possible way of putting things in the Qualcomm messages, which were what we mostly used for communication. A Qualcomm looked like a cross between an Etch-A-Sketch toy and a computer keyboard. Simple messages could be sent back and forth between driver and dispatcher, but all possible abbreviations were used because the company paid by the letter for each message.

I had only called in by telephone because of not being able to get any satellite reception. For reasons that were somewhat mysterious to me, I often had trouble with satellite reception at truck stops with IdleAir, the wonderful service which enabled truckers to have air conditioning or heat without idling the engine overnight. You could also have regular 120 V electricity rather than having to depend on the truck's cigarette lighter for power. I used IdleAir's electrical connection to plug in my oldish laptop computer which could no longer run more than 10 or 15 minutes without outside electricity.

An IdleAir site was strange looking – a large framework erected high above the tops of a row of semis, which bellied up to it like a litter of nursing puppies. Thick yellow tubes were suspended at intervals from the framework, one to be inserted into the passenger-side window of each truck. This necessitated having what was called a template, a piece of black plastic that exactly fitted the passenger-side window of the truck and which had a circular hole the same diameter as the end of the yellow tube. You wedged the template into the window space then, in my case with the help of an IdleAir attendant, manhandled the end of the tube into the hole in the template and locked it in.

1. Pictures of IdleAir. An IdleAir site (above). An inside view of a control console (below)

From there you opened the door on the end of the tube and were greeted by a touch screen which invited you to swipe your IdleAir membership card. The service cost $1.85 per hour, but you didn't need to use it all night, just until the cab cooled down.

I loved IdleAir, only partly because it required driving the truck straight in rather than performing the much harder maneuver of backing into a parking place. It was always a good ending to the day when I could find a truck stop with IdleAir.

That night, though, I cried myself to sleep, albeit in air-conditioned comfort, trying not to scratch the many spider bites I had gotten the night before while sleeping on the edge of a Louisiana swamp.

Why were night dispatchers so nasty? They had a bad repu-tation in the company, but it didn't come across quite so clearly on a Qualcomm somehow. As I waited for sleep, I began to do arithmetic. Suppose I drove 500 miles a day ... and suppose I drove six days a week ... that would be 3,000 miles a week ... very roughly 12,000 miles a month ... and the company gave you a bonus if you drove over 10,000 miles every month of a quarter ... so 500 miles per day should really be plenty. I would talk with Kevin in the morning. I could deal with *him*. Somewhat comforted, but still itching from spider bites, I finally achieved sleep.

The next morning, I woke up before 4 AM and woke, as I always did, fearing to move. It was moving that started the chronic pain in my hip. I lay still for a few minutes, trying to savor the last pain-free minutes which I knew would be followed by an hour or more of torment. Lying still was limited by my need to get out of the truck and hike in to the truck stop's restroom. Hike? Limp was more like it. I stood up, and the pain hit as my weight, not inconsiderable, was taken up by my spine. It was a little like balancing on stilts, with a shard of glass digging into my hip joint and being pressed ever farther in.

Gasping, I bailed out on standing up and, turning, dived back into the bunk onto my hands and knees, where I did several back-stretching exercises, then lay down flat on my stomach. This mitigated the pain, but it was also uncomfortable to lie on a full bladder, so I tried again. This time, standing was a little better. I dressed quickly, putting on my usual jeans and T-shirt, the sort of clothing that had served me as a uniform through the decades of being a mother, a student and a trucker (in that order). Slipping my feet into Birkenstocks, I gathered up kit bag, keys to the truck and enough money for a cup of coffee.

Of course, it was still dark at just after 4 AM in Hurricane Mills, Tennessee. Happily, the temperature was moderate. It was a relief to be a bit farther north where neither heat nor humidity were quite as intense as they had been in Louisiana the day before.

I had two conflicting needs. I was 478 miles from what was called a first-come-first-serve delivery, to be followed by a 4 PM pickup on my next load, but I needed to work out the pain in my hip before I started driving. That would mean at least half an hour flat on my stomach before I could start. And, in any case, I didn't think I could drive 478 miles, deliver the load, and drive to the next pickup, all within 12 hours.

Life these days seemed to be constant stress. It had been so much better during the almost eight weeks I spent with Johnny, the trainer with whom my company, Alan King Associates (or "Alan" as we more often called it), had sent me out. Johnny had 16 years of experience as a driver and could cope with anything that came up. *He* didn't get into these situations, or if he did, he knew exactly how to get out of them.

When I first got onto the truck with Johnny, the only part of trucking I knew anything about, and that only at a beginning level, was how to drive. I had never made a delivery or a pickup, or stopped at a weigh station, had never even fueled a truck. I didn't know much about the daily life of a trucker. How did it really work to live on the road? How would I get food and drink? Where would I sleep? How would I keep clean? All of these matters were routine to Johnny. He did a good job of introducing me to life on the road.

PART I

Out with a Trainer

Map 1

CHAPTER 1

Meeting Johnny – The First Few Days
(March 30-April 2)

Even life with Johnny hadn't been exactly stress free. There was the problem of trying to learn how to back up to loading docks ("bumping the dock" as it's called), something for which I seemed to have no talent whatsoever. But there had been an underlying sense of security. I could always call for help and Johnny would be there within seconds. He didn't sleep very deeply when I drove, having been in more than one accident situation with previous students. I, on the other hand, trusted his driving implicitly and slept very well when he was driving, rocked by the motion of the truck.

I had the impression that the company didn't intend Johnny to sleep at all when I was driving. He was supposed to be there in the passenger seat keeping an eye on me. This would have imposed a limit on the number of miles we could do which was clearly unacceptable to him and which would have reduced his income considerably. So, almost from the beginning, we took turns driving. Johnny slept, or catnapped at least, while I was driving on the Interstates, if nothing much was going on such as construction or challenging hills – and he knew them all.

After I finished a driving stint he would take over, often driving on through the night, but stopping for a three-hour nap when he needed to. It was that stopping that tended to wake me up because he ran the heat full blast for a few minutes before stopping, then slept until the heat dissipated; I commonly woke up with night-mares of heat in a jungle just before the truck halted.

3

Those naps, plus his catnaps while I drove, and some longer naps while the truck was being loaded or unloaded, seemed to suffice him for sleep. But he slept lightly, if at all, when I was driving, so it was always possible to call for help, as I did one night toward the beginning of training when I took an exit, looking for food and a restroom, then found myself staring at a closed gas station – not even a truck stop – with only a dirt road stretching beyond it.

"Johnny?" I quavered. Within seconds he was down off the top bunk, sitting in the passenger seat and looking all around, bleary-eyed, sizing up the situation, while I made what excuses I could, waiting for him to tell me the best course of action.

"You can do a U-turn," he decided. "Remember to use all the available space."

Sure enough, a U-turn was possible, and we were soon back on the Interstate.

Initially, I wasn't very happy about going out with a male trainer. It was my own ignorance, really, plus the press of money problems which got me into it. Another company had turned me down for a job on the grounds that they had no female trainers available. So, when Alan King Associates, a large company with more than 3,000 drivers, offered to fly me to their corporate headquarters in Wisconsin for orientation I assumed that they had women trainers. This assumption lasted until the third day of orientation when all four of us women found notes at our places in the orientation room which stated that there were no women trainers available right then.

To make a fuss about it would have meant paying my own way back to North Carolina, plus the cost of the airplane ticket out which Alan King Associates had picked up, so, without much time to think, I decided I'd better at least give it a try.

The next day Johnny Wattenburg passed through headquarters on his way to pick up a load a hundred miles away. I was called to the back of the room to meet him. My first impression was of a man in his thirties, an estimate which I had to revise upward substantially upon learning that he was a grandfather. He was actually

4

forty-six years old, only seven years younger than I. He looked like an athlete, dressed in sweat pants and a hooded sweatshirt and carrying a clipboard. He had the sort of bouncing-up-and-down-in-place stance which I remembered from one of my childhood swim team coaches. All he lacked was a whistle!

We shook hands and I looked at him, riding out the momentary wave of terror that the sight of him inspired. Was I really going out in a truck alone with this man? Who was he? Would I be safe? Much later he told me that he had seen the fear in my eyes and had thought to himself, "Hoo boy, now what am I going to do?"

I was right. He was, or had been, an athlete. One of the first things he told me about himself was that he had been on the track team in high school and had even tried out for the Olympics, in the 400-meter event. He had the look of a good short-distance runner, being compactly built and with powerful legs. I soon found that he kept a bicycle strapped onto the bottom of whatever trailer he was pulling. Alan King Associates objected to this, but apparently wasn't willing to fire him over it. Whenever we arrived someplace, Johnny was likely to unstrap the bicycle and ride off on it.

On the occasion of this first meeting we went outside to talk for a few minutes, necessary for me. With my hearing problem I couldn't distinguish one voice among many (the orientation was continuing without me). Johnny would otherwise have had to talk loudly enough to bother everybody in the room for me to have any chance of hearing what he said.

Once outside, I explained the nature of my problem. Luckily, I would probably be able to hear him when driving as my right ear, the good one, would be toward him when I drove and he was in the passenger seat.

Johnny told me that he would be back the next afternoon, March 30, to pick me up after my orientation group finished skid pad training, and that he would then be in a big hurry to get to California for an April 2nd delivery of the load he was about to pick up. And he proposed to spend some of the intervening hours using the swimming pool of the motel where Alan King Associates was lodging the new drivers who had come for orientation.

5

The next day, Friday, upon being dropped back at the motel after practicing skidding, I did indeed find Johnny in the motel's swimming pool. I hastened to check out of my room while he got dressed, then, with the help of my roommate and another Alan driver whom Johnny seemed to have met in the pool, we got my luggage moved out to the truck.

This was my first view of an actual working semi – the one I had used in training was old and stripped down. I was impressed with the organizational efficiency of the space within the cab. Besides the two seats and bunk beds there were lots of cabinets, drawers and cubby holes.

It was very clean. Johnny said that he had washed everything in preparation for taking on a new student. There were three folded towels acting as rugs, one each in front of the driver's and passenger's seats and one in front of the bunks. An almost empty plastic grocery store bag hung from the armrest of the passenger seat to be used for trash. Paper napkins, collected from fast food restaurants, and extra plastic bags were stored in one of the netted cubby holes above the windshield. Johnny also collected taco sauce packets of the hottest variety. They were stashed here and there around the truck and sometimes turned up in odd places – I found one on the floor between the bunk and the cabinet.

I was allotted a certain amount of space for my things. I had half of the overhead compartment above the dashboard, the cubbies above the passenger-side visor and seat window and one of the drawers. Also, Johnny was letting me have the lower bunk mostly, I think, out of deference to how difficult it would have been for me to climb up to the upper bunk. This was against the usual practice. It's always the lead driver's prerogative to have the lower bunk.

Once my things were stowed, and Johnny had loaned me a quilt, sheets and a pillow to supplement the sleeping bag and pillow I had brought, we started out. This was the first time I had ridden very far with someone who actually knew how to drive, and I took it all in, fascinated, as we went down the road.

For one thing, he sat in the driver's seat as if he had been born there – comfort personified. He gave the appearance of being wrapped around the steering wheel; I got the impression that he viewed the truck as an extension of himself, an impression augmented by the fact that he drove sock-footed. I had never thought of such a thing! He was clearly an energetic person, almost indefatigable as it would prove, with the same sort of "let's go" air about him as my aforementioned swimming coach. He was acutely alert to the environment. Nothing seemed to escape his notice.

His driving was completely relaxed and self-assured. I could see that much of it was being done without a lot of reflection – very like my driving of a car, really.

It occurred to me that training with a man had certain advantages. For one thing, he had a nice low voice. Women, with their higher-frequency voices were often hard for me to hear. Two of my three daughters seemed to think of me as being practically deaf. Johnny didn't mind speaking loudly. He explained that he had a friend who was hard of hearing, so he was used to having to bellow. The noise of the truck engine made hearing very challenging, though, especially at high speeds, but even an idling semi created quite a high level of ambient noise.

As Johnny drove westward, we used these first hours in the truck for a discussion of ground rules. First, he made what sounded like a well-rehearsed speech, beginning with, "Welcome to the truck. You live here too now." He continued, "I don't care if you wear a seat belt and I don't care about double-clutching."

Double-clutching was the only way I knew how to shift gears in a truck, though I was aware that some drivers could "float" gears, shift them without using the clutch at all (and my husband had demonstrated this to me on his Alfa Romeo many years before). So the double-clutching part of the speech went right by me and just seemed "not applicable." There might be other ways of shifting, but I didn't know them and only used them by accident.

The seat belt part of the speech, however, came to life as I noticed that Johnny himself was not wearing his seat belt. It turned out that he only wore it under two circumstances: 1) when going through weigh stations and 2) if we were being pulled over by the Highway Patrol. This, of course, proved that he was perfectly cognizant of seat belt laws but chose not to obey them. Such disregard for the law troubled me, but I decided that it wasn't any of my business. I always wore a seat belt, both out of respect for the law and from conviction, having been indoctrinated at the age of 15, when an Arizona Highway Patrolman came to our driver's ed class two days in a row to show slides and movies of accident scenes. He made comments like, "This is the man's body here under this bush ... and this is his head which we found under the bridge abutment here (pointing to a spot about 50 feet away). If he'd been wearing a seat belt he probably wouldn't have been ejected from the car and might well have lived."

How this applied to semi driving I wasn't sure, knowing that semis are a lot safer than cars, but I had worn a seat belt for so long that I felt insecure without one. My only complaint was that the truck's seat belts weren't the sort that I could get tight across my lap. On the other hand, the shoulder part of the belt had a clip, like the ones cars used to have, which made it possible to keep the seat belt from pulling at my breasts – a real plus, since it kept me from being tempted to drive with one hand, using the other to hold the seat belt away from my front.

Johnny continued the welcome speech, telling me that I would be living on the truck for the next eight weeks and that I should think of it as my home too. He pointed out that "this is closer than marriage" as, after all, few married couples spend twenty-four hours a day, seven days a week together, much less in a space the size of a walk-in closet. He issued me a set of keys for the truck and the steering gear lock/padlock combination that Alan King Associates gave to all its drivers.

He seemed to feel a need to apologize for making four cents a mile more when he was instructing than when he was driving alone. He explained that he wasn't doing it just for the money, as though I might think I was being exploited. Here I interrupted him to say that my feelings were far otherwise; I had taught three of my four children to drive and knew how very much easier it is just to do the driving oneself rather than sitting in the passenger seat trying to think of everything that needs to be said to a student driver, without even mentioning the burden of responsibility. I had spent almost a whole school year being ferried back and forth to my twins' high school by one or the other of them and had often thought how much simpler it would have been just to do it myself. I added that I was grateful to have a trainer with 16 years of experience and that his being paid an extra four cents a mile didn't take anything away from me. We left it at that.

One of the ground rules Johnny laid out was that when I got out of the truck, I should leave something on the driver's seat so that he wouldn't drive off without me. Another rule was that I should never leave the keys in the truck. Most stolen trucks, he believed, were taken when someone broke in and managed to find a spare set of keys.

I began to appreciate the leaving something in the driver's seat rule in the days that followed when I noticed that the typical end of one of the three-hour naps Johnny took in the middle of the night was a creaking sound in the bunk above as he sat up, then two feet appearing, one on each of the shelves which were about at waist-level from the floor, followed by a thud as he jumped off the bunk, one step which took him to the driver's seat, the turning of the ignition key and the moving off of the truck. All of this happened just about as quickly as a slow reading of the above passage would suggest. Did he even look in the mirror to make sure that the trailer was still attached, I wondered? I was taught to inspect a truck before driving it, looking, at a bare minimum, at the coupling, air lines and tires. Doing that at 3 AM in the cold and dark seemed a bit extreme, but not doing it at all seemed quite chancy to me.

Both rules worked well. We never left each other behind during our time together – and the truck wasn't stolen either. I eventually evolved the habit of leaving my purse on the driver's seat when I got out, thinking that it would speak to Johnny of my existence better than a random object such as a water bottle or magazine.

Johnny himself never bothered to leave anything on the driver's seat, but later on, when I was driving more independently, I found that by studying the bedclothes of the upper bunk carefully I could generally see his left foot (never any more), with or without a sock depending on the weather. I never left him behind either.

Another ground rule was that Johnny didn't want the truck to idle. He turned the engine off whenever he stopped driving. "That's why it has a battery and an ignition." The company rewarded drivers who idled less than 20 percent of the time, but Johnny was running an idle rate of less than one percent.

Many truckers, he told me, idled their trucks at truck stops, and it was sometimes necessary to do this if the temperature was extreme – hot *or* cold – but he avoided it as much as possible.

He was fortunate to be driving a new truck, which they'd given him when he signed up to train for Alan King Associates. There were only 27,000 miles on the odometer when I got on the truck. This represented about two months of driving.

The truck was equipped with a bunk heater – one that could run when the engine was off. Even so, it could be necessary to idle the engine if it got far enough below freezing because diesel fuel "gels" when it gets too cold – that is, it partially solidifies. The engine can't run on gelled fuel, and a driver can waste a lot of time trying to get going again, so it's considered to be worthwhile to idle in very cold weather. A running engine circulates the fuel and keeps all of it warm.

Johnny was hoping that the company would give him an APU (Auxiliary Power Unit) sometime. This was a small diesel engine mounted on the frame of the tractor, which would give him heating and air conditioning without having to idle the engine and would also make it possible to use regular appliances instead of the special ones, sold at truck stops, which ran off the 12 V DC cigarette lighter. A tractor used a gallon of fuel for every hour of idling. An APU used only a tenth of a gallon per hour, or so we were told.

Johnny continued driving westward. We had already been on two different Interstates. Now we took a State route on our way to another State route which would eventually bring us out onto US-30 on our way to Grand Island, Nebraska, where Johnny was hoping to meet up with his brother, another Alan driver, sometime in the middle of the next morning.

I was impressed with this knowledge of State routes. I was accustomed to long car trips and the use of a road atlas. I had learned to read maps at the age of four, on one of the long car trips that were a feature of my childhood. But I wouldn't have had the knowledge to make the kind of use of State routes that Johnny did.

He told me to go to bed whenever I got tired – he wasn't planning on having me drive until the next day. He would pull over and take a nap when he got tired, then continue on.

So around 10 PM I said good night. I thought twice about changing out of my clothes within four feet of a strange man but decided that I couldn't stay in my clothes for the next two months. Johnny was fully occupied driving and it was dark in the cab. I wouldn't have been capable of looking way around in back while driving. Johnny might be able to do it – I wasn't sure – but I was betting that he wouldn't. And he probably wouldn't be able to see anything even if he did look. So, I changed into my pajamas, arranged the covers and lay down on the bottom bunk. It was a cozy feeling, lying in bed as the truck sped through the night. The motion of the truck rocked me to sleep.

Some hours later I awoke, needing a restroom, to find that Johnny was now driving through a snowstorm. The view out the windshield had a hypnotic quality, as groups of snowflakes, lighted by the truck's headlights, seemed to explode continuously against the windshield. Snow was all the more surprising as it had been 80° in Wisconsin only a few days before. I remembered from my Wisconsin childhood what a treacherous month April was – hot one day and the next day snowing a blizzard. It would be April in just a few days.

My husband, in days gone by, would probably have made us stop driving for snow like this, with the continual bursting of clumps of snowflakes against the windshield. I remembered one trip where the two of us, plus children, took refuge in a motel in Las Vegas, New Mexico in similar conditions. Although perhaps the snow had been sticking more on that occasion. It wasn't actually accumulating much, and Johnny didn't seem bothered by it.

I quickly put jeans and a sweatshirt on over my pajamas, then went forward to sit in the passenger seat, noticing how odd Johnny's face looked in the green glow from the truck gauges. My sudden appearance startled him. He jumped but then recovered himself. He must have forgotten that I was on the truck, I thought with some amusement. He was agreeable to my request for a restroom and started searching his memory for the next possibility, which occurred only 15 or 20 minutes down the road at a gas station.

I had heard of woman drivers carrying portable toilets on their trucks. I had tentative plans for getting one later on, but I couldn't possibly use one in this situation, with a man never more than five or six feet away.

Johnny took advantage of the restroom stop to get a snack, then we drove on. He explained again that he would drive until he got tired, then heat the truck up before stopping to nap for a few hours by the side of the road.

The "side of the road" sounded a little ominous to me as it didn't seem to promise restroom facilities. After a moment's thought, and gathering up courage to say something I really didn't want to say but thought I had better get straight from the beginning, I pointed out to Johnny that as a middle-aged woman I needed a restroom rather often – and always when waking up – and that I didn't have the sort of relationship with trees or bushes that men did.

Johnny thought this over for a perceptible amount of time, then seemed to accept what I was saying and promised to stop somewhere with a restroom if it was at all possible. And he always, always did during the almost eight weeks which followed. I was immensely grateful, as I imagined that it sometimes caused him quite a lot of inconvenience.

It was morning when I woke again. I had half-awakened when Johnny heated up the truck – the first of the jungle nightmares – but had quickly gone back to sleep in the now quiet truck. Finding that we were at a rest area, I again put jeans and a sweatshirt on over my pajamas, donned shoes and my coat and climbed out of the truck as quietly as I could, taking care to remember to put something on the driver's seat and making sure that the truck keys were in my pocket.

When I returned Johnny was just waking up. (The sound of the truck's door shutting always woke him, but it was several weeks before I realized that I was slamming the door and started shutting it more quietly.) We drove on toward Grand Island. I drove the truck for the first time that morning, going westward on US-30 from Fremont to the truck stop at Grand Island. Johnny had a cell phone and spoke with his brother at some length several times as I drove. Occasionally, he interrupted his conversation to say something urgent to me, but got the meeting place with his brother coordinated, nonetheless.

When we arrived at the truck stop, he talked me through the procedure for pulling into a fuel island. We bought fuel. As this was only the second time I had seen this done, and the first time I had seen a card reader used, I watched with great interest as Johnny swiped the company fuel card, then swiped his "customer loyalty" card for that particular brand of truck stop, then answered the numerous questions that the machine posed one by one: driver number, tractor number, odometer reading, trailer number, trip number, did he want a cash advance of so-and-so-many dollars? tractor fuel or reefer fuel or both? The questions seemed to go on and on. The company issued each driver with a small trip notebook for writing down load information, one page per trip. Johnny had already showed me the book, and for that matter I had a blank one of my own, given to me at orientation. He made sure to write the odometer reading at the bottom of the page when he stopped for fuel, then took the notebook with him so he could answer all the machine's questions.

Once fueling was authorized, he put gloves on, taking them from the floor next to the driver's seat where they were kept to be handy, and took the cap off the nearside tank, which was located right behind the steps on the driver's side of the truck. Each fuel island had two pumps: the main one on the driver's side, which also had the card reader, and what was called the "slave pump" on the passenger's side. Having started the main pump working, Johnny walked around the front of the truck, removed the cap from the other diesel tank, behind the passenger steps, and started that pump going as well.

Then he cleaned the windshield, first opening the hood of the truck and standing on a tire to reach high enough with the long-handled squeegee which had been waiting in a bucket of windshield washer fluid at the front of the fuel island. He checked the oil and looked at the belts, power steering fluid level, antifreeze level and windshield washer fluid.

Each tank held 100 gallons of diesel fuel, giving the truck a theoretical range of about 1200 miles (!) but Johnny usually bought either 75 or 100 gallons at a time. The truck stops put a free shower on the driver's loyalty card as long as the driver bought at least 50 gallons. Otherwise a shower cost as much as nine dollars. Buying only 75 or 100 gallons came closer to maximizing the number of showers than filling the tanks would have done and also gave him more flexibility, inasmuch as that the next fueling would likely be at a different brand of fuel stop. Showers were sometimes taken right after fueling, but equally often were deferred until another truck stop of the same brand, either later in the day or on another day.

Johnny had half a dozen loyalty cards (TA/Petro, Pilot, Flying J, and Love's plus a few lesser-known ones) and usually had a pretty good idea of which ones held showers, and how many showers they held. A shower only lasted five days on a card, so managing them was a little complicated.

If reefer fuel was being bought, as it was that day, he had to pull the truck forward until the hose could reach the reefer tank, which held either 30 or 50 gallons and was located under the trailer with the filler cap on the driver's side.

In either case, the truck was driven forward after fueling to a line which indicated that the next truck would be able to pull forward far enough to fuel. Then the driver went inside to collect the receipt, and the cash advance if he was taking one.

Johnny explained that it was okay to buy a drink or fast food, and to use the restroom during this time, but that it really made other drivers furious when drivers stayed too long – taking a shower while parked at the fuel island for example.

We had arrived at this truck stop before Johnny's brother, so after fueling Johnny parked the truck in an actual parking place and we went inside.

This was my first experience of a real truck stop, the Grand Island Bosselman Pilot. As it happened it was also one of the biggest and nicest ones in the country. There were 400 parking places for semis. The truck stop itself was built on two levels and contained, besides the usual fuel desk, a huge store selling everything truck stop stores sell: food, toiletries, small items for trucks, such as fuses, lights, tarp straps, etc., etc. This one had all that and a lot more. There were also magnificent restrooms, several dozen showers, two cinemas, four or five pits with televisions so that small groups of drivers could watch whatever shows they wanted. There was a restaurant, two fast food concessions, a large game room, laundromat, various boutiques and even a barbershop!

The first thing that caught my eye was a glass case full of little trinkets, some made of glass, others of crystal. Most truck stops have these, as I later saw. This, however, was my first time of seeing one. "What's that?" I asked Johnny.

"Crap for people who have too much money," he replied, an answer that lives forever in my memory.

Johnny's brother, Jerry, showed up after a while. I happened to run across him as I was walking out an exit on my way back to the truck to get something I needed. I was shocked when I saw him. Johnny hadn't mentioned that his brother was also his identical twin brother. Jerry was a bit thinner than Johnny, and I was sure I'd be able to tell them apart without difficulty, but to see one face was to see the other. And their voices were absolutely identical.

I wandered around, checking out the store, then getting a meal in the restaurant while the two brothers sat at a table in the fast food area and talked. I hadn't known Johnny long enough to want to impose myself on their meeting. My twins were boy/girl twins, twenty-three years old. I always enjoyed their relationship, which consisted of a lot of friendly give and take with many shared jokes and stories.

Johnny and Jerry seemed to belong in a different part of the spectrum of twin relationships. They were highly competitive. They were close: each knew the other's driver's number, PIN numbers and every other number, it seemed. They also knew how far the other one had driven in the last week, month, and year, how many miles per gallon the other had gotten last month (6.7 mpg for Johnny and 6.4 for Jerry) and why. It was all very interesting to me, when I eventually wandered over and got introduced.

We stayed for an hour or so while the brothers visited, then climbed back onto the truck and continued on our way. I drove again, this time on I-80 heading westward toward Wyoming. I was very nervous, hearing in my head the voice of a previous driving instructor who had been critical of almost everything I did.

The first question I asked Johnny was about on-ramps. I couldn't see if a car was coming up one or not but was afraid to look too far backwards down the ramp.

What I said was, "I can't see if anyone's coming or not."

I thought Johnny's response showed an analytical mind. He concentrated intently for a moment, then had the answer: "You'd be able to see if anyone *was* coming."

And this turned out to be true. The height of a car made all the difference to being able to see it. I was relieved.

I also kept looking in the side mirrors, trying to keep the truck centered in the lane and trying to learn, looking forward now, how that might appear. I alternated this with looking far up the center of my lane, which I knew from driving cars would tend to center me in the lane.

After a while Johnny tackled me on the subject of using the side mirrors so much. He said that he had counted me doing it 19 times before he lost count, and he wondered what made me look so often. I explained that a previous instructor had accused me of always being too far right in the lane and that I was trying to correct that. Johnny contended that most things happen in front of a truck and that most of my attention should go there. If I looked far up the lane the truck would be centered, he said, and anyway it was better to be a bit too far right than to be too far left.

Later on, that first full day, I rode in the passenger seat while Johnny drove from Big Springs, Nebraska to Laramie, Wyoming. It was almost more instructive to watch him drive than to drive myself. He was very comfortable about shifting. I had to suppress a feeling of panic whenever I needed to shift. When Johnny drove, shifting gears usually happened silently. Even if the gears made a grinding noise, which he said happened to everyone and anyone who said otherwise was lying, he just calmly tried again. This was an occasional occurrence with him. With me it happened about a third of the time, if I even managed to get it into the gear I had in mind.

I also used my daylight time in the passenger seat to study the inside of the cab more closely. Johnny had a small paper calendar wedged into the upper left-hand corner of the windshield, with the current month displayed. In the center of the top part of the windshield was a built-in clock, about two inches in diameter, apparently part of the truck's original equipment, and which was set to Central Time, the time in which we had to log, that being the time zone of Alan King Associates' headquarters.

The dashboard of the truck was wide and held a lot of books and papers. First in importance was the road atlas, which was a large-print trucker's atlas, each page laminated and the whole spiral-bound to give it longer life. There were also the trip book over on the left, the official list of authorized fuel stops for Alan King Associates, a couple of trucking magazines, free at truck stops, two "USA Today's," the company procedures manual and, strangely, a golf ball sitting in the corner of the far right-hand side of the dashboard.

I asked about the golf ball, wondering what on earth it was doing there. Did it have a truck-related use? Johnny said he had found it on the ground a few days before. There wasn't any special reason for it.

He mentioned that the dashboard of the truck, right up next to the windshield, was useful for heating cans of soup when the defroster was turned on, and that he sometimes used the dashboard for drying socks or underwear, to save the time it took to use a dryer.

In the first days of driving, as we went westward toward Stockton, California, I was nervous about taking my hands off the steering wheel. Picking up a drink from the cup holder, well within reach, was about the most I could do. Even reaching backward to fasten the seat belt clip above my left shoulder was a challenge. Within a few weeks, though, these things seemed much easier. They eventually became completely routine and no challenge at all.

In those first days, when Johnny was usually in the passenger seat if I was driving, we did a lot of talking. He told me stories of the other students he had trained through the years, especially of Stephanie, the student before me, who had often found the truck to be too cold. She had threatened his idling percentage because he had to run the heater so much. "Keeping Stephanie warm," as Johnny put it, had been the hardest part of training her.

He also talked about various aspects of trucking and had an endearing habit of saying, "Trust me!" rather a lot, as in, "Trust me! You don't want to ... " whatever it was.

We exchanged stories of children and spouses. We each had four children, but while I was a divorcee whose husband had subsequently died, Johnny had an ex-wife, a soon-to-be ex-wife and a girlfriend. He also had quite a few grandchildren, one as old as eight, plus another couple on the way. My two grandchildren were infants.

I heard about the many years he had spent driving a bus for a community college in his hometown in northern California, his 16 years as a truck driver, and of the two houses he had built. Construction techniques interested him greatly, partly because he was involved in a project to build a new strip mall in his town.

He told me that he spent a lot of his driving time mulling over ways and means of putting up a pre-stressed concrete-walled building without having to rent a crane. The idea of moving large slabs without a crane sounded frightening to me and I hoped he wouldn't injure or kill himself trying to save money.

At first, Johnny did all the hard driving. Finding a parking place on a Sunday night at any truck stop in Reno or Sparks, Nevada was a real challenge, but he managed it. He explained that a lot of truckers were waiting for early morning to drive over Donner Pass and down into California for Monday morning deliveries, so Sunday night was a particularly hard time to find a parking place. Besides which, one of the Reno-area truck stops had recently closed, which had made an already bad situation even worse.

It was Johnny who drove over Donner Pass the next morning. He talked about power downshifting on upgrades as he went from tenth gear down to ninth, then to eighth and finally to seventh. Power downshifting is the technique necessary for pulling a heavy load up a steep hill or mountain. The truck's RPM's drop as the gear becomes unable to pull the load. You have to shift down a gear without losing momentum and that's hard for a beginner, as there's a narrow band of RPM's that allow you to shift into the next gear down. The nightmare possibility is of missing a gear and coming to a standstill on the hill or mountain. Then you would have to finish the ascent in second gear, going about three miles an hour, presumably on the shoulder of the highway.

I had driven Donner Pass from time to time in a car. One of the reasons I had thought of driving a semi was my enjoyment of long car trips. My most recent car trip over Donner had been in January of the previous year, when a semi and I had had the road practically to ourselves in a snowstorm. After seeing several cars in various stages of being towed out of snowbanks, I had proceeded up the pass at a decorous 30 miles an hour.

Doing the pass in a semi was quite a different experience and I was glad not to be driving as we climbed the mountain. Going down the other side was different too. I watched Johnny and listened attentively as he explained what he was doing in using the engine brake to slow the truck on the steep descent. Once the road flattened out, we had heavy traffic all the way to Stockton, where we delivered the 44,000 pounds of cheese that Johnny had picked up in Beaver Dam, Wisconsin just before I got on the truck.

Delivering a load was another new experience for me. The first step was finding out where to go. We had already asked for directions over the Qualcomm, but when we got near I saw that Johnny was having to size things up quickly to find the right entrance to the delivery site. In this case we were lucky: there was a large sign with the word "Receiving" and an arrow pointing us to the right entrance.

Johnny pulled up to the guard shack and turned off the engine. We both climbed out, Johnny carrying his trip notebook and the bills of lading, usually just called "bills," that he had been given when he picked up the load. The security guard looked the papers over and asked for a confirmation number. The usual situation, I was to learn, was that the dispatch information for the job listed four or five numbers, all of which Johnny had written into his notebook. The challenge was to find out which number the guard wanted.

Once the truck was logged in, the guard told us where to find the receiving office. We climbed back into the truck, then Johnny maneuvered it through the security gate and around a big building. The receiving office was on the far side of it.

Now he had to size up the situation to decide where to park without blocking other trucks while we went into the receiving office to find out which loading dock the company wanted us to back up to.

Some companies had a more streamlined process, fortunately. About half of the time, the security guards from other companies were able to tell us a dock number right at the guard shack, thus saving this intermediate step of parking again. Some companies had designated parking areas for waiting trucks, which was also a help. On the other hand, some smaller companies didn't even have security guards or guard shacks. Sizing things up quickly was often necessary.

In this case, Johnny parked the truck toward one end of a large expanse of loading docks. We climbed down and went into the receiving office, which was in an institutional type of hallway, not very clean, with a drinking fountain and a window set into one wall, above which was painted the word "Receiving." A shelf in front of the window held a clipboard with a sign-in sheet on it and a pen chained to the shelf.

Johnny signed in and waited for someone to come to the window, which happened quite quickly. A loading dock was assigned to us, after which we went back out to the truck. As so often happened, Johnny now had to drive to the other end of the loading docks and turn around in order to be oriented correctly to set up for bumping the dock.

Cheerfully remarking that I should really be doing this, and promising, or threatening, that I soon would be, he made the U-turn, set up for the backing job, then we both got out and opened the doors of the trailer, breaking the shipper's plastic seal, and fastening the doors open by slipping a large chain link on each door over the hook provided for that purpose on each side of the trailer.

The purpose of a shipper's seal is to show that a load hasn't been tampered with. It's a protection for drivers as well as for shippers. There are several different types of the seals. There are plastic strips, almost like the big tie on a large plastic garbage bag. Another kind looks like the plastic one but is made of a thin strip of metal. There are braided wire seals of various thicknesses, which have to be cut off with wire cutters. Finally, there are bolt seals, close to a quarter of an inch thick, which have to be cut off with big bolt cutters.

Once the doors were opened Johnny backed smoothly up to the dock. Even he, competent as he was, had to pull forward a couple of times to get the trailer lined up exactly right. He was backing between two yellow lines painted on the pavement, moving toward a square door which was surrounded by padded buffers a foot wide. The door was about the same size as the back of the trailer. The top and sides of the back of the trailer needed to be centered on these buffers.

In other words, he had to back this 53-foot trailer to the inch. The tires on the driver's side needed to be touching the inside of the yellow painted line in order for everything to line up correctly. This showed, by the way, that the company had done things well. Sometimes you had to be centered between the sets of lines, sometimes you had to ignore the line on the passenger side, and sometimes there weren't any lines. Again, it all depended.

Once the trailer was aligned exactly, Johnny backed until its end touched the buffers and sank into them a few inches, then he set the brake and turned off the engine. We climbed out of the truck one more time to turn off the reefer unit, which had been set to 35 degrees. I was beginning to understand that this wasn't a sedentary job.

Alan King Associates was a reefer company, meaning that they specialized in loads that needed to be temperature controlled, usually some kind of food. A "reefer" is the refrigeration unit on a trailer, a sophisticated machine which I had been told added $35,000 to the cost of the trailer and was capable of holding a load at any temperature from minus 20° to plus 80° F.

2. Loading docks

With the reefer turned off we waited. After about ten minutes there was a bump as the loading dock door was lifted and a hook reached out to grab the trailer's back bumper. This was followed, at intervals, by the trailer and tractor bouncing up and down as someone inside the warehouse drove a forklift into the trailer, lifted up a pallet of cheese, then backed out again. Each pallet weighed roughly a ton. We were carrying 22 tons of cheese, so this maneuver had to be repeated 22 times. Loading or unloading generally took an hour or more. At this place it took two hours.

Johnny soon declared his intention of catching a few winks and climbed into the upper bunk. He told me that someone would bang on the side of the truck when they had finished unloading and hand us our copy of the bills, which we would need, both to get back out by way of the guard shack, and for submitting to Alan later on, in order to get paid for this trip.

I got out of the truck and went to investigate the drivers lounge, up a set of stairs from the receiving window, where I found a restroom and a couple of vending machines. I bought a Diet Coke, then sat down at a table in the very plain, linoleum-floored room to drink my Diet Coke and read a book for a while.

I headed back to the truck after 15 or 20 minutes, being too nervous to concentrate, and afraid of missing the man who would bang on the side of the truck. I needn't have worried. I sat in the driver's seat for more than an hour reading until, eventually, a man did come to the window. He handed me some papers and said we were free to go.

Johnny woke up and told me that I could drive to our next pickup, which was in Vacaville, California, 60 miles away. First, though, we had to pull the truck forward to shut the doors. Before we could do that, we had to wait for enough air pressure to build so that we could move the truck, as the loading or unloading process tended to bleed the air out of the air tanks and that brought into play a safety feature that kept the brakes locked up below 75 psi.

Once the pressure built up to 100 psi, I pulled forward a few feet. We got out and shut one door, leaving the other one open so that the guard would be able to look in and make sure that the trailer really was empty. I drove to the guard shack, got out and handed the guard the exit pass that had been given us along with the bills, then walked with him to the back of the trailer, first putting on the gloves I had brought with me so that I would be ready to shut the door. Later on, Johnny would often leave me to do this alone, but on this first occasion he came too, and pointed out how the inside of the trailer wasn't really clean. Forklifts had a way of breaking big slivers of wood off the pallets which then lodged in the grooves of the trailer floor.

The floor of a reefer trailer is grooved lengthwise so that air can circulate under the pallets as well as over and around them. There are also big plastic "sleeves," or air chutes running the length of the trailer along the top of its interior, one on each side, again for the purpose of circulating air.

The drive to Vacaville was mostly freeway. Johnny had been to the pickup location before, so he was able to tell me exactly what to do. We again checked in at a guard shack, then Johnny was nice enough to back up to this loading dock and we waited while 44,000 pounds of raisins were loaded into the trailer. It went faster than the unloading had, and soon I was back on the freeway, at rush hour now, but happily going against the main flow of traffic, on the way back to Donner Pass.

It was a nerve-racking sort of driving, but after 15 or 20 miles the traffic thinned out. Then it was a question of hauling 44,000 pounds of raisins over Donner Pass. There were some really ugly shifts as I tried power downshifting for the first time. I had trouble figuring out what RPM's this particular truck wanted for a shift. Later on, I became able to hear when a truck stopped being able to pull a load, but for now it was more a question of what the tachometer and speedometer said.

Sometimes Johnny told me when to shift. He suggested going to ninth gear at 57 mph, eighth at 45, seventh at 35. Shifting at the high end of the possible range of mph was easier, he said. I knew better than to let the tachometer go below 1100 RPM's lest the truck stall. It was frightening, though, as the tachometer crept lower and lower and I tried to prepare for the rather complicated downshift maneuver: clutch in, pull it into neutral, rev the engine (but not too much), pull it into the next gear down – heck, *find* the next gear down! And half the time I *did* rev the engine too much and had to wait for the RPM's to fall, then try to catch it at the right range on its way back down in order to complete the shift.

Johnny pointed out that it was a kinesthetic sort of knowledge, really (he didn't phrase it that way, but that's what he meant). The feet and hands just had to work together in a very particular way. Eventually, but not that day or week, it got easier. By the time I got my own truck I didn't even find it particularly hard. And, with 330,000 miles on it rather than the 27,000 mi. of Johnny's truck, my truck could be downshifted much more smoothly.

"Bottoming out" a gear was a new concept to me. It meant that you just weren't going to be able to go any faster without shifting up a gear. Eighth gear seemed to bottom out at about 45 mph; ninth gear at 60 or so.

I was tired out by the time we got back to Reno. Johnny parked the truck, then got picked up by a daughter to go to his home in Susanville, California, 80 miles away and conduct some business, so I had the next day off in which to recuperate and had the truck to myself that night.

Sometimes, as on that evening, I looked back at the truck as I was walking away from it, on my way in to the truck stop – 53 feet of trailer plus the cab, maybe 73 feet in all. It was as big as a house! The thought that came to me at such a time was, "I've been driving *that*?!"

As I waited for Johnny the next day, I had plenty of time to think and remember. I always noticed trucks from a huge company called Mueller because I had trained with them before coming to Alan King Associates. The company was so big that there were always a lot of their trucks around. When a Mueller truck hauling a tanker came and backed into a parking place just a few holes down from where Johnny had parked our truck it started me reminiscing about my weeks at Mueller trying to learn to haul the very sort of tanker I was watching now.

Before going to Mueller, I had attended a CDL (Commercial Driver's License) school in Yadkinville, North Carolina while staying with Hungarian friends who lived in Elkin, not far away. Successfully completing the school and getting my CDL just before Christmas left me needing to go out with a trainer for six or eight weeks as the next step in learning to be a trucker. Pretty much only the largest companies offered this sort of apprenticeship. I signed

25

on with Mueller after I returned from spending Christmas in England, visiting my oldest daughter and her British husband and meeting my first grandchild, who had been born the previous September.

CHAPTER 2

Mueller Flashback

It was only a few months before, late in the month of January, when I drove from North Carolina up to Pennsylvania in a small Toyota, borrowed from my friends, to start training with Mueller. It happened to be just a few days after an ice storm had closed the Pennsylvania Turnpike for several days. Apparently, every place except the northwest corner of North Carolina where I was living had gotten snow. Almost every truck that passed me, coming from farther south, was covered in snow. The trailers of passing trucks had about an inch of hard-packed snow or ice on their roofs. Big chunks of snow or ice fell off and exploded on the road in front of my car from time to time, as a passing semi hit a bump on the Interstate.

Then, about 100 miles short of the small city in Pennsylvania where I was going, I began to notice ice on the trees. The fields were even more interesting. I had never seen anything quite like it. All the fields were covered, or coated, with ice. They reminded me of the thickly iced Christmas cakes I had seen in England a few weeks before. Like an English Christmas cake, the fields of Pennsylvania were very smooth, and the color was the matte white of snow rather than the glitter of ice. The coating looked thick – anything with a corner had a blunted appearance. It was an amazing sight, on a much vaster scale than any ice storm I had seen in 53 years of life. Every place, *every place*, that hadn't been shoveled or plowed, was ice coated.

The driving school for Mueller was also outside of my experience. It ran from 6:30 AM to 6:30 PM, seven days a week. By

27

6:10 in the morning a couple of dozen rather morose-looking men, and a few women, had assembled in the foyer of the very decent motel where the company lodged its students.

Looking at them collectively, I thought that all but one or two of the younger ones looked like people whose careers had gone wrong somewhere. That was my case, too, of course. Too much staying home with the children, even homeschooling them some of the time, and not enough attention, in fact, none at all, to building a career. Raising the children had seemed to me to be the higher priority in the sight of God; I still thought that was right, and the children had turned out well, but it did leave me pretty well stranded in the world of work.

This crowd was clearly a blue-collar bunch on the whole, though I was to meet other people with BA's, or even MA's occasionally, everywhere I went in the trucking world. And I heard rumors of erstwhile lawyers or doctors who were now truckers.

The bus came punctually just before 6:30 and we all shuffled out into the cold and dark, trying not to slip as we walked down a steep, icy hill to file onto the repainted school bus which Mueller used as a shuttle.

On the advice of a North Carolina recruiter I had signed up to be trained for driving tankers rather than the more usual dry van trailers. This meant that I wouldn't have to sign a promissory note to pay back $3,000 dollars in tuition if I left the company in less than a year.

Everything was well organized. The course lasted two weeks. A new course started every week, so on this first day the bus was filled with about two-thirds new students, one-third previous week's students who hadn't dropped out or been washed out, and a couple of more experienced drivers who were catching a ride back to the terminal, having spent the night at the motel.

Our days were divided into academic instruction, practice on the driving simulators, and driving lessons, both on the driving range and on the surrounding streets and highways of this Pennsylvania city. Matt, the only other tanker student, and I were pulled out from time to time to go for specialized instruction in various aspects of hauling tankers.

On the first day, the two of us were taken to the driving range by the tanker instructor, a very heavy man who must have weighed more than 350 pounds. He was going to make sure that we could climb up on top of a tanker and walk around on it without panicking.

There was a spare tanker trailer sitting at one edge of the driving range, surrounded by an area of glare ice, apparently some three or four inches thick. This troubled our instructor, who explained that this was his first day back to work after six weeks of medical leave occasioned by his having tried to catch a student who was falling off a tanker.

We all walked rather gingerly across the ice field, which didn't show any signs of breaking, even under the great weight of the instructor. The other student was a man of about my own age, well over six feet tall but slim. None of us slipped on the ice as we walked up to the tanker, which was itself mysteriously free of ice.

The instructor spoke to us at some length about how to climb around on a tanker safely, mostly by the same technique used to climb into and out of trucks, namely to maintain three points of contact at all times, either both feet and one hand or both hands and one foot. We were to climb up the ladder which was situated halfway along the tanker, and maneuver carefully around a big hollow square, or box, about four feet across with an eight- or nine-inch rim. It was right at the top of the ladder, protecting a manhole cover and a vent. After negotiating that obstacle we were to walk the length of the catwalk which ran from the box to the valve at the front of the tanker, reach down and touch the valve cap, then stand up again, walk back along the catwalk to the box, maneuver around it again and descend the ladder.

I was to go before Matt. The instructor asked me what I wanted him to do. Should he go up first or come up behind me? Having in mind the accident that had sidelined him for six weeks, I asked him if he could promise not to try to catch me if I fell.

He answered that, no, it didn't seem to be in his character not to try to break a student's fall if he thought he could help.

"Well, then, you'd better go up first," I decided.

I climbed after him, making sure I had a good foothold before putting my weight onto the next step. Once on top, I clambered gingerly around the box. The instructor watched to make sure I maintained three points of contact at all times. Then I stood up, not mentioning to him that my hearing loss had left me a little dizzy all the time. As I walked the catwalk, I pushed serious reservations about my sanity to the back of my mind. The actual thought was, "Have you lost your mind, woman?" I found the walk tolerable as long as I didn't look down at the ground, fifteen feet below. I crouched down and touched the cap, stood up again and walked back to the box and climbed down the ladder, all without incident.

Matt, also, had no trouble with the exercise. Afterwards we walked back across the ice, which again showed no sign of giving way, and went back to the main building for the next activity.

By the time the bus dropped us back at the motel that evening I was tired out. We had filled out forms, heard lectures on the company's procedures and practiced shifting gears on the driving simulators. The company had given us lunch, but if I wanted dinner, I would have to go get some. I blessed the chance which had made me say that I would drive rather than take a Greyhound bus to Pennsylvania and blessed the kind friends who had insisted on lending me their third car.

The next two weeks passed quickly. The cold held, so the ice didn't melt, but the weather didn't actually get bad again until toward the end of the two weeks.

The quality of instruction at Mueller's school was very high. The company clearly had a lot of practice teaching people how to drive trucks. I was one of only two students who already had a CDL, so I didn't feel the pressure of a looming CDL test as most of the others did. I still had to pass the company's tests, though, before being sent out with a trainer. There would be three: a written test, a driving test and a backing test.

Learning to be a trucker is partly an apprenticeship. After getting a CDL a student is sent out with a trainer for six or eight weeks to learn the myriad things that a trucker needs to know, and to practice driving.

Two weeks hardly seemed long enough for learning how to drive a truck. I felt fortunate to have attended a school where we had had six weeks in which to learn and even that didn't seem very long. I was sure I could not have passed the CDL test on only two weeks of lessons.

A number of people dropped out. One of them was a black man from Jamaica. He had struggled from the beginning, both because he had trouble with the rapid-fire English of these Easterner instructors, and because he apparently wasn't very literate. Some of the instructors spoke very quickly indeed. I was working pretty hard to follow it all even as a native speaker of English. I would have liked to help the Jamaican, the more so because my master's degree was in TESOL (Teaching English to Speakers of Other Languages) and I could see what was going wrong for him. I was drawn to him because he reminded me of people I had met during my year as an English teacher in Africa. Just looking at him made me feel as though I had come home. Africa wasn't home for a white woman, of course, and never could be, but I had felt the pull of it, as did so many people from Europe or the US who went there. I sometimes thought that I would never feel at home anywhere else, and a quote from Isak Dinesen's *Out of Africa* would come to me:

"You woke up in the morning and thought: 'Here I am, where I ought to be.'"

I talked with the Jamaican, after I heard that he was planning to quit, and came to understand that he had taken in very little of the information that was being given out. I concluded, sadly, that there just wasn't enough time to tutor him in all he needed to know; it would take weeks rather than hours.

The most grievous part of the whole situation for this man was that he had been working an awful job washing out the insides of tankers and would now have to return to it. It saddened me that he had tried to improve life for himself and his family but couldn't get enough help to do it. The man, himself, had a humble attitude about his failure, which grieved me even more, somehow. He wasn't angry with the teachers but said, instead, that he had let himself down. "I didn't practice my reading enough," he said.

There were half a dozen driving instructors for the class. My instructor, Mike, was the head of the team, a big man with a curly beard and thick jowls. At first, I rather liked him. Two of us went out with him on the second day for our first Mueller driving lesson.

Mike drove first, demonstrating some aspects of what he wanted from us. For example, students were required, not only to put the truck into neutral before starting the engine, but also to prove it to the instructor, whether he was in the truck or out of it, by flicking the low/high range switch up and down. This made a popping noise that was audible to the instructor's trained ear even if he was outside of the truck. The low/high switch was normally used to go from fifth to sixth gear or vice versa, that is, the switch was in the lower position for the first five gears, but to shift to sixth gear the driver first flicked the switch up, then hit the clutch, pulled the gearshift lever into neutral, hit the clutch again and pulled the gearshift all the way over and down into what would have been first with the switch down.

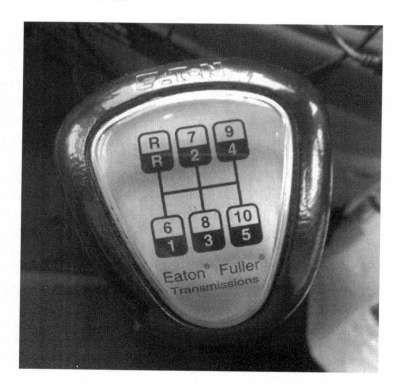

3. Gearshift pattern

One of my early problems with shifting was that I would find myself trying to shift from sixth gear, say, into ninth rather than fourth because I had forgotten to put the switch down. Or I would try to start out from a dead stop in eighth rather than third gear, again because I had forgotten the switch.

We were required to put the truck into first gear before shutting off the engine. This made trouble for me later, once I was out with Johnny, when I absentmindedly left the truck in first gear. Johnny wanted it left in neutral and noticed that it wasn't when he started the truck. We always stepped on the clutch before starting the engine, so it didn't really matter, but of course Johnny noticed. I wondered whether it wasn't wiser to leave the truck in gear before shutting it down, as it gave one more line of defense against the truck rolling, but I switched over to Johnny's way, holding a mental reservation about the matter, but deciding not to decide what I would do when and if I got my own truck until I learned more about it.

At this first lesson, Mike announced that he was going to drive us, the two students, by remote control. This was exactly what happened. I went first, and by following Mike's instructions I didn't have any major problems. I already knew how to shift, so after a few circuits of the driving range we went out into traffic. Mike's voice came at every decision point, reminding me to steer wide at corners, telling me when to shift up or down.

When the other student had his turn, he shifted beautifully, never once grinding the gears. He seemed comfortable driving, something that certainly wasn't true of me at this point. Mike, too, noticed the difference immediately. Upon questioning, the student admitted to having a CDL B license (for slightly smaller trucks than semis) and lots of driving experience. Sadly, he washed out of the school a week later for defying one of Mike's commands and almost wrecking a truck, or so I heard.

Starting with day three of the program, I spent two and a half hours of every day driving the streets and surrounding highways of the Pennsylvania city with Mike. I began to have troubles of my own with him. The school's procedure was to ease off on telling the student what to do bit by bit, in order to see if the student would

33

still do the right things. Unfortunately, Mike added to this by yelling at me whenever I didn't do something he thought I should have.

After a particularly difficult morning, when I was constantly on the verge of: a) crying, b) quitting, or c) telling Mike exactly what I thought of him, we pulled over to the curb at a coffee shop and Mike suggested a 15-minute break. I sat outside on a curb alternately praying and sulking, when an idea came to me.

"Listen," I said to Mike as soon as we got back into the truck, "if you aren't going to tell me what to do, I'm going to talk it myself. Then you can tell me if I say something wrong. Do you think that might work better?"

"Try it," replied Mike.

This new technique made the lessons bearable again. I still had problems sometimes. On two separate occasions I started a left turn so late that I couldn't complete it. Mike had to hop out of the truck and stop traffic so that I could back the truck up enough to get around the turn without running up onto the far curb.

But on the whole, the technique worked. I just kept up a running patter. "This is a right-hand turn so I'm putting on the turn signal 100 feet away and slowing down to 20 for sixth gear ... now 10 for fourth gear. I'm going to start my turn halfway across the intersection ... I'm looking in the right-hand mirror to make sure I've gone far enough to start the turn ... now I'm looking in the left-hand mirror to make sure there aren't any cars. I'm turning all the way into the right-hand lane and looking in the mirror to make sure the trailer is clearing the curb," etc., etc.

One of the harder things to remember to do every single time was what is called high-siding a curve. With any articulated vehicle the back tires don't follow the same path as the front tires on a curve or turn.

How much difference there is between the two sets of tracks depends on how sharp the curve is. A lot of effort has to be spent "driving the trailer," as it's usually called. In other words, the tractor has to be driven in such a way that the trailer doesn't run over curbs or crash into lampposts or other obstacles. High-siding a curve means running the tractor tires along the outside edge of the curve so that the trailer tires will stay within the inner lane lines.

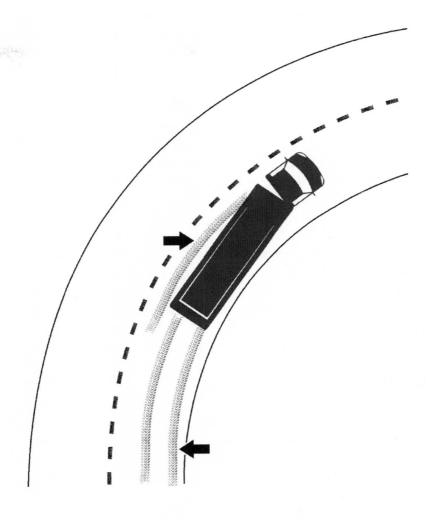

4. Diagram of off-tracking

Mike taught me that I had to look at the trailer tires at the beginning, middle and end of any sharp curve or turn, and this became part of my "spiel," as I called off what I was doing or was about to do.

I became less and less fond of Mike's smart-aleck manner. One day, as we were approaching an underpass that was labeled "14 feet," I mentioned that the sign said there was enough clearance.

"How do you know the sign's right?" asked Mike.

"Well, I don't, but a truck just came through from the other direction, so I assume it's safe."

"Do you know what you're doing when you assume?" asked Mike, in a deceptively sweet tone of voice.

I knew that one, so I snapped back, "Making an 'ass' out of 'u' and 'me.'"

After an interval, and once I had gotten control of my temper, I asked, "How *am* I supposed to know that the underpass has enough clearance if I can't trust signs or another truck coming through?"

"Look at it."

"I can't tell by looking, for goodness' sake!"

But backing was the real nightmare. Even at my North Carolina CDL school I had had a lot of trouble with that – and the school was only trying to teach us one very limited maneuver – a specific angled backing from one place on the school's dirt track into a set of cones. The setup was always the same.

Even so, it was not often that I could do it. I had spent hours of my driving school lessons practicing. Sometimes the instructor would just get out of the truck and sit in his car while I tried to work out a reliable method for myself.

Part of the problem was trying to back an articulated vehicle. Compared to backing a car it was necessary to do the opposite thing with the steering wheel. If you wanted the trailer to go backwards to the left you had to turn the steering wheel to the right. But if you already had a leftward angle between the cab and the trailer, then the only way the trailer was going to go would be to the left. Turning the steering wheel could only determine how sharply left the trailer would move. I found the total effect completely disorienting.

The problem had to do with a strange sort of dyslexia that I seemed to have. I wasn't dyslexic for anything to do with letters or reading, but when I looked in a side mirror the world just spun around until I didn't know which way was which.

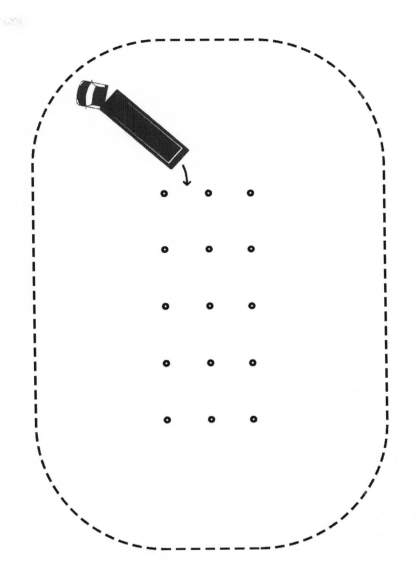

5. Diagram of CDL school's backing setup

It reminded me of my first visit to Africa, to a country that had kept the British practice of driving on the left after achieving independence. I had gone to visit my oldest daughter who was serving in the Peace Corps in Malawi. What I found was that I absolutely could not cross the street safely in Malawi's capital city of Lilongwe. I would try to look "right-left-right" instead of "left-right-left" as at home. Even so, I'd wind up somehow looking the wrong way. In the end I had to take my daughter's arm whenever we crossed a busy street and say, "Please, don't let me get run over!" This backing problem gave me the same feeling of frustration – trying to do the opposite thing but finding that I wasn't, somehow.

At the CDL school in North Carolina I just barely passed the backing portion of the CDL test. I got out of the truck twice, which I should not have done, and it was probably only because the examiner was paid by the school that I squeaked through. I found out later that paid examiners were, on the whole, quite corrupt and often passed students whom they really should have failed. Even at that I lost five out of the six points allowed. I had to pull forward once to try again and I never did back in far enough.

So backing was a nightmare, except for straight-line backing, which I could do fairly well, although I was terribly, dreadfully slow at it.

Things didn't improve much at Mueller's driving school. The school held a backing lab on the first Saturday. There were five stations set up around the driving range, each with a different instructor. The stations replicated the setup at an ideal loading dock, in that there was lots of space in front of the line of trailers. But the trailers were parked close together. Great precision was needed to back into an empty space between two of them.

Each student would go once around the course, meaning five opportunities to try backing. The basic technique was called alley dock or "12-9" backing, using the clock for orientation. The setup for it was done by driving up at right angles to the hole where the trailer was to be put. We were taught to "clear" the hole, that is, stop and look down the empty space between the two other trailers, making sure that there weren't any overhanging obstacles or sharp objects on the ground. Then we drove forward beyond the hole almost two trailers in width, turned the truck sharply to the right until "12 o'clock" (90 degrees from its previous position), then sharply left, back to "9 o'clock," or, in other words, the former orientation, except that the trailer, which always lagged behind, would be left at an intermediate angle, ideally about 45 degrees and lined up in such a way that it could be backed into the space between the two trailers.

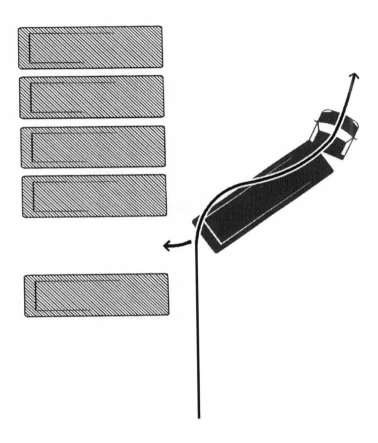

6. Diagram of alley dock or "12-9" backing

It was a complicated procedure even after that, trying to get the trailer headed exactly into the hole and, and the same time, get the tractor worked around until it was straight in front of the trailer. Only then could the trailer be backed straight into position between the other two trailers.

This never happened for me. For one thing, I almost always

turned the steering wheel the wrong way first. Or I'd turn it the right way but not far enough. The trailer took eight or ten feet to react to whatever I had done and by then I had usually despaired and done the opposite thing, which then caused trouble after the first reaction finally occurred, and also left me not knowing which of my actions had caused which result. It was a nightmare!

But what really finished me off, as far as this particular lab was concerned, was that each of the five instructors at the driving range had his or her own favorite method of backing – and they were all different. I would finish at one station, having paid very careful attention to the comments the instructor for that station made. But when I moved on to the next station, I would find the new instructor telling me something completely different.

The worst was one of the women. I set up for the maneuver, started backing up, and immediately was stopped by the woman, who walked up to the window and demanded angrily, "Why are you doing it that way?"

"That's the way Dan told me to," I replied, giving the name of the previous station's instructor.

"I don't care what Dan told you. That's not the right way." Then the woman told me yet another way.

It reminded me of being sixteen, just learning to drive a car, when five different people (my father, two instructors, one aunt and one uncle) each told me a different way to parallel park. Any one of the methods might have worked separately but trying to combine them had led to disaster every time. In the end I picked my uncle's method as making the most sense to me and worked with it until I got good at it.

I was immensely grateful that I didn't have this yelling woman for my regular instructor. According to one of her students, she issued angry orders for the whole two and a half hours of a lesson and was quick to accuse a student of defiance even when no defiance was intended. One of her students had quit and the other one, an older hillbilly-type man with long gray hair who always wore striped Oshkosh overalls, was struggling, determined not to let her drive him from the program but suffering daily from her temper. He seemed like such a nice man, planning to team drive with his nephew, who also was in the class, after they both learned to drive. I hope they made it through, but never found out.

Much of the time that wasn't spent driving was spent in class. After the first morning of filling out forms, other days were spent on such topics as logging, route planning and safety.

Our instructors were experienced and knowledgeable. The handouts were well designed too. One of the major strengths of the program was the use of various acronyms to help drivers remember procedures.

The funniest one, I thought, was GOAL – Get Out And Look – before backing a trailer. The alternative, we were told, was GOALS – Get Out And Look Stupid – after hitting something. Another one, used daily, was FCOB. Free Case Of Beer was the way to remember it, but it really stood for Fuel, Coolant, Oil and Belts, a list of the most minimal check to be done before driving a truck.

Another one that I found useful was for coupling or uncoupling a trailer. It was PAL for coupling: Pin, Airlines, Landing gear. In other words, first you backed under the trailer to lock the kingpin into place in the fifth wheel, then you connected the two air lines and the electrical plug, called a "pigtail," to supply compressed air and electricity to the trailer and finally you wheeled up the landing gear – the supports that held the trailer up when it wasn't coupled to a tractor.

For uncoupling the procedure was reversed: LAP. First the landing gear was put down, then the air lines and pigtail disconnected, then the kingpin release pulled so the tractor could be driven out from under the trailer. By using these mnemonics, the trailer would never get dropped before the landing gear was down and the air lines would never get ripped out either.

I was impressed with these acronyms, which made it so easy to remember necessary procedures and, above all, to stay safe and keep from making big mistakes.

Logging was the most difficult subject. We spent time every day studying how to log correctly. I had already studied this in CDL school, of course, but welcomed more instruction as I certainly hadn't mastered it. It surprised me initially to learn that truckers have to account for all of their time, filling out a logbook whether or not they are working on a particular day. The logbooks have four lines. All of a trucker's time can be divided into: 1) off duty, 2) sleeper berth, 3) driving, or 4) on duty, not driving.

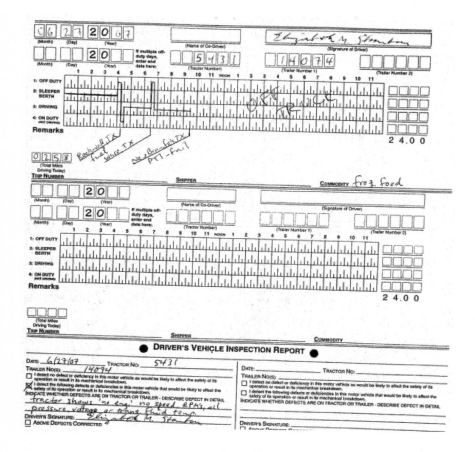

7. Logbook page

What makes logging so complicated is a set of federal rules called HOS (Hours Of Service) regulations. Three rules apply simultaneously:

1) A trucker may work no more than 70 hours in eight days.

2) After working 14 hours a trucker must rest for ten hours, or
3) After driving 11 hours a trucker must rest for ten hours, whichever comes first.

There are a lot of ramifications to these rules. Calculating how many hours a driver has left to drive involves figuring out how far away from the 14-hour limit one is and comparing that to how many hours are left of the 11-hour limit.

In effect, from the moment of coming off line one or two of the logbook, a 14-hour clock starts. During these 14 hours a trucker tries to drive for 11 hours. The extra three hours are used for fueling, pre-trip inspections, deliveries, pickups, all of which have a 15-minute minimum log time with paper logbooks. Meals, and even naps come out of this same three hours, but you can't have much of a nap.

These rules had been in place for several years, replacing a more liberal set of rules which I didn't ever study, but which apparently had allowed truckers to drive for five hours, rest for five, then drive another five. The current rules were pretty brutal. Driving would be much easier with a nice long nap in the middle. Driving 11 hours out of 14 was grueling. And keeping track of the whole thing was a challenge too.

The "Fairy Godmother Department" of the federal government had thrown truckers one bone in the form of what was called a "34-hour restart." The hours toward the 70-hours in eight days provision could be reset to zero by taking 34 hours off. There was a recap page on the cover of logbooks where those hours could be tracked.

It was no wonder we needed to spend some time on logging every day. The whole thing was so complex that I wondered how people with only a high school education, or less in some cases, coped with it. I was having a hard-enough time, even with a background in economics and lots of accounting classes.

Day of mo.	(Total of lines 3 & 4 on graph)	A Total hours on-duty last 7 days -OR- Total hours on-duty since restart	B Hours available tomorrow 70 hours minus col. A	C Total hours on-duty last 8 days -OR- Total hours on-duty since restart
(Last 7 Days of preceding month)		7 days	8 days	
		S.3		
		7.5		
1	10.0	22.5	47.5	22.5
2	9.25	31.75	38.25	31.75
3	8.75	40.5	29.5	40.5
4	7.75	48.25	21.75	48.75
5	9.0	57.25	12.75	57.25
6	0	57.25		
7	7.0		6.0	9.0
8	9.25		51.75	17.25
9		.5	43.5	26.5
10	8.5	35.0	35.0	55.0
11	8.0	43.0	27.0	43.0
12	10.5	53.5	16.5	53.5
13	10.25	63.75	6.25	63.75
14	6.75	61.0	9.0	70.0
15	10.5	67.25	—	71.5
16	5.75	59.75	10.25	69.00
17	4.75	56.0	14.0	64.5
18	7.75	55.75	14.25	63.75
19	10.0	55.25	14.75	65.75
20	10.25	55.25	14.75	65.50
21	4.75	53.75	16.25	60.00
22	5.0	48.25	21.75	58.75
23	3.25	46.75	23.25	52.50
24	4.25	45.25	24.75	50.00
25	6.5	44.0	26.0	51.75
26	7.75	41.75	28.25	51.75
27				
28				
29				

SUMMARY SHEET

Month _____

If you operate on the period of 70 hours in 8 days, use the summary sheet on the left.

The figures 1 to 31 represent calendar days, and entries should be made for each day -- even when driver does not work. If no work is performed, enter zero (0) in first column and compute other columns as explained below.

70 HOURS – 8 DAYS

Enter the number of working hours (on duty & driving) for each of the last seven days of the preceding month in the first seven spaces under the column headed "Hours Worked Today". Enter in the first space under Column A the Total of the number of hours worked during the last 7 days. Subtract the figure entered in Column A from 70 hours and enter this figure – hours available for tomorrow – in Column B.

At the end of each day, complete the first three columns adjacent to the days of month in the same manner as explained above. Total the number of hours worked during the last 8 days and enter in Column C. If any number in Column C exceeds 70, no driving should have been done. Any driving that was done is a violation and should be circled for easy identification.

34-hour restart: If you took 34 consecutive hours off duty, you have 70 hours available again. You would then begin your totaling on the day of the restart and not go back the full 7 or 8 days.

DRIVERS ONLY

Day of mo.	Today (Total of lines 3 & 4 on graph)	A Total hours on-duty last 7 days -OR- Total hours on-duty since restart	B Hours available tomorrow 70 hours minus col. A	C Total hours on-duty last 8 days -OR- Total hours on-duty since restart
		7 days	8 days	
1				
2				
3				
4				
5				
6				
7				
8				
9				
10				
11				
12				
13				
14				
15				
16				
17				
18				
19				
20				
21				
22				
23				
24				
25				
26				
27				
28				
29				

8. Recap page

Truckers who had been driving long enough to have operated under both sets of rules thought that the new rules were unreasonable and hampering. There were even people who had quit trucking because they couldn't operate under the new system. I had been thinking about logging for several months now and had come across a survey in a trucking magazine which claimed that 66 percent of truckers admitted to lying on their logs. That seemed awfully high. Most people were more honest than that, weren't they?

I had determined to be totally honest myself, but wondered if, perhaps, there was more to it than I knew... As usual, Mueller taught us very thoroughly. I came out of the classes feeling competent to log – if only I could remember it all!

It was Mueller's classes that gave me the solution to my worst fear in driving. Several times at CDL school I had "missed" a gear and found myself flying down the road in neutral, unable to get the truck back into any gear. Every time it happened, whichever instructor I had for that session eventually was able to reach over and pull the truck into a gear or else tell me which gear to put it in, but I was terrified. It seemed so dangerous, and probably illegal, to be coasting down the road in neutral. And it drove me to the verge of panic, turning me from an unsafe beginner into a driver very likely to have an accident within seconds.

But Mueller had the solution to the problem. On only the second or third day of class we were given a list to memorize of gears and speeds for 1300 RPM's. The way it worked was this. If you found yourself out of gear, you looked down at your speedometer. Suppose it said 40 mph. The gear associated with 40 mph was ninth. So if you revved the engine to 1300 RPM's you could put the transmission into ninth gear. Or suppose you were out of gear and looked down to find that you were going 25 mph. The gear associated with 25 mph was seventh. Again, you revved the engine to 1300 RPM's but this time you put it into seventh.

I knew immediately that this was the answer to my problem. I didn't just memorize the list, I internalized it, reciting it over and over until I was absolutely sure. What a relief!

The driving simulators were as impressive as everything else at Mueller, though they were still a bit temperamental – not totally reliable. There were four of them, big machines like glorified arcade games, but more complex, involving several computers per simulator.

It was possible to practice all sorts of maneuvers, from something as simple as shifting to something as complicated as skidding, without actually risking life, limb or a real truck. Nothing more serious than embarrassment or humiliation could happen on the simulators.

45

There was one exercise where we "got lost" in a suburb and found ourselves on a residential street – where a semi had no business to be – needing to find the way back to a truck route. For this exercise the students had to ask passersby for directions, which really meant interviewing the instructors who were running the lab.

Another exercise had us practice weaving around in a parking lot, going between various imaginary trucks and cars that looked as though they were parked there.

Then there was the highway obstacle course. It simulated road hazards that a student might encounter, ranging from bears and moose to accident scenes and construction, complete with flashing lights and blocked-off lanes. There were also slow-moving construction vehicles, cars ("four-wheelers" in truckers' parlance) zipping here and there, and debris in the road. On this one the simulator went bad on a couple of the students, including me. We found ourselves running off the road and crashing for no reason whatsoever.

The instructors were amazed, and all gathered around the machine, making remarks like, "Look at that!" "She didn't do anything!" "Wow!" The machines quite often needed fixing, apparently. They had cost more than a quarter of a million dollars each.

We practiced straight line backing on a virtual plain, marked with lane lines and a tree to show its back edge. Most interesting, perhaps, was trying out a virtual skid pad where we tried to learn how to react to the truck going into a skid. I turned out to be rather good at it on the simulator, though I hoped I would *never* have to put what I had learned into practice.

The last exercise was driving a mountain road in snowy, icy conditions. I was hauling a virtual tanker. The speed recommendations for tankers were even lower than for a normal semi; where a semi would slow down to 15 or 20 mph on a curve posted at 25, a tanker needed to go no more than 10 mph because of the possible sloshing of liquid inside the tank, which could make the whole rig roll over on a turn. I played it cautious, just like the middle-aged woman I was, and did the whole course in third gear. I didn't slide on the ice, even, much less crash, but in real life would probably have had a mile-long tail of angry four-wheelers by the end of the route. In the simulation I merely ran out of time before finishing.

The most curious aspect of this exercise was that I was ninety percent sure I recognized the route as being on US-24 in Colorado, west of Colorado Springs. I had driven it a couple of times as a scenic way to get from Colorado Springs to Salida, Colorado where a friend lived.

Besides driving lessons, classroom instruction and the simulator there were also a few labs, held at the driving range. These were rather difficult because temperatures were hovering in the 20's all day every day. We had been advised to bring insulated coveralls, but I had priced them at $100, which would have been hard to afford. Also, they were unisex garments, meaning that in order to buy them big enough to fit around my hips I would have had to buy a size suitable for a six-foot man – and I am only five three. So I decided that my wool long underwear would have to do. And it worked very well. Most of the students didn't have coveralls. The few who did were comfortable in the cold weather – but so was I. Besides my wonderful merino wool long johns, I wore a Shetland wool sweater, wool socks and a wool hat, along with my more usual jeans, turtleneck, polar fleece and snow boots.

A chilled group of us huddled around a chilled instructor listening to explanations of pre-trip inspections, for example, then practicing the Free Case Of Beer (Fuel, Coolant, Oil, Belts) minimal inspection which the company required before moving a vehicle.

One of the two lab instructors was a young man whose behavior mystified me considerably: he kept turning aside and drooling onto the frozen ground every few minutes. It made me wonder if he had an obscure medical or dental problem of some sort. After the second session with this instructor, I asked one of the other students, an older man, if he understood what on earth all that drooling was about and learned, to my surprise, that the young man was chewing tobacco. For one thing, there didn't seem to be any chewing involved. For another, I had always thought that people chewing tobacco spat rather than drooled. I had even imagined them spitting great distances with accuracy and panache, possibly into spittoons. It was a disillusionment.

I thought the most interesting lab was the demonstration of how to slide tandems, as the double axles of a trailer are called. Both lab instructors took part in this; it's much easier to do with two people. The box of a trailer can be moved along a track called a slider rail while the tandems stay still, creating more or less distance between the front of the trailer and its back axles. When the back axles are even with the back of the trailer, the stability of the trailer's back end is maximized, valuable for when a 3,000 lb. forklift is moving back and forth from loading dock to trailer or vice versa, carrying a one-ton pallet.

Many companies where drivers pick up or deliver loads require drivers to slide the tandems all the way to the back before they will load or unload a trailer. On the other hand, it's not really possible to drive the truck with the tandems all the way back, both because it's illegal (each state has what is called a "bridge law," which specifies the maximum legal distance between the kingpin and back tires) and because it increases the turning radius of the truck and makes turns, especially on city streets, difficult or impossible, like the difference in turning radius between a small car and a stretch limo, only more so.

Driving with the tandems all the way forward isn't ideal either. It makes the ride maximally rough as the trailer bounces up and down. Also, loads in the trailer have to be balanced to comply with legal limits. These are 12,000 lbs. for the tractor's front (single) axle and 34,000 lbs. each for the double axles of the back of the tractor and the back of the trailer. The legal limit for all of these put together is thus 80,000 lbs.

It is quite possible to have a load that is illegal because one of the double axles is at more than 34,000 lbs. even though the total weight of the vehicle is well under 80,000 lbs. Loading a trailer properly is an art. A partial remedy for a poorly loaded trailer is to slide the tandems. Sliding them one way puts more weight on the front (or "drive") axles; the other way takes weight off the drives, anywhere between 250 and 500 pounds per hole, depending on the distance between the holes on the track.

There are several systems in use and at least three different locking mechanisms for the pins that hold the back axles in place. None of them works well in terms of sliding the tandems, but some are worse than others. Also, the pins tend to get wedged in the holes of the slider rail, making it impossible to get them to retract so the tandems can be slid.

9. Slider rail and tandem pins

This was my first opportunity to see it done, though I had studied the theory of sliding tandems in CDL classes. The two instructors were both very experienced (they sometimes took time off from instructing to drive as a team) and very strong. And this trailer was cooperative, so they were able to demonstrate sliding the tandems all the way back and all the way forward without any difficulty. It was amazing to see the box of the trailer moving 10 or 12 feet while the back axles stayed still. Until I studied trucking, I had never known that such a thing was possible.

The instructors also gave advice on how one person could slide tandems alone, some of which I didn't understand, but one part of which, the idea of dropping something on the ground by the driver's door as a marker in order to be able to estimate how far the trailer had moved, I stored away in my mind for later use.

Driving lessons continued. We went farther afield each day, exploring the State roads around the Pennsylvania city extensively. It was interesting to drive in the country – I had never seen so many farms. It was an ugly time of year, though, with the gray sky, leafless trees and empty fields. They were as bleak as death, not giving any promise of the rebirth of spring.

The tanker which Matt and I took turns hauling now had water in it. We got to experience the sloshing effect which comes from stopping too abruptly. In a quick stop the truck comes to a stop before the liquid in the tanker does. Then the liquid sloshes forward. It feels like being rear-ended. You stop and then, a perceptible moment later, the surge of water hits the front of the tank with a bang. In extreme cases this phenomenon is capable of shoving the truck out into an intersection.

I was told that most companies wouldn't train people to drive tankers until they had several years of experience with regular semis. This made more and more sense to me.

Worse, we had been shown several films now, in the special tanker classes to which Matt and I were sometimes sent. The films showed nightmare industrial complexes, science-fiction-looking cities of concrete smokestacks, metal pipes and bright lights where tankers had to deliver loads of dangerous chemicals. Some of the loads were "heated in transit," meaning that they were kept hot. These were substances that would solidify if they cooled to a normal air temperature.

Tanker students were required to wear chemical gloves and a hard hat whenever they were working around the tanker. The hard hat wasn't so bad, though it generally fell off if I looked up, but the gloves didn't fit me. They weren't available in smaller sizes, at least not at Mueller's school, so the ends of the gloves' fingers stuck out a good inch beyond the ends of my fingers. This made it impossible for me to do anything that required manual dexterity – pulling the ring to drain water from the air tanks of the tractor, for instance.

Now we began to learn some of the procedures involved in transferring liquids into or out of a tanker. With some of the chemicals a single drop hitting the ground constituted a reportable chemical spill. Drivers were required to duct tape hose joints – while wearing chemical gloves! I had trouble enough using duct tape even under the best of conditions, i.e. with scissors and without gloves that stuck out an inch beyond the ends of my fingers.

Then, too, the idea of driving into one of the brightly lit "works" – which looked to me like something out of Dante's *Inferno* – and piping a whole tankful of hot goop into a tanker while wearing a protective suit, boots, gloves (possibly duct taped to the sleeves of the suit) *and* goggles *and* a hard hat with the face shield down made me quail. I wore glasses, but didn't yet have safety glasses, so I had to wear all three things: glasses, goggles and face shield. In the brief minutes that I had tried out this magic combination, I had noticed that the goggles had a very great tendency to fog up, leaving me pretty much blind.

What if I couldn't see? Or what if it was 95° outside and I had to wear all that protective clothing? Was I strong enough at an unfit middle-aged 53 to do this job? Or what if I made a mistake which led to a chemical spill? Some of the procedures had 30 or more steps which had to be done in the right order. And there were half a dozen different procedures. It seemed all too likely to me that I would eventually do something out of order.

One of the movies was of a man who had not bothered with protective clothing one day – doing a task he had done a hundred times before. He had been burned over two-thirds or three-quarters of his body!

As the last day, "graduation" day, approached, I became less and less confident at the prospect of driving a tanker. Matt was an ideal candidate. He had decades of experience working in industrial complexes and was pretty well educated about chemicals and engineering procedures. He couldn't shift very well yet, but I was sure that he would soon learn. The chemical gloves fitted him!

As I mentioned earlier, all of us had to pass three tests in order to graduate: a road test, a backing test and a written test. I had already passed the road test, Mike told me. And I wasn't worried about the written test. The only real question was whether I would get a hundred percent or whether they would manage to dock me a few points.

But the backing test! Mike spent the entire lesson time of the next-to-the-last day working with me on backing. And I just couldn't get it. The world spun whenever I looked in the mirror, I didn't know whether to turn the steering wheel left or right, or for how long, and I always wound up in the same position relative to the hole I was trying to put the trailer in, that is, short of it. Finally I decided that it might be instructive to be sure that I didn't end up short of the hole again, so I deliberately turned the steering wheel the wrong way and held it there. This turned out to be the worst disaster of all, according to Mike, because I went past the front of the trailer and found myself with the trailer bent at the opposite angle. Mike immediately stopped me and exclaimed that what I had done was very dangerous and might well have caused me to hit one of the trailers I was trying to back between. The reasons for this were obscure to me but I obediently went back to the other method, with the same result of always coming up short.

At the end of the session Mike pointed out, as if I didn't know, that I was doing the same thing over and over and getting the same result. "Kind of like bashing your head against a wall repeatedly, isn't it?" he asked. Then he told me that the next day I would have to back in correctly three times in a row to pass the backing test. That was clearly impossible.

That night, taking into consideration the movies about nightmare industrial complexes, the gloves and the impending backing test, I decided that I had better quit. I took all the company's training materials with me when I rode the shuttle bus the next morning. When Mike came for me, remarking that the first thing on the docket was to give me the backing test, I replied, "What's on the docket for this morning is that I'm quitting."

"Oh, that's what's on the docket, is it?" he asked, rather snidely I thought.

"So, would you please help me to do it in the least irresponsible way?" I asked.

He led me into the administrative part of the building and down a hallway to a small conference room, not saying one word to me about my decision or anything else. "Wait here," he ordered, pointing into the conference room. Then he walked away.

I sat down and waited. After about ten minutes the man in charge of training came in. I had seen him before – he had given several speeches to the class and had conducted one feedback sort of meeting. He had struck me as being a nice man, smart and competent too. We were able to talk frankly. The man said he was sorry I was quitting and asked if moving out of tankers would change my decision. I pointed out that tankers were easier to back than dry van trailers, and yet I had no chance of passing the backing test, even in a tanker.

At that point he accepted the inevitable, thanked me for not just sneaking out of the motel in the middle of the night as many people did, and for returning all the materials, which I was required to do anyway. I said good-bye to the tanker teacher, giving him a copy of a "New Yorker" article about a "tanker yanker," as they are called, which I thought might interest him. The tanker teacher was very nice, shook my hand, and expressed the hope that I would be back. I replied that I would certainly consider it if I ever learned to back because I thought this would be a good company to work for.

Then I was free! It had been a long almost two weeks of 12-hour days. It felt as though a large weight had dropped off me, even though I didn't know what I'd do next. The immediate future was fixed though: drive back to North Carolina and start looking for another job. And at least I didn't owe Mueller any money, though I felt a bit guilty about that. I had had some excellent training for free. Maybe someday I could pay them back, or go to work for them...

I had to wait around for half an hour until the motel's shuttle came at its regularly scheduled time, but then was soon back at the motel. It seemed like no time at all before I was on my way back to North Carolina, not even calling the family with whom I lived until I reached a rest area in West Virginia.

CHAPTER 3

Orientation Flashback
(March 26-30)

Still waiting for Johnny to come back to Reno, I remembered the more recent events of the last week and orientation with Alan King Associates. After returning from the abortive Mueller training I applied for jobs with several other companies and was accepted by this one. My plane had landed in Wisconsin, just a little over a week previously, on a day that was surprisingly warm for being near the end of March – 80-some degrees.

I was to take a shuttle van to a motel in a town near Alan's corporate headquarters. The van was packed. I had to share a three-person bench seat with two men who were even fatter than I. I felt squeezed and a bit claustrophobic, as well as not being able to hear very well because of the noise of the shuttle van's engine.

I tempered this unpleasant hour-long ride with my usual practice of reading two books chapter for chapter, alternating this with enjoying the Wisconsin scenery. It was a long time since I had been in Wisconsin, probably more than 25 years, I thought. As I had lived in Arizona for 12 of the intervening years, I found the beginning of spring with all the trees leafing out to be a beautiful sight.

The shuttle dropped us off at a nice motel. I was given one bed in a double room, shared with a woman of about my own age who had already arrived. We enjoyed chatting. This woman, Bess, was a more advanced student than I but would be sent out with a trainer for a week or two because she had less than a year of experience.

The first morning of orientation was nerve-racking in the extreme. There were twenty-five or so new hires, most of them men of experience. I was one of four women. After a welcoming speech, we were given physicals and drug tests. Anyone who didn't pass both of these tests was sent home.

Probably because the stakes were so high, the situation so stressful, the six or eight of us who had blood pressure issues found ourselves seeing numbers higher than we had ever seen before when our blood pressures were taken. We were sent outside to sit down for fifteen minutes or so and calm down, then had better readings the second time around.

There was also an awful test involving a plastic milk crate loaded with weights. We had to lift it down from a chest-high shelf to the ground, then back up to the shelf fifteen times. The first five times the crate contained 25 pounds of weights, the second five times 50 pounds, the third five times 75 pounds.

Seventy-five pounds was more weight than I had ever tried to lift, other than, perhaps, a really upset 10-year-old child? The woman doing the test was as helpful as she could be. She couldn't let me off the test but told me exactly how to position myself for lifting, then critiqued each lift, warning me not to let my back get involved, but to lift with my legs alone.

Somehow, I passed the test, though I was almost crippled with leg pain when I woke up the next morning. I could hardly walk. The other three women of this orientation group were in much the same condition. One of the men explained to us that it was lactic acid buildup and that a hot bath would be a good thing, but the pain would ease up over time.

I also made it through the driving test, which happened after lunch. Those of us remaining, which was most of us, were photographed for ID badges.

I was impressed by this company's organization. First thing in the morning, upon being herded into the orientation room, we had each found a name tag on the table in front of our assigned seat. Each name tag classified us as either "student," "advanced student," or "experienced driver."

Next to each name tag, was a brand-new green canvas briefcase with the company's logo painted on it in gold letters. The briefcases were full of interesting and useful things: a pen, a highlighter and a key ring, each with the company's logo. There were also the company manual, a list of authorized fuel stops, a pad of trip report forms, trip envelopes, trip book, logbook, and a ruler for drawing straight lines in the logbooks. There were paperback copies of the official hazmat book and the FMCSR, (the Federal regulations book), a packet of T-cheks (used to get advances or to pay for company-reimbursed expenses such as getting the trailer unloaded), a short book of procedures. It was all very well thought out.

The second and third days of orientation were spent watching movies and having classes to learn about Alan's ways of doing things. There was a session on how to run the three or four different models of reefers that Alan used. There were classes on payroll, logging, truck maintenance. It was something like the Mueller school, but much shorter, smaller in scope — the difference between orientation and a driving school. We were already supposed to know how to do these things. This was just to orient us to this company's ways of doing them.

The heads of different departments took turns coming to teach the group of us. The most entertaining speaker was Chip Walsh, currently the Driver Trainer Coordinator, but formerly a driver himself, with more than thirty years of driving experience. He was a man of medium height with a large beer belly and a slight lisp, who really knew what he was talking about and was able to present what he had to say in a humorous way.

For example, he talked about the importance of not swerving to try to miss an animal such as a deer, pointing out that the consequences of hitting a deer were much less severe than what happened if a truck rolled or went off the road into a ditch. It was better to hit the animal squarely and keep control of the truck.

He added that if a truck was wrecked over a deer incident, there had better be blood and fur on that truck somewhere, to show that the driver hadn't swerved, as deer were notorious liars. If the company went looking for a deer that had almost been hit, the probability was that the whole herd would deny any involvement whatsoever!

Everything Chip said was highly relevant and most of it was new to me. He posed the problem to us of what to do if someone passed you then cut back in too soon, in such a way that you found yourself tailgating the vehicle that had just passed. The class as a whole seemed to think slowing down was the answer. And what if a whole series of people did it, one after another? Slow down and practically grind to a halt?

"No," said Chip, quite surprisingly. "If they've passed you they are going faster than you are, so you just keep your speed up and wait for them to pull away, which they soon will." That made sense.

After attending classes all day Wednesday and most of Thursday, the experienced drivers were given trucks and dispatched to pick up loads.

The two groups of students, eight of us in all, had an extra session Thursday afternoon to learn about our trainers. I had already met Johnny, so I just hung around. On Friday we spent most of the day at a local community college, for skid pad training. This turned out to be very worthwhile. Besides skidding, we practiced weaving between cones, making sudden decisions, similar to the one to be made at weigh stations, to cut left or right when a green arrow lit up at the last moment, and getting back onto a road from a shoulder an inch or two lower than the road. Surprisingly, the best way to do this was to jerk the truck abruptly back up in order to minimize the chances of rolling it. We took a written test at the end of the day, then were given certificates of completion.

I formed the impression that this community college would have been a wonderful place to study truck driving. It had a semester-long program dedicated only to that, in addition to extra programs like skid-pad training. The teachers here really seemed to know how to teach.

CHAPTER 4

From Reno to Chicago
(April 3-6)

But back to Reno and waiting for Johnny after driving 44,000 pounds of raisins over Donner Pass. (It seemed such a picturesque thing to do, somehow.) Johnny was dropped off the next day by the same daughter who had picked him up. He had spent his day off signing papers and consulting with a lawyer about his impending second divorce. We spent much of the rest of the day driving to Salt Lake City. Johnny was doing something clever with our logbooks.

Logging for the trainer/trainee situation was different from the more straightforward solo driver situation which was all that I had studied. For one thing, Johnny was running two sets of logs: his and mine. All I ever did was write place names into the logs and sign them. Johnny drew the lines.

This sort of logging was different, not just from logging for a solo driver but even from the more normal team driver logging of two people taking turns driving, but I didn't know in what ways. For one thing, I didn't think Johnny was allowed to log that he was sleeping when I was driving, but I wasn't sure even about that.

So, I didn't know how Johnny was running the logs, but I didn't think it was worth trying to learn. I was so far away in time from being a trainer that if I ever became one, years in the future, I would worry about logging it then.

Moreover, Johnny belonged to the 66 percent of drivers who lied on logbooks. He sometimes tried to teach me aspects of how to do this, but I couldn't seem to take it in. It just confused me, and most of it would go against my conscience anyway.

The fundamentals seemed to be that fueling, toll booths and getting pulled over at a weigh station had to be logged accurately, because the company received information from those sources and checked them against the driver's logbook, but anything else was fair game. "Sliding hours" was a term Johnny used pretty often. It was all a matter of weighing probabilities. If we were to be involved in an accident, or even if the company just decided to do an audit, it was possible for them to figure out exactly where we had been at any given time. So Johnny was taking the risk of getting into big trouble.

It was all rather mysterious to me, but what he was doing now, logging the time we had spent in Reno as being in Salt Lake City, or vice versa, meant among other things that I had time to go out to dinner with my mother and youngest daughter in Salt Lake City. Johnny dropped me off across the street from a Village Inn restaurant, doing the most amazing "button hook" turn that I had ever seen to get into an Office Max parking lot. I felt terrible about inadvertently putting him into a position where he felt he had to make such a turn; I had really intended him to enter the parking lot by the second entrance, farther down the street, and had forgotten about the first entrance, near to the corner. Anyway, he succeeded at the difficult turn, only running the back tires of the trailer over the curb a little bit.

A button hook (or "jug handle") turn is used in tight situations when a normal turn would have no chance of getting the trailer around the corner without hitting the curb because of off-tracking.

Besides having dinner with my relatives, I also had time to go to a used bookstore in Salt Lake City, having run short of reading material. I was blessed to find five or six interesting books for a total price of only $12 and arrived back at the truck very content with my purchases.

Johnny professed himself to be amazed at the amount of reading I got through – and I was equally surprised to hear him say that, to his conscious knowledge he had never read a book outside of school. Never? I had trouble taking this in. I was a bookworm (bibliophile? bibliomaniac?) who had read every moment that I didn't have to do something else ever since I learned to read.

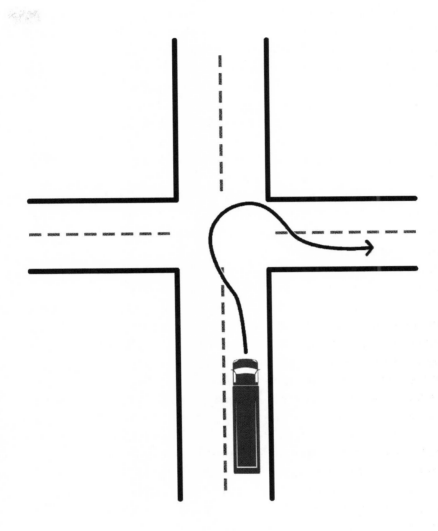

10. Diagram of a "buttonhook" or "jug handle" turn

Never to have read a book? It wasn't that he was illiterate or stupid. He seemed well able to handle the paperwork and other reading that went with the trucking job. He read newspapers and an occasional magazine article. For that matter he had graduated from high school and done a two-year associates degree at a community college, so he wasn't even uneducated. But not to read!

I had a friend, years before, who claimed never to have read a book. She had dropped out of school in the tenth grade, though. And eventually I found a book that interested her so much that she read it straight through and felt very proud and happy afterwards. I wondered idly if there might somewhere be a book that Johnny would read.

Reading was the joy of my life. As Anthony Trollope wrote:

"This habit of reading, I make bold to tell you, is your pass to the greatest, the purest, and the most perfect pleasure that God has prepared for His creatures. It lasts when all other pleasures fade. It will support you when all other recreations are gone. It will last until your death. It will make your hours pleasant to you as long as you live."

Even more, though, I treasured what Phyllis McGinley had written in her introduction to *The Secret Garden*, speaking of reading as a magic carpet that enabled a small girl growing up in Wyoming to know something about life in the 1800's on the moors of Yorkshire.

Most of the history that I knew came from reading, which had helped to fill in the gaps in a somewhat inadequate late 1960's high school education. Over the years I had been, in thought, to so many places and times. I knew something of the London blitz of WWII and what it was like to live through it as a child, or as an adult; I had read numerous, numerous books about life in England, whether poor, middle-class or rich, and from the points of view of a number of different decades. I had been to the outback of Australia, to Norway in the 1300's. The examples could probably have been multiplied a thousand-fold.

As a child I read so avidly partly to counter an unhappy childhood. Stories of happy families were my favorites or, more accurately, stories of unhappy children who eventually worked their problems out and became happy largely because of the kindness and reasonableness of one or more adults who came into their lives.

Johnny and I were opposites in almost every way, really. I loved books, foreign languages and classical music. Before my hearing loss I had played the cello and violin. I had often sung in church choirs. Johnny liked NASCAR races, basketball and amusement parks, especially the sort of ride that jerks you from 0 to 60 mph in three seconds flat! He reminded me of the fourth-grade boys I had taught one year in California in the way that he was so alert to his environment, always observant. Whereas I was not at all observant and rather often didn't notice a thing until I either tripped over it or banged my head on it.

This tendency caused me some trouble in driving a truck. The trick of sizing up a truck stop or delivery site, with a view to being able to leave it later on and get back to the highway, going in the right direction, was difficult for me. I also had to learn what I needed to look for as a trucker. I tended to be oblivious to various things that were crucial for truck drivers but uninteresting for drivers of cars, such as weigh station signs and low-hanging tree branches.

Remembering which side of the highway a truck stop fell on and the direction of the turn into it became matters of great importance. One night, Johnny parked at a truck stop after I had fallen asleep. The next morning, I had to drive the truck out while he slept, and found that I simply had no idea which direction to go. The freeway sign didn't give information about direction, just listed two different towns. I had never heard of either one of them. In the end I had to do a "flip" (taking an off-ramp, turning left, then left again onto the on-ramp for the other direction of travel) when I realized that I had inevitably guessed wrong. I hoped that Johnny hadn't noticed this from his place in the sleeper berth, but of course he had, and pointed out that the direction of the rising sun would have given me the information I needed!

It might be that how unobservant I was surprised Johnny quite as much as his not reading surprised me. One day, when I was beginning to notice black skid marks on the freeways and to realize that each set told a story, I mentioned some to Johnny – a long set of marks that eventually trailed off onto the shoulder of the road.

He agreed that the marks always told a story, then asked if they had been single or double, in other words, made by a car or a semi. And I couldn't tell him, although I had just seen them. A look crossed Johnny's face which told me that this sort of lack of observation was beyond his ken – he found it amazing.

I made a small mental note to notice whether skid marks were single or double in the future.

I was now learning about the basics of trucking life apart from driving. Besides learning how to stop at a weigh station, fuel a truck, and make a pickup or delivery, I was learning how it really worked to live in a truck. How and where to eat, drink, sleep, find restrooms and keep clean on the road were routine to Johnny but new to me.

Showers were fast becoming the high point of my day, an oasis of sybaritic luxury in what was proving to be a pretty hard and dirty life. Johnny arranged showers for us every day. Often the shower one day might be in the morning and the next day in the evening, but that was the longest we ever went without one.

The truck stop showers, which at one time had usually been communal, for men only, were now contained within individual rooms, each provided with clean towels, a sink and a toilet as well as the shower itself. Going into that room and shutting the door was about the only privacy I had. It was lovely, I found, to stand under a stream of hot water, washing away all the grime of the last 24 or 36 hours. Showers were cleaned, and dried even, between each use. I always left a dollar tip, if I had one, for whatever poor soul did the nasty job of cleaning up after strangers. I wasn't sure if others tipped or not but reasoned that if everyone left a dollar it would add up to quite a lot for the hardworking cleaner. So, what with being cleaned between each use, the showers were always pretty decent – indeed, some of them were truly nice.

After a refreshing interval with soap and water, I would come out and wander around the truck stop store for a while or go back to the truck and wait for Johnny. I found that it took him about half an hour longer to shower than it took me, and figured it was because he shaved too. It was only later that I learned he was using shower time to do between 50 and 100 pushups in preparation for a rematch of a competition he had won the year before with one of his stepsons.

The 44,000 pounds of raisins were due to be delivered two days later to Niles, Illinois, a town near Chicago. There were lots of hours of driving over the next two days. I was already beginning to be a little less panicky about keeping the truck in the center of the lane, and shifting was becoming less intimidating too, but only when conditions were good.

There were high winds as we drove eastward through Wyoming. Johnny was napping, and I bore it for a while but was beginning to feel thoroughly unsafe. Finally, I called to Johnny and said I didn't think this was beginner's weather. He agreed and gave me instructions about pulling off the freeway onto the shoulder of the Interstate.

We switched places, with a prolonged hissing sound as Johnny put the driver's seat up and I put the passenger seat down – I was beginning to think of this sound as marking "the changing of the guard." It would have looked pretty funny to a bystander, I thought, this "one goes up, one goes down" that always happened when we switched seats, almost like elevators crossing.

Johnny took the opportunity to instruct me in how to get off a shoulder and back onto the freeway preferably, when possible, by getting up to 40 mph before pulling off the shoulder into the highway's rightmost lane. He also told me that he decided whether to stop on an on-ramp or off-ramp primarily by choosing whichever one was on a downhill slope, as this made it much easier to get back up to speed.

Once we were back on the freeway I lay down to rest for a while. Conditions were getting worse and worse, I noticed. It was snowing now, in addition to the wind. In fact, conditions got so bad that Johnny decided to stop for a while. He pulled off of I-80 at Wamsutter, Wyoming, a small place with several little truck stops all in a hodgepodge. Johnny parked in the fuel island of an out-of-business truck stop. Parking was a real challenge because lots of truckers had had the same idea of getting off the road. More than that, there seemed to be a lot of mud on the ground and finally, just to add interest to the situation, three half-grown steers had gotten loose from somewhere and were roaming all over the truck stops, their progress limited by a cattle guard and a fence at the edge of the property.

The weather cleared a bit so we went on, only stopping late that night at an even smaller place where I parked with great difficulty at one end of a dirt lot, fearful of being in everyone's way and hoping that Johnny could get the truck out in the morning, which of course he could and did.

That was the night the bunk heater didn't work. We never knew why, and it never happened again. In the middle of the night I woke up because I was so cold. I put on my wool long underwear and a sweater, got under both layers of the sleeping bag that I normally used as a mattress pad, and was able to warm up and go back to sleep. How Johnny coped I don't know, but we may have started earlier than usual the next morning.

Johnny began to have me practice the kind of angled parking that larger rest areas often have for trucks. It was easier than backing into any kind of parking place, but that didn't make it easy. The trick was to come into the parking lot as far as possible to the side away from the angled parking then, depending on how wide the lot was, to drive until the front of the truck was even with the far side of the hole beyond the hole where I wanted to put the truck. When I had gone far enough, I had to turn the tractor more than 90 degrees and run up the near side of the parking place I wanted. If all went well, this brought the rear end of the trailer neatly into place. When I misjudged it, though, I risked side-swiping any trailer parked in the next space over.

As always, the back of the trailer took eight or ten feet to react to any change made to the steering wheel and again, as with backing, I often despaired of seeing the trailer react to what I had done with the steering wheel and did the opposite thing – usually just as the first reaction was starting to take place.

Johnny was patient about telling me which way I should be turning the steering wheel. Going slowly was essential. I occasionally saw drivers just sweep into parking places, but knew that if I tried such a thing, I would hit something.

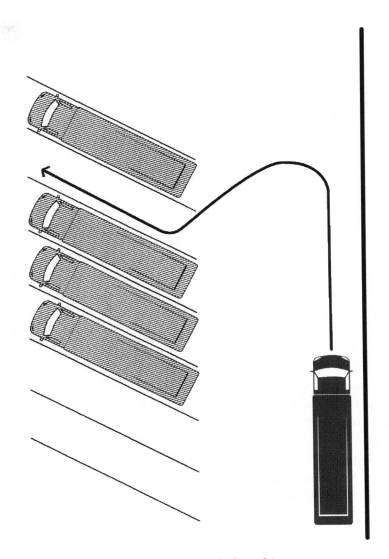

11. Diagram of setup for angled parking at a rest area

Many rest areas were too small to have angled parking and late at night those that had it were often full, so if we were just stopping for five minutes so that I could use the restroom, Johnny sometimes pulled into the car section of the rest area, or told me to if I was driving.

We got into trouble with this one night, though. The rest area wasn't in any of the common patterns. When Johnny told me to drive into the car part, the truck section being full, I had to make a sharp right turn. It quickly became apparent that the car part of this particular rest area ended in a cul-de-sac. Johnny took this in and began to reassure me that I shouldn't worry: he would get us out. Once I got back on the truck, he carefully turned around in the cul-de-sac; mercifully the car area was entirely free of cars. I was sometimes surprised at how little space could be used to do a U-turn with a semi. The way back to the freeway now lay through the full truck parking area, but Johnny had to turn a sharp right coming out of the car part.

This would have been difficult enough in any case but was rendered virtually impossible by a truck which had parked next to the last legal truck parking space. For a minute I thought Johnny would wake the trucker up and ask him to move, and Johnny told me later that he had thought of doing that but hadn't. Making all possible use of the available space, he turned the truck by running up on a small concrete island with a stop sign embedded in it which was planted four-square in the middle of where we needed to be. He succeeded in making the turn without hitting the illegally parked truck, but he scraped the front left fender of the truck against the stop sign and it left about a four-inch mark on the fender. Of course, the back tires of the trailer ran over the opposite curb, but not too badly. Johnny got out and examined the fender closely, but there wasn't anything to be done about it. The stop sign was still standing, so we drove on. I thought we had come out of a trying situation relatively well but was sorry for the scraped fender of what was almost a new truck.

Overall, I found these early days with Johnny to be pleasant. There was a lot to learn, but the two months of training stretched out before us. I was making progress. I was grateful to Alan King Associates for sending trainees out for a whole eight weeks; many companies had shorter training periods.

Once we got to Illinois, Johnny drove, taking State routes to avoid any congestion on the Interstates around Chicago. It was very early morning, so we hoped to be ahead of the rush hour. We drove for several hours, past field after field and farm after farm, finally arriving at the outskirts of Chicago to make the delivery.

I was relieved that Johnny was still doing all the backing up to loading docks. He kept threatening that I really ought to be doing it, and promising that we would do some practicing at truck stops, but so far we hadn't gotten around to it. I was undeniably relieved, but knew he was right that I ought to be practicing. I knew, better than he did, how bad my backing was, and how hard it might be for me to learn it well enough to go out on my own, even if I did nothing else but practice backing for the remaining seven weeks of training.

We went through the same sort of procedure as in California, checking in at the guard shack of the company in Niles with bills of lading, trip notebook and pen in hand. Johnny did his usual neat job of bumping the dock, while I watched.

One of the last steps in backing was often to pull all the way forward to open the doors once the trailer was lined up exactly, or once you were morally certain that you could move it over the last inch or two. This pulling forward was often necessary because the trailers on both sides of the hole could prevent the back doors from being opened. Modern loading docks were often spacious enough to make this unnecessary, and if the load was not being temperature controlled, or was being kept at a temperature somewhere near the temperature of the outside air, then the doors could be opened at the beginning of the backing maneuver. But with a load at, say, minus ten degrees, door opening was better done at the very end.

Also, opening the doors made it even harder to see exactly where the trailer was going to bump the loading dock because the doors stuck out about four inches on each side of the trailer even when they were hooked into place against its sides.

I always got down to help with the doors, though Johnny obviously didn't need my help. I thought it showed a better attitude and, after all, it wasn't as if he needed my help with anything. Indeed, part of the reason he got extra pay for training was that he could have done the whole job more easily himself.

CHAPTER 5

A DOT Inspection
(April 6-11)

After the raisins were unloaded, we headed for a noon appointment in the nearby city of Romeoville, Illinois, 35 miles away, to pick up almost 40,000 pounds of frozen McDonald's food, the start of my third trip with Johnny. The food needed to be delivered to a company in Phoenix, Arizona three days later. The dispatch said to keep it at minus ten degrees, so Johnny showed me how to precool the trailer by adjusting the reefer temperature before we left the raisin place.

There isn't any good way to get from Niles to Romeoville. Johnny had me drive straight south on a road which was, technically, a truck route, but which just seemed like endless city driving. My toes curled in my shoes as I waited for the scraping sound and tugging feeling which I imagined would accompany sideswiping a car or signpost on the narrow road. I got what seemed like endless practice in running up and down the gears as traffic lights came and went.

Finally, the road degenerated into being only two lanes in each direction. Johnny told me to hug the lane line to the left because of overhanging trees. Trees on a truck route are always supposed to be cut so that no branch hangs down below 14 feet above the road, but this isn't something you can count on, if only because trees are always growing. I hugged the center line and didn't hit anything, whether trees, cars or signs. After what seemed like a very long time we eventually arrived at I-55 and proceeded to Romeoville where we changed seats at the guard shack and Johnny backed up to the loading dock.

The trip to Phoenix went well. I hadn't driven across Texas for years, decades even, and was surprised at all the huge windmills that had been installed to generate electricity. Johnny pointed out that the windmills were made in sections which were trucked in on oversize flatbed trailers. Each trailer carried either one blade of the windmill or one section of the windmill's tower. They were then assembled on site, using a crane.

And he helped me go to Mass for Easter Sunday in Amarillo, Texas. In what I still thought of as my real life, I was a daily communicant. I had missed Mass the previous Sunday when we were driving across Nevada. It was the first time I had not gone to a weekend Mass, at least without the excuse of illness or a blizzard, for years. Johnny seemed surprised at how many Catholic churches there were and how easy it was for me to find one. I got on the Internet at a truck stop Saturday night and located several churches that were near our route. As I was trying for the earliest Mass, Johnny was actually able to park at one end of the church parking lot, something I was very sure I would be unable to do on my own. I went to Mass while Johnny took a nap, then we drove on.

I enjoyed driving across the wide-open spaces of Texas and New Mexico. Johnny drove from Flagstaff into Phoenix early Monday morning when it was still dark. The three long hills, as the elevation drops more than a mile, were difficult to drive, so he did it, but talked about the necessary technique as we went along.

When the sun came up, I was charmed to find that the weather in Phoenix was perfect. I had lived in Tucson for 12 years, often visiting my in-laws who lived in Phoenix, and had developed a real loathing for the summer heat of both places. Phoenix was always said to be five degrees hotter than Tucson and with a higher humidity because of the irrigation canals. But in early April the high temperature was only in the 70's and we arrived during that magic period when many of the cacti were blooming. I remembered a lot of the different kinds of cacti from my years of residence. The ocotillos were my favorites, with their fiery red blossoms looking like small birds perched in the cactus. The saguaros were blossoming too. I had forgotten that they grew north of Phoenix, but there were quite a few. I even saw an old "plantation," apparently, of 30 or 40 saguaros planted squarely in rows and columns, with their beautiful waxy white blossoms. Once we got into Phoenix, I started to see jacaranda trees, which bloomed a lovely purple color at this time of year.

We dropped the frozen food off in Tolleson, a suburb of Phoenix. This was what was described as a "drop and hook," as opposed to the live loads or unloads we had been doing. It meant, in this particular case, putting the trailer into a storage yard, leaving the reefer going so that whatever was in the trailer wouldn't spoil – it would be unloaded at the receiving company's convenience – disconnecting from the trailer, then hooking up to an empty trailer so we could drive to Tempe for our next pickup and the start of trip number four.

I was sorry to say good-bye to trailer 14032, which had been with us ever since I got on Johnny's truck, but realized that this was a completely ridiculous sentiment, and one for which Johnny would have no sympathy. I had already heard him be moderately sarcastic on the subject of women being sentimental about animals, for instance.

The drop and hook was my first chance since the Mueller training school to try out dropping a trailer. Johnny backed the trailer into place but told me to unhook while he unstrapped his bicycle from underneath the trailer. The "L" for landing gear part of the LAP acronym went fine. I turned the crank until the landing gear was solidly on the ground. The "A" part of the acronym stood for unhooking the air lines and pigtail from the trailer.

This was harder. Unhooking the air lines was easy enough. They have what is called glad hand couplings. When these lines are being hooked up, the center of an air line has to be exactly matched up with the center of its opposite number on the trailer, then the line is twisted into place, being sure to catch its edges under the projecting lip of the other part. It gave me lots of trouble from time to time.

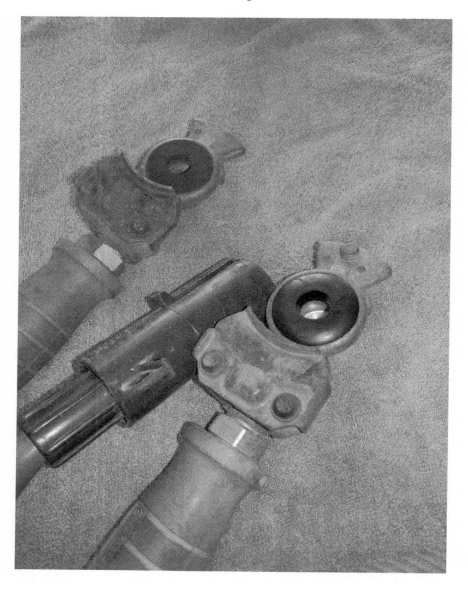

12. Glad hands and a pigtail

But unhooking one was easy, just requiring a twist of the line. The pigtail, or electrical connection, is a big plug that fits into a corresponding hole in the trailer. Plugging it in or pulling it out sometimes requires almost more strength than I have. I began to

74

realize as I pulled on this one that the connection was particularly stiff on Johnny's new truck. In fact, I couldn't get it out from my position on the ground. I climbed up onto the back of the tractor and pulled on the line, putting some of my weight into the pull, just as Johnny reappeared at my side, having dealt with his bicycle.

He sized up the situation and warned, "Be careful of doing it that way. If it suddenly lets go you could fall and hurt yourself."

No sooner were the words out of his mouth than the plug came out suddenly and I fell backwards, scraping my arm against a sort of standpipe or conduit that stood at the back of the tractor. This conduit was bent from some fooling around with the truck that Johnny had done on the first day he had it. He had jackknifed it in the terminal yard while doing figure eights to show off. The plastic or rubber cap, about an inch in diameter, which was supposed to seal the end of the standpipe, had been ripped almost in half and the rip was jagged. It cut the underside of my forearm for about an inch and a half.

I grimaced and clutched my arm, remarking to Johnny, "You're right; that's exactly what happened."

The cut, almost more of a scratch really, seemed to become infected instantly, whether because of what the cap was made of or because the whole thing was dirty I don't know. It didn't look that dirty. I washed the cut and put Neosporin on it as soon as I could, but I had to spend the next two weeks treating it with Neosporin and hydrogen peroxide alternately, as it seemed constantly on the verge of becoming a real problem, bright red around the edges of the cut and with a thick scab that eventually came off bit by bit but left a scar.

The rest of the procedure for dropping the trailer went fine. The company used an electronic system for releasing the fifth wheel jaws from the kingpin, so I didn't have to worry about the rather strong, straight pull that was required on other companies' trucks.

I bobtailed over to the empty trailer we were going to take away, had my usual amount of trouble backing up to it. This was a very simple process relative to the angled backing of a tractor and trailer, but still a problem for me when I looked in the side mirror and couldn't tell which way was what – and somehow *always* guessed wrong the first time.

Hooking up to the new trailer went well. I followed Mueller's rather lengthy procedure of inspecting everything. Johnny watched this impatiently, seeming to find what I was doing to be unnecessarily time-consuming. It did make me very slow, but I didn't feel safe doing it any other way for fear of making some big mistake, like dropping the trailer on the ground or ripping its underside out somehow.

Having finished my inspection, and finding that height and alignment looked acceptable, I backed under the trailer until I felt the collision that signified, possibly, that the fifth wheel jaws had locked around the kingpin. I put the truck into second gear and revved the engine a bit, tugging at the connection to see if it remained secure. This tug test was done twice, then I shut the engine down and climbed out of the truck, keys in hand, to walk back and take a look. "Keys in hand" was a safety measure to make it less likely that anyone would move the truck while I was under it.

First, I checked to make sure there wasn't any space visible between the fifth wheel and the bottom or "apron" of the trailer. There wasn't. So I crouched down and half crawled under the trailer to look toward the front and see if I could see the fifth wheel jaws in their locked position. And I couldn't. Everything just looked black, compared to the non-electronic locking bar to which I was accustomed. With one of them I would have been able to see an inch-and-a-quarter wide steel bar behind the kingpin. It was frustrating. I peered at the blackness for a few seconds, then asked Johnny to check it. He pronounced it to be fine, on what basis I didn't know, so we were ready to go as soon as I hooked up the lines and wheeled up the landing gear.

First, though, we inspected the new trailer, walking once around it. It looked good except for a missing mud flap on the offside, which Johnny pointed out. This was illegal, he explained, and we would have to get it fixed as soon as we could. He didn't seem to interpret "as soon as we could" literally, because we went on with our day rather than going in search of a new mud flap.

13. A fifth wheel hitch

We drove to Tempe for the next pickup. Johnny had two truly difficult backing situations in a row. First, he backed the trailer between a telephone pole and another waiting semi. He was only an inch away from the telephone pole as he backed the whole length of the trailer next to it. Then, when it was our turn he had to back up to a dock without hitting a concrete pylon which the company had seen fit to place right in the middle of the area in front of the loading docks.

This was a dairy, as indicated by the several tankers waiting in a different part of the yard to deliver milk. We were picking up a load of 43,134 pounds of cheese (going to Green Bay, Wisconsin) and were invited into the warehouse after we checked in with the Shipping Department. It was the first time I had been in such a place. It was a vast cold room, filled with storage racks. A number of forklifts were scooting around, each with its driver, picking up pallets or large drums, then disappearing into the caverns of the semi-trailers, which had backed up to the loading docks in a long row.

14. Loading docks from the inside

Johnny and the forklift operator who was going to load our trailer discussed how Johnny wanted the weight distribution for this load. Did he want it loaded evenly or with more weight here or there? I couldn't hear what they were saying very well because it was so noisy. Once he and the man had come to an agreement, we walked back outside to the truck and waited through the thumping and bumping of the loading process. As usual, Johnny took a nap.

When we were loaded and had our bills, I drove to Flagstaff. Forty-three thousand pounds of cheese was quite a load to haul up the three stiff grades as the elevation went from 2,000 feet to 7,000 feet. I practiced power downshifting, and it went okay. At least, there were still some ugly shifts, but I never actually missed a gear to the point of bringing the truck to a standstill on a steep grade. Again, the recurring nightmare of driving the rest of the way up the hill in second or third gear, at three or four mph, didn't happen.

It was bad enough, I thought, to inconvenience all the cars by going only 25 or 30 mph. I noticed that the signs saying, "Warning! Slow trucks next two miles" gave me warning of the steeper parts of the hills and how long they would last. And I began to experience what it meant to "take a run" at a hill, starting up it at the highest speed I could achieve.

I had noticed this on the way to California too, of course, but now I was a bit more relaxed and began to practice more consciously as well as observing overall effects as they happened instead of the just the minutiae of keeping the gears and speeds matched.

Although the road tended upward, there were downhills too, when I could shift back up to 10th gear. If the downhill was steep enough, I could get up to 70 or even 75 mph.

Alan's trucks were governed to 65 mph, but that didn't keep the truck from going faster on a downhill, when gravity, rather than the engine, was giving the truck its speed. Johnny had already explained that one of the truck's computers noticed, and recorded, any speed over 75, so I used 74 as an upper limit, braking if the truck looked as though it was about to go faster than that.

And it made a real difference to the next hill if I could start up it going over 70. The speed limit was 75, so there was no legal problem with going more than 65. Once or twice there was a slower four-wheeler or another semi in just the wrong place so that I had to start up a hill going 65 mph or even less. This meant that every downshift happened earlier and seemed to drop my maximum speed on a hill by a disproportionate amount.

We stopped for a meal in Flagstaff. Johnny was planning to get the trailer's mud flap replaced in New Mexico, at a truck stop where he knew that Alan King Associates would authorize the work to be done.

After lunch I continued driving but had hardly reached the outskirts of Flagstaff before I saw a Highway Patrol car sitting in the pine woods that covered the tract of land that was the median between the eastbound and westbound lanes of I-40. I pointed him out to Johnny, who was standing up in the back of the cab doing something with his TV set then, about a minute later, had to report that he had turned his lights on and was pulling us over.

Johnny's immediate response was to jump into the passenger seat and fasten his seat belt. There was a broader-than-usual shoulder ahead, so I signalled, then eased the truck off the road onto the dirt and came to a stop, setting the brake and shutting off the engine.

After a minute the highway patrolman appeared at the passenger window, greeted us, then announced that he was going to do a "level two" DOT (Department of Transportation) inspection. I had frankly forgotten what a level one, two or three inspection was; this one seemed pretty thorough. We explained my student status and gave him our licenses and physical cards.

Johnny and the patrolman had a short, sharp debate about the patrolman breaking the shipper's seal on the trailer. He undoubtedly had the right to do this but would have to sign the bills and write onto them the number of the new seal which he would put on to replace the one he had broken. Shippers hated it when their seals were broken; drivers weren't allowed to do it except under the most unusual circumstances, and always with permission from headquarters.

Once Johnny had established that the highway patrolman knew the right thing to do about the seal and would do it, he seemed to relax a bit. The patrolman had thawed slightly when he realized that I was a student. He was now treating the inspection as an educational exercise. He took bolt cutters from his patrol car and cut the bolt seal off the back of the trailer. Then he helped me open the back doors of the trailer. Johnny had disappeared after the seal discussion, but he now joined us again. I suspected that he had been making sure our logbooks looked okay.

It was a beautiful mid-afternoon in Flagstaff, neither too hot nor too cold, with a fresh breeze wafting the smell of evergreens about. I stood looking around at the rich, red dirt and numerous pine trees, while the two men talked and traffic roared by on the Interstate. It was quite an embarrassing position to be in, but I tried not to mind.

The trailer inspection was soon over; I shut the trailer doors, then the patrolman put on a new seal and wrote its number onto the bill of lading, which he also signed and stamped. He then retired to his car to go over the documentation he had collected from us, including the logbooks which Johnny now handed him.

This stage of the inspection took a good twenty minutes. The highway patrolman eventually appeared at the passenger door again, and didn't have any complaints about the logbooks, which he returned to us along with our licenses and DOT physical cards.

Then he led me through an inspection of the truck including all the brake lights, turn signal and flashers. I had to sit in the driver's seat and turn the various signals on and off at his command, as well as stepping on the brakes when he told me to. There seemed to be quite a lot to it.

The truck passed the inspection with the single exception of the missing mud flap on the back of the trailer. I explained that we had just picked the trailer up in Phoenix a few hours before, had noticed the missing mud flap and that Johnny was planning to have it replaced before the end of the day.

The patrolman got ready to leave. He and I wished each other a Happy Easter, causing Johnny to mutter that Easter was over. (He clearly didn't know that Easter is a season, not just a day.) Then the patrolman turned to Johnny and asked, "Do you want to know why I pulled you over for the inspection?"

Johnny nodded.

"It was the mud flap," said the patrolman.

We reiterated our commitment to getting a mud flap before

nightfall, and the man got back in his car and left. The whole inspection had taken almost exactly one hour.

The route from Arizona to Wisconsin was interesting, involving as it did more than 500 miles of US highways, rather than the more usual Interstates. After buying a mud flap in Moriarty, New Mexico, Johnny had me cut off at Tucumcari onto US-54, a northeast diagonal route that took in a corner of Texas and cut across the narrow part of Oklahoma before bringing us out in Kansas. We drove through Greensburg, a small town in Kansas that was soon to be flattened by a tornado.

I was learning how to pull into or through fuel islands safely. This involved a technique of oversteering to make the trailer come back into line more quickly than it otherwise would have, not unlike the technique for parking at rest areas with angled parking. The stakes were higher here because the concrete fuel islands were protected by yellow-painted metal pylons. These pylons almost always had scrape marks and often stood at odd angles, like the Leaning Tower of Pisa, from being sideswiped by trucks.

Pulling through fuel islands was also harder because it was a question of a 90-degree turn rather than the lesser angle of rest areas. There were a number of variables involved: how nearly straight was the truck when entering the truck stop and how close to the fuel island was it?

Usually it was sufficient to head for the second fuel island over from the one I really wanted, then cut back sharply and run up the imaginary line on the side of the fuel island away from the turn I had just made. So, if I came in from the left, I aimed to the right of the island, then brought it back and ran up the left side of the island. Or conversely if I came from the right. As always, going slowly was crucial. So was listening to Johnny. He would tell me which way to turn the steering wheel. I never actually hit anything but came very close once or twice.

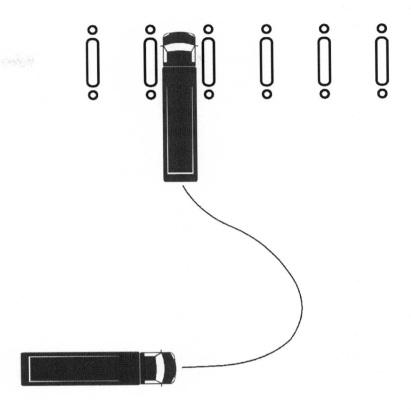

15. Diagram of a fuel island pull-in

We finally started to practice backing into spaces at truck stops whenever we found a sparsely populated lot, usually in the middle of the morning. This went just about as badly as I had expected it to. One of the more confusing aspects was Johnny telling me to turn the steering wheel "the other way." The other way relative to what? I never knew which way I had been turning it to begin with. And it seemed hard for Johnny to call out "right" or "left" on the spur of the moment. Even if he did, I wasn't sure which way was right and which way left. Right with the top of the steering wheel or the bottom?

One basic misunderstanding I had brought with me from Mueller did get cleared up at least. Johnny was telling me that I had to turn the steering wheel sharply to the right to make the trailer back up sharply to the left and I just couldn't take that in – thought it was the opposite really.

Finally, Johnny, with characteristic energy, said to me, "Hop out! I'll show you!"

He jumped into the truck, roared around the half empty parking lot in a circle, set up for the backing and started to back, doing all of it about ten times as quickly and efficiently as I had.

He yelled out of the window, "Watch now!" and turned the front wheels of the tractor sharply to the right. To my amazement, the trailer turned sharply to the left as he backed up. Seeing it happen from the ground that way drove it deeply into my mind.

Mirrors were still a terrible problem to me. I couldn't tell by looking in a mirror which way was left and which way was right. I had to twist around and look back down the side of the trailer to try to decide which way I wanted it to head, whether more left or less left, and even then it often got turned around in my head and I would make the wrong decision about which way to turn the steering wheel.

Then, too, it generally happened when I climbed out of the truck that I would suddenly be struck by the backwardness of what I had just done. "Oh! the tree was on *that* side and the yellow truck was on *this* side!"

After several practice sessions, Johnny was beginning to promise me lots more work on backing. I had thought from the beginning, had even said to Johnny, that my success in the program probably hinged on whether or not he could teach me to back well enough and that it would be no easy task. Now he was beginning to see the truth of this for himself, or so I surmised when he commented about backing, "I have to tell you that right now it's kicking your butt!"

The middle weeks of training passed very pleasantly. Johnny and I were used to each other by now and were able to talk or not talk, feeling comfortable either way. The "rules of the truck" were working. No one was getting left behind, nor was anything else going noticeably wrong.

There was a relaxed feeling, for me at least; there was plenty of time left. Though there was still much to learn, I had a lot of time ahead with Johnny before I needed to think about driving on my own.

One surprise about trucking was the sheer amount of time that the truck moved every day. The great majority of our hours were spent driving. For Johnny, driving seemed to be the normal state of life, the state in which he spent, not just the majority of his waking hours, but the majority of all hours, waking or sleeping. Well, that couldn't be quite true, I thought. I was driving quite a lot too. But when he was on his own it probably *was* true.

Were most truckers this way, I wondered? Long car trips had always been a feature of my life, but this was something more, something quite other, to move so fast so consistently. True, we took a couple of hours each day for eating and showering. There were shorter stops too, most often just driving "through" a rest area or truck stop in 10 minutes or less. And the truck did get shut down for a certain number of hours out of the 24 while we both slept.

Still, it was moving most of the time. This was one of the things that I hadn't imagined about trucking life, the almost constant driving. Equally, it amazed me how much could go on while one person drove. Johnny could read and send Qualcomm messages. Although we weren't supposed to, it was really completely impossible to stop every time a message was received, and some of the messages needed a quick reply. Johnny could, while driving, have a snack, pick a drink up off the floor, study a map and plan a route, reach back into the body of the cab and slam a drawer shut behind him – one of them having a tendency to come open unexpectedly. I had even seen him lean out of the open window and slam the driver's side windshield wiper up and down on the windshield to clear it of ice, all the while holding the truck steady on the road.

I was much more limited. I could snack, up to a point, drink a drink perhaps, but not pick one up off the floor. I didn't do the rest of it yet, and never would do the windshield wiper trick. My arms were much too short.

Naturally, the person not driving could do all sorts of things: sleep, read, watch TV, make cell phone calls, have a meal, write a letter. All the routine tasks of life were carried on, but in a truck roaring down the highway at 65 mph.

Another surprise was the poor condition of many of the nation's highways, even the Interstates. Trucks seemed to be more affected by rough patches of road than cars were, which I never would have guessed. Johnny sometimes told me to switch to the left lane if conditions were really bad, but this made me nervous, as car after car passed me on the right. Even semis sometimes ran up my righthand side, which was far worse.

One day when I was driving in the right lane of a very bad stretch of Interstate highway Johnny, who had been trying to tune in a basketball game on his TV set, suddenly jumped into the passenger seat and announced, "I've got to tell you that I'm working up a sweat back there just trying to stay upright!"

Johnny had put two restrictions on me as a beginner: I wasn't allowed to use cruise control or to listen to the satellite radio. Now these two restrictions vanished. One evening he invited me to use cruise control and showed me how. It was a relief not to have to keep my foot on the accelerator all the time. And it made it much easier to stay up to speed. I had noticed that I couldn't manage to go 65 mph by the end of a long driving stint. Sixty mph was about as fast as I could manage.

A few days later I received permission to listen to the satellite radio on an evening when the Interstate was pretty flat and empty. From then on Johnny would help me get the radio going before he climbed into the upper bunk for one of his naps. I was able to stop reciting songs and poems in my mind while I drove, though I still did it occasionally just for fun.

I was afraid of driving without having some minor activity such as listening to music, or making it, to focus my attention. My thoughts took me so far away sometimes! If I grew so preoccupied that I forgot where I was or what I was doing, it could be dangerous. Mueller called this Driving Without Awareness (DWA).

I had often been troubled by it as a car driver, suddenly "coming to" and realizing that I hadn't noticed anything for at least two miles. My psychologist daughter assured me that my mind would "call" me if anything came up that couldn't be handled automatically, without awareness, but I was unconvinced.

Then there was Praying Without Awareness (PWA), a term I had invented myself. Praying the Rosary, for example, could be done with or without awareness. And what about driving without awareness and praying without awareness simultaneously? I had already managed this several times. Where in the world *were* my thoughts on such occasions? Far, far away certainly. It was a mystery to me.

Sometimes Johnny sat beside me and we talked, in between him having to give sharp directions or explain some aspect of driving. I was interested to notice that he knew nothing, and cared less, about classical music. He didn't seem to mind whatever I chose to listen to, but upon being asked, remarked that all violin pieces sounded like the instrument was being tuned. He couldn't ever actually have heard a violin being tuned, I decided.

Johnny himself, in between basketball games and NASCAR races, listened to the 60's or 70's hits channels, but generally only at night with headphones on. I couldn't seem to persuade him that it wouldn't bother me to hear his music – if I even would be able to hear it, which I doubted.

Johnny was interested in the fact that I speak varying levels of five other languages. I am fluent in French, pretty fluent in Swahili, and speak decreasing amounts of Hungarian, German and Spanish. Johnny didn't speak any language but English. Having only a native language, he was accustomed to the idea of understanding language only as a Gestalt – an either/or proposition – you did or you didn't. He couldn't understand anything I said in French, for example. I almost always made comments or remarks to other drivers, from the safety of the cab, in French. It kept me polite and gave me an opportunity to practice pronunciation. I had never learned how to swear or be obscene in French.

Was it, Johnny inquired, necessary to memorize the meanings of hundreds of words in order to learn a different language?

"Hundreds, certainly," I replied, "thousands even."

"Oh... Well then I probably never will," he declared to my

considerable amusement.

I didn't like memorization either but speaking different languages and being able to think of five or six different ways of saying the same thing were a joy that made it worthwhile. Or so I thought. It seemed to me a sad limitation to have only one language. I had sometimes thought that monolingual people were so deeply bound to their native language that they lacked perspective. As though God had decreed that the word "cat" signified the animal, when in fact the word used for anything was essentially arbitrary and only a matter of agreement between those of one language group. It could just as easily be "*le chat*," "*paka*," "*macska*," "*die Katze*," "*el gato*," or any of a myriad of other terms.

I had even heard of an American somewhere saying that English "had to be *the* international language" because it was the language in which Jesus wrote the Bible! A young Frenchman, with whom I had worked as a translator years before, heard this said at a conference and came to me for an explanation of it. Was it a joke? It didn't seem like a joke, somehow, he said, though it *was* pretty funny. But what else could it be? Trying to explain to him that Americans really could be that ignorant was rather difficult.

Another thing Johnny and I talked about was mathematics. My father was a research mathematician, with a Ph.D. from Harvard. My husband had called himself a "frustrated mathematician" who worked as a hardware designer in Silicon Valley (electronics with him was "a hobby which had gotten out of hand," he sometimes said), but who had taught himself calculus in the ninth grade and who eventually had a master's degree in math. My son had majored in math for his B.A. and was about to start graduate work in mathematical logic.

I had studied calculus in high school but lacked the sort of passion for math that I had observed in my father as well as in the mathematicians with whom he socialized, so I had made the decision rather early not to go into math.

And here was Johnny, who told me that he had never been able to understand what a variable was in algebra. He had not been able to make sense of such a concept, had demanded over and over to be told what number the "x" or "y" stood for. Johnny was an entirely new kind of man to me, very different from the mathematicians and scientists of my previous life. It was odd indeed to meet someone who liked sports. And I had never met a NASCAR fan or anyone who liked the frightening amusement park rides.

Some of his strangeness was probably a matter of extroversion. He was clearly a raging extrovert. I had heard that extroverts were in constant need of stimulation, while introverts such as myself were more in need of soothing activities such as reading, to calm and regulate the ceaseless stimulation of our own thoughts.

Johnny had said when I met him that he wasn't going to take any home time during our time "out" together, but he did have plans to spend a few days in Phoenix, with one of his daughters who was flying in, to watch a NASCAR race that was to take place there.

We talked a bit about what I would do in Phoenix while he was at the race. He offered to get me a ticket, but also admitted that NASCAR races were very noisy. This didn't appeal to me at all. My hearing problem made me leery of anything that might threaten the hearing in the one ear I had left.

Besides, the little bit I had seen of NASCAR races on TV, plus the movie "Cars," had not led me to think that I would enjoy attending a real race. My plan was to figure out bus routes so I could see the Thorne Miniature Rooms at the Phoenix Art Museum and also get to another used bookstore. I was almost out of books again. For the rest, I could read or get on the Internet or listen to the satellite radio in the truck. Johnny promised to park the truck at a truck stop in Phoenix that had a drivers lounge with free Internet, and we left it at that for the time being.

But back to trip number four. From Kansas we drove up through Des Moines, Iowa then skirted Madison, Wisconsin and on to a food manufacturing plant in Green Bay, Wisconsin where we delivered the cheese that we had picked up in Tempe, Arizona.

There were a couple of toll booths on this route. It was my introduction to toll booths in a semi. I couldn't understand how it was that Johnny managed not to sideswipe either side of the toll booth. There were only a couple of inches between the tires and the curbs of the toll booths – on each side!

He was reassuring about them, advising me that if I looked far ahead as I came up on the toll booth, just as I normally did to stay centered in a lane out on the Interstate, I wouldn't find it particularly difficult. I wasn't so sure. It *looked* difficult. But I made it through my first one without hitting anything. Johnny had made sure I had money to pay the toll and told me just to drop the change and the receipt on the floor of the cab rather than distract myself by trying to put any of it away.

The Green Bay plant where we delivered the load was again a new world to me, a sordid, gray-painted concrete block building filled with old machinery, redolent of sour milk and peopled with gray-haired, gray-skinned men wearing hairnets and white lab coats and driving forklifts under the glare of the many fluorescent lights with which the ceiling was lined. A lot of what went on seemed to be automated. The machinery was working in ways that weren't immediately apparent to me.

The scene was quite shocking. It gave me thoughts about the value of an education in procuring work in more pleasant environments – not that my MA seemed to have availed me much. Still, with or without a degree, I was grateful to be able to drive away from the place. It might, for all I knew, be a good company for which to work, beloved of its employees and a model of employer/employee relations, paying fair wages, etc., etc., but it looked more like my idea of a prison.

CHAPTER 6

NASCAR Race and Bobtailing around Phoenix
(April 12-22)

The start of trip number five was at Appleton, Wisconsin the next morning when we picked up more cheese, in a different form than the 600 lb. barrels we had brought from Tempe to Green Bay. These were ordinary cases on pallets, shrink-wrapped to keep the cases from falling off the pallets.

As in the factory of the night before, the process was largely automated. This place gave more the overall effect of one of the cartoons of my childhood. Machines did almost everything – boxes progressed slowly along elevated conveyor belts which ran only a few yards below the high ceiling of the factory. The boxes were then sent down one of three diagonal conveyor belts, which one being decided in some arcane fashion not obvious to the observer, and accumulated in layers on a pallet until a critical mass had been reached, at which point they were shrink-wrapped by a machine which spun the pallet around and around, winding it up in multiple layers of cellophane. Finally, the whole group of shrink-wrapped cartons was deposited, with its pallet, onto the floor. The forklift operator then had two or three minutes in which to pick the pallet up and stage it somewhere else before the next shrink-wrapped bundle was ejected from the machine.

After our trailer was loaded, Johnny drove to Racine, but I drove through Chicago. Even at 10:30 in the morning it was nerve-racking. Traffic on the freeway often slowed to a crawl, or even came to a standstill. I got lots of practice in idling along in third or fourth gear, and learned, to my surprise, that the truck could idle in any gear. It was neither necessary nor desirable to slip the clutch a lot, as I would have done in a car to keep it from stalling.

It was tedious work, though, made worse by cars darting in and out in front of us, striving to gain an advantage by jumping into whichever lane looked like it was moving better at the moment. I was a sitting duck for this, not able to ride close enough to any vehicle in front of me to prevent a car from jumping in front of us, but during one stretch where I was crawling along even with another semi in the lane to our left, Johnny pointed out that as long as I kept beside the other semi, cars would be unable to lane weave. I could let the other semi get ahead or behind as long as I didn't let a gap big enough for a car develop between us. He added that truckers often use this technique deliberately, both as a safety measure and a remedy for the annoyance of having four-wheelers dodging all over the place.

Eventually we got clear of Chicago. Johnny would rather have gone through Chicago, or any other big city, in the small hours of the morning when there really wasn't much traffic, but the pickup time on this load had dictated otherwise. I could see the wisdom of such a practice, considering that even 10:30 AM, which should have been a time of very light traffic, was so crowded. If the middle of the morning was this congested, maybe 3 or 4 AM would be a good idea.

Once we were clear of Chicago, we found ourselves in what Johnny told me was the heaviest truck traffic in the whole country – the I-80/I-90 corridor that runs along the south side of Lake Michigan. We stopped in Gary, Indiana for a few hours, then I drove again, all the way to Tennessee. It was a 532-mile day, the farthest I had yet driven.

Johnny took over and drove on through the night, but I did the last 90 minutes of the trip the next morning. We delivered the cheese to a place in McDonough, Georgia, then "deadheaded," that is drove with the trailer empty, 74 miles to pick up a load of Bud Ice at Anheuser-Busch in Cartersville, Georgia for the start of trip number six.

This load had a temperature of 99 on the dispatch, Alan's shorthand for a no-temperature load. The reefer didn't need to be turned on. The load could travel at whatever the ambient air temperature would be. This was the first load without a temperature set point that I had encountered. I found it restful not to have to listen to the running of the reefer, which up to that time had been a frequent background irritant.

Anheuser-Busch had strict shipping procedures in place. We had to weigh the truck empty as we went in to pick up the load, then weigh it loaded on our way out. Also, Johnny warned me to drive smoothly. Any sudden movements could have a very bad effect on a beer load.

This was also a shorter run than we had been having. It was only 503 miles to the delivery site, near St. Louis. We delivered the beer the next afternoon, then deadheaded 37 miles to Edwardsville, Illinois, to pick up a load of Hershey chocolate going to Chanhassen, Minnesota – the start of trip number seven.

The Chanhassan load was 559 miles and delivered at eight in the morning a day and a half later. Then we drove to Gaylord, Minnesota to pick up a load of frozen food. This was the start of trip number eight, going to Phoenix and the NASCAR race for Johnny.

We drove back pretty much the same way we had come from Phoenix, that is, cutting across 500 miles of Kansas, Oklahoma and Texas on US-54, emerging onto I-40 at Tucumcari, New Mexico.

Johnny again drove down the big hills of I-17 between Flagstaff and Phoenix. We were a day early in Phoenix and were there two days before he had wanted to be – something he resented as a waste of time, both because he didn't want an idle day and because I would have that much less training.

The delivery in Phoenix was made unpleasant by one of the rudest women I had ever encountered. It was another ugly warehouse – I wasn't yet used to this industrial world – with a lumper service right by the entrance, then the receiving windows some yards farther on.

"Lumping" in trucker parlance means the loading or unloading of a trailer. Alan King Associates didn't want its drivers doing the loading or unloading, so we always used a lumper service if the shipper or receiver's own personnel didn't do the lumping themselves. (Parenthetically, is this the origin of the phrase "like it

93

or lump it"?)

In such a case, the lumper service was a bit like fleas on a dog, or perhaps more accurately, like the birds that live on the back of a rhinoceros or crocodile and are tolerated in return for the service they provide of eating parasites that would otherwise infest the animal. The lumpers were a separate company that mediated between the carrier and the shipper or receiver.

The receiving windows of this plant had a large sign posted telling drivers to form a line "to the right." To the right of what, I wondered idly as I stood in line with four or five men, including Johnny, waiting our turn at the one window where anyone seemed to be processing deliveries. I soon found out what was meant by the sign. After we had waited ten or fifteen minutes, the monotony was broken by a woman who stormed out of a door that I hadn't even noticed until then and began to berate us all.

"Can't you read?" she asked, shrilly and sarcastically. The sign said form a line to the right. We needed to form a line to the right immediately. She went on at some length on this same theme, then stood and waited while all of us shuffled around sheepishly into the desired orientation. When we were positioned to her satisfaction, she let out one or two more huffs, then slammed back through the same door, where she sat down at a desk, but seemed to find something more worthwhile to do, in her own eyes at least, than processing deliveries. She shuffled papers very busily for the rest of the time that Johnny and I waited in line, but never did get around to helping anyone at her window. Perhaps it was just as well.

The men in line and I all looked at each other with raised eyebrows, but nobody said anything. I committed a trifling act of vandalism, à la Dorothy L. Sayers in *Busman's Honeymoon*, and with Johnny's permission took a pen and corrected a misspelling on one of the other signs posted near the receiving windows. It relieved my feelings a bit.

I could see the point, upon reflection, of creating a line that headed away from the lumper's table rather than toward it. The procedure was to check in at receiving, then go deal with the lumpers. If the line went the wrong way, there would probably be chaos and confusion as the line waiting for the receiving window got mixed up with the line waiting to talk with the lumpers. Still! She could have been nice about it. And posting a clear, unambiguous sign would have prevented the problem in the first place.

After this ordeal, and once the trailer was unloaded, we were given some local work to do for Alan with one of our extra days in Phoenix, doing a couple of yard checks and shuffling empty trailers from one shipper to another.

"Doing a yard check" meant checking on all the Alan trailers at a particular location, writing down their numbers, the fuel level of the reefer tanks and whether they were empty or loaded, then sending this information to Alan.

I had a lesson in watching for overhanging tree branches during this time in Phoenix. For some reason Phoenix seemed particularly bad in this respect, or perhaps it was just one particular street along the edge of Tolleson, a street down which we seemed to drive perpetually in the Phoenix area. I hit the CB antenna against various branches along that road until I was so embarrassed and humiliated that I began to notice low-hanging branches and avoid them.

We bobtailed down to Casa Grande and moved a couple of empty trailers from one place to another, giving me lots of practice hooking up to trailers and dropping them. It was also my first experience of driving bobtail for any distance. It was surprisingly easy after dragging a trailer around for so long.

With a trailer, passing another vehicle on the freeway is much harder than it is in a car. Unlike a car, when the front part of a semi gets past another vehicle there are still 53 feet of trailer to go before it's safe to pull back over into the other lane. This is why truckers "flash each other over," as it's called, by blinking their headlights as soon as it's safe for the passing truck to pull back in. The usual response to this is for the driver who has just passed to flash his lights in turn, thus thanking the first driver.

I got lots of practice doing this, because Alan trucks were governed to 65 mph. A lot of trucks could go faster than 65. One entertaining aspect of flashing truckers over was the variety of ways they flashed back to say thank you. Most drivers contented themselves with flashing their own headlights a couple of times, making their taillights blink too. But some of them had worked out a whole little routine. My favorite was the occasional driver who blinked the right turn signal twice, then the left turn signal twice, then did something that made the trailer's three central marker lights blink twice. I laughed out loud sometimes.

My least favorite way was when a driver just blinked his left turn signal once or twice to acknowledge being flashed over. I had already seen a couple of four-wheelers take fright at this phenomenon. It had frightened me more than once, as a driver of cars, when I had thought, "Oh no! He's coming out again!" after a truck changed lanes then flashed his left turn signal. I hadn't understood it then. Now I did, but I still didn't like it and thought the practice was unsafe.

Because we ended up without a trailer at the Phoenix truck stop, Johnny now offered to let me bobtail around Phoenix by myself while he went to the races. This was against Alan's rules for trainees. He pointed out that we would probably both get fired if I had an accident but didn't seem to think it at all likely that I would.

The prospect of not having to waste hours trying to take buses was too tempting – I decided to take Johnny up on his offer, but to be extremely careful.

The next day, Johnny took his bicycle down from the back of the tractor, where he had fastened it in the absence of a trailer, and rode off toward the Phoenix airport. His daughter was flying in that morning, and he had reserved a rental car. It would be a 15- or 20-mile bike ride to get to the airport, but the prospect didn't seem to worry him.

I watched him go, then started up the truck's engine to drive to the Phoenix Art Museum and its Thorne Miniature Rooms collection, which I hadn't seen for nearly 30 years. Most of the collection is housed at the Chicago Art Institute, but Phoenix has sixteen of the rooms. I had been in Chicago the previous fall and had enjoyed seeing the rooms at the Chicago Art Institute so much that I was eager to see the rest of the collection in Phoenix again.

I had mapped out the route ahead of time, even writing down the directions. What I hadn't counted on was construction in downtown Phoenix. The speed limit was 15 mph and rows of cones led traffic from one side of the street to the other. I drove the maze, my heart in my mouth so to speak, but managed not to hit anything or anyone and arrived at the museum just before its ten o'clock opening, when the parking lot was still more than half empty.

I parked carefully, in a double row of parking where I could take up four spaces and in such a way, I hoped, that I'd be able to get out later, even if the lot filled up.

Then I got out, raised the hood and inserted the steering gear lock into the lower U-joint on the steering shaft, padlocking it into place. Alan issued each of its employees with a steering gear lock and padlock. Employees were supposed to put the lock on any time they weren't in the truck, even when they pulled forward at a fuel island and went inside to sign for the fuel they had just purchased.

If a driver had the lock on and the truck was stolen, which it probably wouldn't be, and in any case the thief wouldn't make it out of the parking lot because it was impossible to steer with the lock on, Alan wouldn't hold the driver responsible for the theft. If, on the other hand, the truck was stolen and didn't have that lock on, the driver would almost certainly be fired.

I was beginning to realize that this was typical of the trucking industry. Drivers were required to do something time-consuming and fundamentally unreasonable – putting a steering gear lock on at a fuel stop? When putting it on would double the amount of time needed for what they were doing? Besides making them look like total fools? As an older driver had said, "Ah!... They're not living in the real world!"

But that really wasn't the point. It wasn't that Alan thought anybody would actually use the lock at a fuel island. The point was that this was Alan's way of holding a driver responsible for a stolen truck. They put you on notice that you *would* be blamed. It seemed that almost anything that went wrong would either lead to a fine or to being fired. I was coming to see that the trucking industry was vicious, unlike anything I had ever experienced or even heard of.

Johnny rarely used the steering gear lock. Paradoxically, he used it most consistently at Alan terminals where it was well known that mechanics were sometimes sent to check on all the trucks parked there and report on anyone who wasn't using the steering gear lock. I found that to be nonsensical. If a truck wasn't safe at its own company's guarded terminal, where on earth would it be safe?

I hadn't thought it right to criticize Johnny's practices in this area or any other; he was, after all, the trainer, I was the trainee. I had questioned him about using the steering gear lock. He had explained that he used his own judgment about the matter. This seemed to come down to using the lock only at certain truck stops, especially in the East, and virtually never for short stops. As he had already told me, it was his belief that trucks were usually stolen only if the thief found a spare key when breaking into a truck. He was very careful to make sure that no key was ever left on the truck. That generally covered the case as far as he was concerned.

It was my intention to use the lock a lot more than Johnny did, and I was determined not to have the truck stolen while I was in charge of it this first time. I was afraid of forgetting that the lock was on, though, so I took the precaution of leaving the driver's side of the hood unlatched, in hopes that seeing it would remind me of *why* it might be unlatched. I also laid the spiral notebook Johnny kept in the truck on the steering wheel, opened to the page where I had taken a green highlighter and made a bold, big-lettered sign which read: "STEERING/GEAR/LOCK!"

After putting the steering gear lock on for the first time on my own responsibility, I went to get in line for the museum, which was now opening. It was a popular place on that Saturday morning, so I had quite a long wait, but the time didn't drag because of a display in the front lobby of an unusual car, a "Silver Beetle" dating from the 1930's. The museum had a temporary exhibit of very fine old cars, some of which might have been unique, I thought. I wasn't willing to pay the extra money required to see the whole exhibit but was able to study the Silver Beetle at some length. It had what my husband had taught me to call "suicide doors," that is, doors that were hinged toward the back of the car. If such a door came unlatched in motion the wind would tend to rip it open, hence the name. There was also a bright red Thunderbolt, a 1941 Chrysler concept car, which was in the general area, on the way to the Thorne Miniature Rooms. It was interesting to see that retractable headlights had already been thought of so long before.

16. "Steering Gear Lock!" sign

The Thorne Miniature Rooms were completely satisfying, as always. I was able to buy some postcards of them in the museum gift shop. This was disappointing, though, as the rooms were so well done that the postcards just looked like pictures of nice rooms of various periods and places. It wasn't at all obvious that they were on a scale of an inch to a foot.

By the time I left the museum, close to noon, it had warmed up a lot and my long-sleeved shirt had become oppressive. Also, the parking lot had filled up completely and several cars were cruising around looking for parking places.

One particular car, holding three older women, pulled up beside me as I walked across the lot toward the truck. A refined-looking woman opened her window and asked if I was leaving. I replied that I was about to drive the semi out of there and free up four places if they would give me a couple of minutes to change my shirt. The woman's eyes widened in surprise. Evidently, I didn't look like the

99

average trucker, I thought in amusement. I remembered to take the steering gear lock off, climbed into the truck, changed quickly into a T-shirt and pulled carefully out of the parking place(s).

I headed across town toward a used bookstore that I had found in the truck stop's phone directory. The next challenge, apart from finding the store, would be where to park. There was a left turn onto the street of the bookstore's address. I made the turn, had a moment of near panic as I saw from the number on a building that the bookstore must be right there and also saw that the street ahead of me didn't go straight through but seemed to have some complication in it about a block up.

There was a U-Haul dealer on my right, with quite a large yard at the back of it. I made an instant decision that I could probably at least use the lot to make a U-turn and pulled in. The yard was half empty, so I carefully turned the truck around, childishly simple when bobtailing compared to running with a trailer attached and backed into a parking place.

Then I climbed down, noticing that the bookstore was indeed almost next door, put the steering gear lock on again and walked into the U-Haul store. There were a couple of men working there. I greeted the nearer one, who greeted me back, then remarked, "That was very pretty backing."

Highly gratified, I thanked him, then said, "I wanted to ask you for a favor. Could I possibly park it here for a few hours while I go to the used bookstore and get some lunch?" Seeing agreement in his eyes I concluded, "I'd be back for sure by three, or even earlier if you want."

The man nodded, "That would be fine."

I thanked him profusely, then headed for the bookstore where I spent a happy hour and a half or so, browsing the store's large collection of fiction, children's books and a few other categories. I bought a dozen books, including one I hadn't seen for years but which had been a favorite when I was about ten. It was called *Sandra of the Girls' Orchestra*, a really junky book, in its way, about a girl who eventually discovers that the violin she has inherited from her grandfather is a real Stradivarius.

I spent my childhood studying cello and wishing I was studying violin. My school library owned *Sandra of the Girls' Orchestra*, which I read as many times as the librarian allowed. The librarian at my elementary school was not like most librarians, whom I have always thought of as the "salt of the earth." Mrs. Gant was a woman who seemed to view her main job as being to protect "her" books from the children. One way she accomplished this was to limit the number of times a child was allowed to read a book. Another way was by making difficulties if a child wanted to read a book that was intended for older or younger children.

Mrs. Gant didn't like *Sandra of the Girls' Orchestra* and eventually discarded it while my family was away for a semester, to my very great dismay. I hadn't seen it since, so this book was a real find. A number of the other books looked promising too. With jubilation in my heart, I found lunch at a fast food restaurant – "eating to live" rather than "living to eat." Then I returned to the truck and drove off to find a church I knew of on Campbell Avenue. I went to confession, then to Mass.

The rest of the two days passed rather quickly, between reading three of the books, spending time on the Internet and playing computer solitaire. Johnny and his daughter dropped by once in his rental car to make sure that all was well with the truck but stayed only a few minutes.

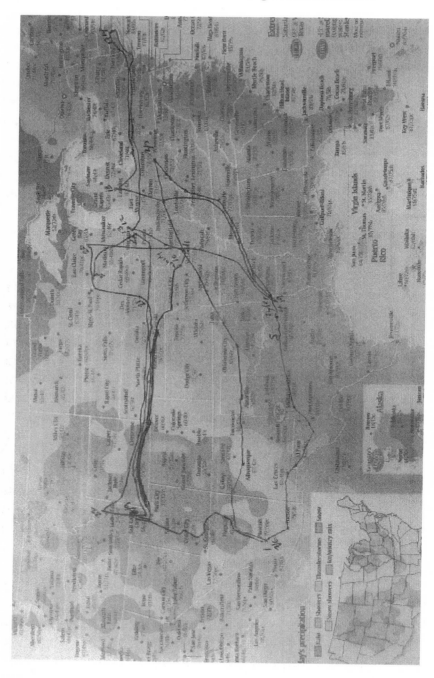

Map 2

CHAPTER 7

Grandma?
(April 23-May 3)

On Monday morning Johnny came back to stay, looking, as he so often did, sleek and well-satisfied, something like a skunk, I sometimes thought, searching for the right metaphor. This one didn't quite satisfy me, somehow. He had a distinctive walk, though, like that of the athlete he had been. He sometimes reminded me of the Superior General of the religious order where I had worked in Africa, a big Tanzanian man who always entered a room as if to say, "I'm here! Now things can begin." The African Superior General really was important, of course, very important indeed in his own society, and Johnny wasn't at all prominent in ours. There was a similarity in their walk though.

I couldn't decide if Johnny really felt the kind of confidence his manner and walk seemed to portray or if it was a front. There was some evidence to suggest that it was a well-practiced front. He had once remarked to me that he was just a very ordinary fellow, "a dime a dozen" he said, following this up with, "probably a dozen *for* a dime," not seeming to notice that this was the same thing.

As soon as Johnny was back on the truck on this Monday morning, he sent a Qualcomm message to say that we were ready to go. While we waited for a dispatch, he told me about his weekend. The bike ride to the airport had indeed been a challenging one, along some major streets. At a certain point he had been so hot and thirsty that he stopped at a bar and ordered a beer. (This was perfectly all right, as I understood Alan's rules. He was off duty, on "home time" – which could be taken anywhere – not "under a load.") From what he said, he drank the first beer so fast that he didn't even taste it, then then drank another two beers in a more leisurely way.

It worried me enough to think of anyone riding the major streets of Phoenix on a bicycle but doing so on three beers! However, as usual, he seemed to have gotten away with it.

Johnny's daughter, he said, had felt strongly that the wrong man had won that weekend's race, but Johnny seemed perfectly happy with the result. He had enjoyed watching the race, had bought T-shirts for both of our dispatchers as well as for some other friends, and had had a really good time.

Now he was eager to get back to work, hoping for a load back East, where the driving was harder. He was determined that I should experience this before he turned me loose. Even so, he told me, with his last student, Stephanie, he had told Alan that they shouldn't send her to the Northeast for at least six months. He would do the same thing for me, he said, because the Northeast really wasn't for beginners. I was happy about this and hoped it would work. I preferred the West and didn't care if I never drove the Northeast, except possibly for going to Quebec and speaking French.

After an hour we were dispatched on trip number nine to pick up a load of Similac and Ensure at Ross Laboratories and drive it to Columbus, Ohio. I was the driver as we went to Sara Lee in Tolleson to pick up an empty trailer, then continued to the Ross plant, where we arrived well before our 3 PM appointment time and had to park along the street, on the wrong side of it, and wait, as the Ross yard was very small. Just to make things more difficult, there was something like a miniature traffic circle, or cul-de-sac, at the entrance to the yard, complete with a small curb-lined and landscaped circle four-square in the middle of it. Johnny took his bicycle off the trailer and rode it up and down the street while we waited. When word came on the CB radio that we could pull into the first loading dock, he was two blocks away, visible only as a small speck in the distance. This gave me an uncomfortable few minutes while I waited for him to make his way back to within hailing distance.

Johnny was determined that I should back up to this loading dock myself. Apparently, he had made a resolution during his time off that I had better be doing more of the backing. He helped me set it up, but then, as I began to back, he was able to size the situation up better and to realize just how difficult it was going to be.

The problem was that although the yard was new, and beautifully landscaped with trees and other vegetation, it was poorly designed from the standpoint of backing trailers up to its loading docks, with limited space in front of the docks. Dock one, nearest to the entrance, was the hardest space of all. Worse yet, there was another Alan truck already in dock two, which had the effect of making the job nearly impossible.

With an abrupt change of plan, we switched places, first opening the back doors of the trailer. Johnny began to back the trailer up to the loading dock, watched by the other Alan driver and me. It took him four tries. He kept needing to run over the curb in front of the loading dock then nearly tangling with the tree that was planted between the curb and the wall. One of the doors of the trailer came unfastened at one point and the other driver and I hastened to stop Johnny so we could fasten it back again.

Finally, he made it in. The other Alan driver remarked to me that he wasn't at all sure he could have done that backing. He had had trouble enough getting into dock number two, he added.

After getting loaded up, I was the one who drove out of the yard, without any particular difficulty. Hard to get into didn't always equal hard to get out of, partly because the other Alan driver had already left. I headed for Flagstaff, up the big hills again.

I was now conscious of being in week four of the eight-week training program. The days seemed to be flying past. I felt strongly that I wanted to wring every last bit of instruction out of the program and resented anything that might prevent me from doing that.

Johnny had made the commitment to not going home for the whole eight weeks, so we could fit in more trips. I wanted to do the same thing but was now subjected to the united pressure of my family, which was about to gather for the graduation of my youngest daughter from college. This would mark all four of my children having BA's. All of my children and both of my brothers were planning to meet at my mother's house in Salt Lake City and they wanted me there too if it was a possible thing. Was it possible, they wanted to know? I railed against fate, but Johnny urged me to go too, so we asked to be routed through Salt Lake City for home time on the relevant dates, at the beginning of May.

But that was in the future. In the meantime, we arrived in Ohio and did a drop and hook at Ross in Columbus, trading the Similac and Ensure for a load of Zone bars and Similac going to Tyler, Texas and the start of trip number ten. This was only 970 miles away, so we arrived two days later, dropped the load and, unusually, bobtailed to Ft. Worth, where we had been dispatched to pick up a load from Kraft and take it back to Phoenix, trip number eleven.

Johnny and I were both rather unhappy about having to go back to Phoenix yet again. This wasn't the "back East" trip that Johnny wanted, and I already had a good working knowledge of Phoenix, had started off with one, actually, as I had visited my in-laws there for many years. But clearly, we were being set up, though it seemed a bit prematurely, to be routed through Salt Lake City for my home time, so there wasn't much to be said.

That was bad enough, but when we reached the Kraft plant in Ft. Worth, an unpleasant surprise awaited us. The woman at the guard shack, a tiny little grandma of a woman, white hair done up in a bun, who had a little lap dog lying on a blanket in the guard shack to keep her company, consulted her lists, then told us that we weren't expected until Sunday.

"Friday – today," asserted Johnny.

"Sunday," repeated the woman, and made it stick.

We had to get back into the truck and leave. Johnny picked up the Qualcomm and started a series of messages with dispatch, but there was really nothing to be done, again because of the necessity of me being in Salt Lake City in five days.

In the end, we spent the night at a very nice nearby truck stop. It was my introduction to IdleAir and I was enthralled. Johnny had described IdleAir to me, but I hadn't seen it in action until now. This was also the first time we had needed the air conditioning that

IdleAir could supply. With the bunk heater in Johnny's truck, staying warm was never a problem.

We drove, still bobtailing, into Arlington, Texas the next day. Johnny had decided to spend the day at the Six Flags amusement park there. I wanted to go to a Saturday vigil Mass and do my laundry.

We went first to the information center for Arlington, located next to the baseball stadium, so that I could find out about churches and laundromats and get a map. The senior citizens who staffed the center seemed surprised to find themselves dealing with truckers and were more than a bit hesitant in trying to answer questions about where a semi was allowed to park. But I got the addresses and Mass times for a couple of churches as well as recommendations for laundromats, found them all on a wall map in the information center and was set to go.

Johnny took his bicycle down from the truck and rode off in the direction of the amusement park, visible in the distance, after we agreed on a meeting place and time. By now it was late morning, so I drove over to the laundromat, but passed it on the left and found a place to eat lunch.

After lunch I went back to the laundromat and washed all of my clothes. On the spur of the moment I took the three towels that Johnny kept as mats for the truck, and which were filthy by now, after four solid weeks of use. I made a separate load out of them because they were much too dirty to put in with my clothes.

Trucking is a dirty business and while Johnny and I each kept a pair of shoes to wear only in the truck, we still had to step into the truck to change our shoes. We had been in ice and snow, mud, dirt and various kinds of grease, tar and miscellaneous goo, these last usually on the ground at fuel islands, and had tracked some of all of these things into the truck.

I put the towels into a machine, added quite a lot of bleach along with the detergent and set the machine on hot, but the towels weren't very clean when I started to pull them out to put them in the dryer. So, I washed them again, again with hot water, detergent and bleach. They still looked awful when I pulled them out, but this time I ran them through the dryer anyway.

When Johnny and I met up again that evening, I confessed to him that although I understood perfectly well why, with 16 years of experience, he could drive a semi and back it up much better than I could, I was totally humiliated to find that he was better at doing laundry than I was with more than 30 years of experience as a housewife. He roared with laughter and informed me that the towels had been new when I got on the truck. He never washed towels, but just threw them away when they got too dirty and bought new ones. They were cheap.

Sunday morning finally arrived, and we picked up a load, though it took two more tries. The same woman wouldn't let us in when we arrived at 6 AM for an 8 o'clock appointment, but made us go sit for an hour, so that we wouldn't be more than an hour early. I remarked to myself that the woman might *look* like a sweet little grandmother, but her behavior was quite otherwise.

Finally in possession of the load of Kraft Lunchables, we drove out of Ft. Worth, taking a more southern route than I had ever been on, I-20 westward until it merged into I-10. Once we got to El Paso the route became familiar, though it was many years since I had driven that way. I greatly enjoyed driving across southern New Mexico and Arizona.

There was an odd independent truck stop out in the middle of nowhere in New Mexico, where we stopped late one night. It was like being back in the Third World, I thought: a dirt parking lot, crumbling concrete walls and peeling paint on every painted surface. Blankets in loud colors were draped over the dirty walls. There was a lot of cheap plastic junk for sale. The whole place looked worn out and dirty. Johnny's opinion was that it was tolerated by local authorities, even though it clearly could have been condemned, because it was the only place for truckers to stop for many miles around.

Having to wait two days to pick up this load had made things tight for delivering it on time. Johnny sent a Qualcomm to the dispatchers to say that we could still do the load but we would drive it as a team. Now, at the end of the fourth week out, this was a permissible thing. I was about to discover how the truck could move twenty-two hours out of twenty-four, the typical team driver practice.

Johnny was driving when we came to Tucson and turned north. I had lived in Tucson for 12 years. On the whole, I hated the city, but not having been back for many years I was eager to get a look at it. Many cities don't look their best from the freeways that pass through or around them. Tucson was rather an extreme example of that.

Thinking back to my years of living in Tucson, it was being pregnant and terribly hot all one summer that had really finished me off on it, that plus the atmosphere of "suppressed violence." Tucson was too near the Mexico border, so there was lots of drug-related crime. When I lived in Tucson, I tried to appreciate the "subtle beauty" of the desert, the dull green colors and different earth tones. Sometimes I could and sometimes I couldn't, but I was always thrilled when I got away and saw the beautiful green vegetation of other, lusher, parts of the country. Actual lakes and rivers of real water just lying around in the open seemed amazing after a long period of residence in Tucson. Even ten years later another Tucson-refugee friend and I would exclaim over open water whenever we saw so much as a pond.

On this day we didn't stop in Tucson, but just stayed on I-10 as it turned northward. I enjoyed seeing Picacho Peak for the first time in many years. It's a lone mountain, covered with saguaros, rising out of the flat desert and is supposedly the site of the one Civil War battle to take place in Arizona. There was a rest area there, as I well recalled, having stopped at it many times on my trips back and forth to and from my in-laws' house.

From the rest area it looked like about a 15-minute walk to the top of Picacho Peak, but it was actually much, much farther. In the 1960's and 70's, when my family lived in Tucson, we saw newspaper stories almost every year about a tourist family getting out of their car at the Picacho Peak rest area and deciding just to walk up the "hill," usually in sneakers and not even carrying water. The ones who knew enough to cut the top off a barrel cactus for water might survive, but sometimes people died.

We delivered the Lunchables in Tempe, then went to Tolleson

for a 6 AM pickup at Sara Lee and the start of trip number twelve. The man at the Sara Lee guard shack inspected the trailer, then insisted that it be washed out before he would let us bump the dock. He and Johnny seemed to aggravate each other, unusual for Johnny, who was usually "hail fellow well met" with security guards. This guard got off on the wrong foot by demanding to see Johnny's CDL – always left in the truck. I produced mine instead, having formed the policy of carrying it into guard shacks. It was required only occasionally.

Johnny guarded his CDL and was never happy about moving it off the truck, which he regarded as risky. He explained to me that his livelihood depended on the CDL; he was afraid that he would eventually lose it if he took it off the truck very often.

So, to save trouble, I pulled mine out of my jeans pocket and let the man write down its number. He was noticeably nicer to me and struck me as the sort of man who might want to flirt, though he was clearly impeded by Johnny's presence. He was middle-aged with a long, sallow face. What hair he had was combed over the top of his head in a vain attempt to hide a large bald spot.

Johnny was annoyed at having to get the trailer washed out, but it couldn't be helped. We drove up the street to a truck wash business right next to the truck stop where I had stayed while Johnny went to the NASCAR race.

A trailer washout turned out to be comparatively easy, if only because we were paying someone else to do it. Johnny had me drive to the right of the truck wash building and park beside it, then we opened the trailer doors. I waited at the wheel while a man climbed into the trailer with a hose and washed it out.

Once the man had finished washing out the trailer we went back to Sara Lee. This time Johnny let me cope with the security guard alone. He seemed kinder in the absence of Johnny (and, yes, quite flirtatious). He explained that he knew Alan employees weren't allowed to get a trailer washed out unless the shipper demanded it, so he had been trying to do us a favor.

He was right, or almost right. Alan policy was that trailers could only be washed out at company expense before or after produce, meat or hazmat loads, or when the shipper demanded it. Drivers were expected to do the washing out themselves if they went through a terminal, a sort of "branch office" where Alan kept mechanics and which offered some services to drivers, such as a lounge, showers, vending machines, cheap or free laundry, and free Internet. Alan had half a dozen terminals scattered across the country.

You could also get fuel at Alan terminals, but Johnny never did if he could help it because it would deprive him of a truck stop shower, and he hated the terminal showers which didn't provide towels, weren't as nice as most truck stop showers and weren't cleaned any oftener than once a day.

Finally having gotten loaded in Tolleson, we headed north toward Flagstaff and the start of an interesting day as we went through Page and saw the Glen Canyon Dam. This had been one of my favorite routes for years, being the way that my husband and I used to drive from Tucson to Salt Lake City to visit my parents. I wasn't sure if it was suitable for trucks, having a vivid memory of turning right off of one highway, then climbing a cliff in a series of hairpin turns.

Johnny decided that it was the best route, after studying the truckers' atlas and searching his memory. He wanted to see the Glen Canyon Dam too – said he hadn't been that way since he had been in training himself, 16 years earlier.

He told me about his trainer, a nice and competent man, but one who chain smoked and the inside of whose truck resembled a pig sty more than a human habitation. After finishing training with the man Johnny had called his boss and recommended that he not be allowed to train anymore because his truck was six inches deep in trash!

I had settled into the way of life on Johnny's truck. We kept things pretty tidy. Johnny shook the towel mats out every few days, oftentimes by holding them out the window one by one as I drove.

Johnny was using most of the truck's cabinets and cubbyholes for his own clothing, so I lived mostly out of my suitcase. I had divided it into quadrants: socks and other underwear here, pants there, shirts the other place. The suitcase had a place to lie flat between a lower and an upper cabinet. I dragged it onto the foot of the bed whenever I needed something out of it, foraged around in it, then put it back in its place.

My Alan briefcase and the laptop computer fitted in the space between the mattress and the wall of the cab at the foot of the bed. The head of the bed had a set arrangement too. On the left-hand side of the pillow I kept my prayer books, plus whatever two books I was current reading, usually one fiction book and one nonfiction book about some aspect of Christianity or Catholicism.

A water bottle or two could be wedged into the space at the head of the bed, between the mattress and the wall of the cab. I felt fortunate indeed to have the lower bunk. Once or twice in Johnny's absence it was necessary for me to climb up and open or shut the window vents at each end of the upper bunk. I found that the bed, besides its obvious use as the place where Johnny slept, was also being used as a sort of storage overflow. The neatness of the rest of the truck didn't extend this far, and Johnny must be sleeping curled around various boxes and other miscellaneous objects. After seeing the condition of the upper bunk it no longer surprised me that things occasionally fell down onto my bed.

My purse, which I had stopped carrying on the theory that it might be contributing to my hip pain, was on the right-hand side of my pillow. Apart from using it to store things, I used it to keep my glasses safe at night, slipping one of the sidepieces of the glasses into the purse's outside pocket. In my wallet were my new truck stop loyalty cards. I was working on accumulating one of each brand: Petro/TA, Pilot, Flying J, Love's, Sapp Bros., and Ambest.

Although we had driven out of Phoenix on the now-familiar I-17, after Flagstaff we cut north on US-89, off the beaten path. It was Johnny who drove the switchbacks that I remembered. He enjoyed the unfamiliar scenery after we departed from the normal route and didn't seem at all bothered by the steepness of the hill.

We stopped in Page and visited the tourist information center there, then drove across the dam. To Johnny's disappointment, the parking area on the other side of the dam was prohibited to truckers, but then he came on another place, just a little farther, where he was able to park the truck. He walked back to get a closer look at the dam but I (typically for me – I'd been doing it all my life) stayed in the truck to read, having seen as much as I wanted to of the dam when we drove across it.

Then I drove, while Johnny took one of his naps. He must actually have dozed off because he didn't say anything when I got tired of driving US-89, with its frequent changes of speed limit and small towns. I cut west on I-70 to pick up I-15 northbound instead of continuing up US-89 until it crossed I-15 as Johnny had planned.

This was a real mistake, as I found out when Johnny woke up. It added at least an hour to the day's drive. It was also an assertion of independence, and a poorly chosen one. The route had been explained to me, and I knew the way Johnny intended us to go. Johnny didn't visibly lose his temper, but he did seem surprised and I felt that I had been untrustworthy and would have to work to get back in his good graces again.

We reached Salt Lake City in the evening, a couple of days early for the graduation. After taking ten hours off we drove up to Alan's drop yard, north of Salt Lake City, where I practiced backing for a couple of hours. Sometimes I succeeded in getting the trailer into the "hole" between two other trailers and sometimes I didn't. I still wasn't getting it.

In the afternoon, we delivered the load of Sara Lee frozen food to a Walmart distribution center in Corinne, Utah, where Johnny made me do the backing. Walmart distribution centers always had spacious loading dock areas. In this case it was possible to do an easier type of backing than the classic alley dock setup. Johnny talked me through sweeping a large semicircle with the truck which, when stopped at the proper point, left the trailer straight in front of the loading dock. Even I could back it straight into a hole by this time.

After delivering the load, we went back to the same drop yard, where we were supposed to leave our now-empty trailer and pick up a full one, which another driver had left there for us, then deliver the full one to Costco's Salt Lake City distribution center at 5 AM the next morning. We didn't reach the drop yard until almost 10 PM. The first thing we did was walk across the street to eat a late dinner at a restaurant there.

After dinner, when we walked back across the street to the drop yard to hook up to the new trailer, it quickly became apparent that there was a problem with the new load. The reefer was set at -10° F, but the gauge temperature was reading +10 F., too large a discrepancy to be normal. Johnny immediately phoned road service and began trying various things to correct the problem, first by doing a manual defrost.

Alan monitored its reefers by satellite, so Johnny's activities set off alarm bells at headquarters and we soon received a Qualcomm message warning us that the reefer had problems. There was no easy answer to why it was malfunctioning. After talking with road service several times, Johnny was told to take the trailer into Salt Lake City, to a Thermo King dealer there, for diagnosis and repair.

At this point I again let Johnny down. I had been up since 9 AM and it was now almost midnight, but of course Johnny had been up since 9 AM too. He was driving, as I had done all the driving I could legally do that day. I simply went to bed and fell into a deep sleep, missing all the subsequent events of driving to Salt Lake City and waiting while the reefer was repaired. Lack of coolant was its problem. I didn't wake up until the delivery at 5 AM.

When I woke up we were at the guard shack for the Costco delivery. My first thought was to feign further sleep and let Johnny bump the dock, but then my conscience kicked in, so I got up and dressed, then slipped into the passenger seat of the truck. I was pretty sure Johnny would make me do the backing, and so it proved.

He climbed back into the truck after dealing with the guard, glanced over in my direction, looked away for a second then, turning back to me gave a devilish little grin and asked, "How would you like to be the one to back up to the dock?"

I sighed and responded, "Sure. That's why I got up – in case you wanted me to," which seemed to surprise him. With the usual struggle, the trailer was backed up to the dock. Then I went in to deal with the paperwork while Johnny was finally able to get some sleep.

Later in the day I was picked up at a Salt Lake City truck stop by one of my daughters and her family who were driving into town from California. Johnny had made various plans for the next few days, so we agreed to communicate on the Friday and I got off the truck, first giving my family a tour. They were interested, never having seen a semi up close. They took my picture, with and without a grandchild in my arms, both inside the truck and standing beside it.

Some members of my family seemed to think I was being brave to drive a semi, whereas several friends were frankly afraid for my life.

CHAPTER 8

Pleasant Days
(May 5-8)

Two days later, after the graduation celebration was over, I got back on the truck, when Johnny stopped by the same truck stop to get me. He had previously been up to Logan, Utah to pick up 32,000 lb. of frozen cookies for delivery to Moberly, Missouri, and had taken the southern route through Salt Lake City rather than "cutting the corner" on I-84, which would otherwise have been the better choice.

As we drove Parley's Canyon on I-80, east of Salt Lake City, we got caught up on each other's lives. I told Johnny about my daughter's graduation. He told me about an abortive trip back home that he had tried to make to see his youngest daughter play softball. The airplane to Idaho had broken down, causing him to miss a connection and the game was cancelled anyway. A series of frustrations! He had managed to see an NBA game in Salt Lake City, though, and was happy about that.

After the graduation, my training with Johnny was more than half over. Time seemed to move faster and faster and I had a greater sense of urgency about trying to learn everything. There was so much *to* learn!

I was getting comfortable with truck stops, truck stop showers and laundry facilities, rest areas, and the rhythm of a trucker's life, besides all the technicalities of picking up and delivering loads, passing through weigh stations, sliding tandems, using the Qualcomm and doing all the necessary paperwork. Johnny had a very efficient way of dealing with paperwork, which I watched closely and determined to use when and if I went out on my own.

Alan provided trip envelopes and a trip book. Johnny stored all the papers related to one trip in that trip's envelope as we went along, writing relevant statistics into the spaces provided for them on the front of the envelope. That way there were never stray papers floating around the cab to get stepped on or misplaced.

All of these other things were in addition to driving the truck, which was really only one aspect, though admittedly the most important one, of the trucker's life. Driving was going okay for me. If only I could learn to back!

And I was appalled at how hard Johnny worked. Of course, he was training me on top of trying to make as many miles as possible. I knew we were doing more than Alan intended. I had noticed a paragraph in Johnny's training manual which seemed to indicate that I should be doing *all* of the driving instead of only half. And we were moving pretty far, pretty fast, having gone more than 13,000 miles in our first month out together.

Alan gave a performance bonus to drivers who averaged more than 10,000 miles per month for a given quarter, but Johnny seemed dissatisfied even with the 13,000 miles. He had hoped to get over 15,000 miles, he told me. Having to wait two days in Texas, plus a few other losses of time, had kept us from reaching that goal.

The normal trucking life, as I was beginning to understand it, consisted of working 14 hour days, 7 days a week. It was what truckers called a lifestyle rather than a job. This seemed to mean that you couldn't do much else but run when you were out on the road. Some people who had been doing it for a long time had evolved a livable schedule of three weeks out then one week at home, or even two months out and one month home. They could earn a good enough living that way, once they were being paid at the higher rate that drivers made after they had a few years of experience.

The bad part was that with all that work, a total commitment really, hours spent getting loaded or unloaded, doing paperwork, route planning and all the rest, drivers were only paid for the number of miles they drove, which was usually expressed as, "If the wheels aren't turning you're not making any money." This "came with the CDL" as Johnny explained it, but I wasn't so sure. It seemed like a systematic pattern of exploitation to me. If you divided the money by the number of hours actually worked to get it, the hourly rate wasn't very good.

Johnny's was the reaction of the super-competent piece worker. If they only paid for miles he'd drive a ton of miles. If they expected him to drive 500 miles a day, he'd drive 650 instead. Let them see how they liked them apples! He'd make lots of money, log it whatever way he could get away with and beat them at their own game. He'd laugh all the way to the bank. The only problem was, as I saw it, that Alan King Associates was laughing all the way to the bank too.

It seemed certain that the drivers were making lots of money for the company, but the company paid drivers less than it spent on fueling the trucks – a lot less. There was something wrong with this picture, but I couldn't solve the problem in my own mind, and I put it away to ponder later once I knew more about it.

Alan was supposed to be one of the good companies. I was learning the company culture. Drivers normally waved to each other when they crossed on the highways, and sometimes greeted each other on the CB, especially if they were off the beaten path a little, on a State route or in a small town.

An Alan driver who broke down could expect, at the least, a series of inquiries on the CB from other Alan drivers going past. Alan drivers helped each other out. They were often called "Alan," both by other companies' drivers and among themselves. "Hey, Alan, how's it going?" or "Come on over, Alan," on the CB when a truck was letting another truck change lanes in front of him. The usual answer was, "Thank you, driver."

Using the CB was yet another thing that I learned from Johnny. I was old enough to remember some of the CB slang that everyone had learned in the 1980's with the movie "Smokey and the Bandit." "Ten/four" was an acknowledgment. "Smoky" or "Smoky Bear" or "Bear" all meant the Highway Patrol.

Johnny rarely used the CB. He complained about the language used by what he called "CB Rambos." As early as CDL school I had heard complaints about the bad language used on CB radios these

119

days, as well as the sort of harassment that a woman might run into.

"It's as though they had never talked to a woman before," Johnny once said.

But he used the CB when he wanted information, and I was interested in how he did it. He would turn the radio on, tune it to channel 19, then pick up the microphone and say one of two things into it, either "Have you got a copy?" or "Have you got it on?"

So, for example, if we were headed east and he remembered that there was a weigh station not far ahead and wanted to know if it was open, he would say something like, "Westbound, have you got it on?" or "Westbound Alan, have you got a copy?" if he saw one of our own trucks. Then he'd ask about the weigh station until somebody gave him an answer.

Or if we were in bad weather, he might use the CB to try to find out how far a storm extended and how bad it got, offering information about the weather where we had just been in return.

One of the more important uses of the CB was to find out why traffic had jammed. Was it construction, or had an accident occurred? I had never realized as a car driver that whenever traffic jammed, the airwaves around the spot were filled with the voices of truckers talking on their CB's, finding out what was going on and how to get around it, if possible. As soon as the truck had slowed down enough, and he was sure no one was going to run into us, Johnny would turn the CB on and listen to the talk. Occasionally he put in a question, but more often it was enough just to listen.

"Westbound, what's the problem here?" (often phrased considerably more strongly than that).

"You've got a four-wheeler turned over in the median and about three bears on the scene. Keep to the right to get by," or

"It's just a construction slowdown. They've got it down to one lane at mile 122."

One day in Tennessee the traffic ground to the sudden and complete halt which usually indicated an accident. As we sat waiting, engine turned off but CB on, truckers all around us were complaining and swearing. Drivers nearer the front explained that it was a bad accident and that a helicopter was arriving to take some injured people away.

"Why the #@!* can't they let us by?" came a question from a frustrated driver.

"Wa'al," drawled the original informant, "if you get too close to a helicopter, you'll get your head blowed off. You just wait patiently, driver. They'll let us go when they can."

Soon after that the traffic did begin to move.

CB's were useful in big cities, too, where we often heard interesting news about construction or other slowdowns. The satellite radio had stations devoted to traffic and weather, but only for the dozen or so biggest cities.

I liked Alan's logo. It consisted of the capital letters "AKA" for Alan King Associates in script, the two "A"'s balancing each other, the "K" surmounted by a gold crown. In some places, on the company's letterhead for example, the words "The King of Transport" were written underneath the logo. Trucking firms were not noted for their modesty.

There were so many different colors of trucks on the road. Alan's trucks were a particular shade of green, somewhere between forest and apple, which I was beginning to find easy to pick out, so that I could wave to other Alan drivers. The Alan trucks looked distinguished, I thought, with the shiny gold AKA on the door and on top of the cab against the darkish, but not too dark, green background of the rest of the tractor. I especially liked the crown, which was stylish.

The logo showed up well against the white trailers that Alan pulled too. Here the gold letters and crown were highlighted in the same green color, making them stand out. Most other companies pulled white trailers too, though there were other possibilities. A few trailers were aluminum, which Johnny said was hard to make paint stick to, and a few were of completely other colors. One of the biggest companies pulled blue trailers, for example, and another pulled orange ones.

Once in a while I saw trailers with pictures, or even whole murals, on them, such as Budweiser cans or bikini-clad young women drinking Pepsi. My favorite was the one covered all over with images of huge jelly beans, a real rainbow of colors.

But most trailers were just white, usually with some kind of writing on them. One rather large company had trailers with a wide blue stripe which turned up toward the front to end in a flying bird. Drivers from this company were sometimes called "Bluebird" on the CB. I admired their look but thought the crowns on the Alan tractors and trailers were equally good.

Although the majority of tractors were red, white or blue there were tractors of every conceivable color. I particularly liked the bright yellow tractors which carried a huge picture of St. Michael the Archangel on each side. I had seen green tractors, of course, purple ones, orange, maroon, even one painted a bilious shade of yellowish lime green.

Johnny and I were company drivers. The truck we were driving belonged to Alan King Associates, not to us. The owner operators, who owned their own trucks, did all sorts of things to them, adding chrome and extra lights. Some of their trucks had bumpers that seemed to be only a couple of inches off the ground, and usually showed it in various sorts of damage from being scraped against dips in driveways or on other low obstacles.

The older truckers, quintessential or "real" truck drivers, as I tended to think of them, considered the kind of truck Johnny and I were driving to be a "toy," hardly real. They preferred tractors with massive engine compartments sticking out in front. They would sometimes say that the Freightliner Columbia Johnny and I drove was too small and "plasticky," as in not made of metal. I liked the Columbia, though, for the amount of storage space inside the cab – the well-thought-out design for people who lived in a truck. The few times I had gotten to look into a Kenworth or a Peterbilt they had seemed to have noticeably fewer places to put things. The Peterbilt's dashboard wasn't even flat enough to lay things on.

I thought privately that Johnny put a little *too* much on his dashboard, and hoped to run a neater truck if and when I got one of my own to drive, but you couldn't put anything onto a Peterbilt dashboard – it would just slide off onto the floor.

As we took turns driving, we sometimes amused ourselves by noting the hazmat numbers on the placards of passing trailers, then looking them up in the hazmat handbook that we carried.

Hazardous materials were listed by class, and by number within that class. So if a passing tanker was placarded, say, with a "Class 8 Corrosive" sign listing it as number 1837, one of us could look in the handbook and find out that the product being hauled was "thiophosphoryl chloride," which really told us nothing – as neither of us knew any chemistry – but which sounded pretty deadly.

Time did, indeed, seem to be speeding up in the second half of training. Johnny seemed to feel it too. He was leaning on me harder about backing. Whereas he had previously been a little too indulgent sometimes, "treating me like a woman" and doing a backing himself, he was now arranging more frequent practice sessions as well as having me do all the backing at shippers and receivers. This made more work for him, of course. It took him a lot longer to talk me through a backing than it would have taken to do it himself. But he grudged no effort!

After one particularly difficult session, where it seemed that Johnny was always telling me to turn the steering wheel "the other way" (he never stopped thinking that I ought to know which way I had been turning it in the first place – probably true, but I simply didn't), I looked at him in near despair.

"Why do I *always* turn it the wrong way first?" I asked. "Wouldn't you think I'd have a fifty-fifty chance of doing it right? But I always do it wrong! Even when I think to myself that I'm probably wrong, so I turn it the opposite way to what I think, I'm *still* wrong. Why?!"

"I don't know," replied Johnny. "That's something I haven't figured out about you yet."

I was liking life as a trucker, enjoying the wide-open spaces and beautiful scenery of the countryside between cities. I liked driving a semi, now that I was getting better at it, as I had always liked driving a car. I still had moments, though, of thinking that semis were absurdly large and that it amounted to criminal insanity for anyone as small as a person to drive anything as large as a truck.

And I liked life on the road, no domesticity, no guilt for not cooking or vacuuming or dusting. I liked taking a shower after working hard enough for the shower to make a real difference. The best moment of the day was stripping off and sluicing myself off under hot running water, feeling the sweat wash away.

I liked being with Johnny, listening to his trucking stories. There were endless things to learn; clearly I wasn't going to plumb the depths of his knowledge in this short space of time. He'd been at it for 16 years, after all. But I soaked up all I could from his stories.

We usually ate one meal a day in a restaurant or fast food place. We talked and looked at newspapers. I bought whatever local paper I could find, mostly for the sake of the comics and the crossword puzzle. Johnny always bought a "USA Today." It had very good national weather maps and Johnny followed some sports as well.

One of the unpleasant things I noticed about the blue-collar world and being surrounded by truckers was a way some of them had of looking at a woman, any woman, and seeming to strip her naked with their eyes. This happened quite often in the truck stop restaurants we frequented. One day I was doing my daily crossword puzzle and came across a clue that said "strip bare with the eyes" — and the answer was "ogle." Was *that* what ogle meant? About a week later a crossword puzzle clue was "check out and then some." Again, the answer was "ogle." I had thought I knew what ogling meant, but somehow hadn't imagined it being as ugly as what some of these truckers were doing.

How did they do it? I didn't know. I recognized the look but didn't think I could have done it myself. As the weeks of training passed, I found that some truckers ogled every woman who passed by. They didn't seem ashamed of it. It was never done in such a way that the woman being ogled — if that was indeed the correct term — could see, but they didn't hide what they were doing from the rest of us.

Sometimes they almost seemed bored by the whole thing, as if performing a tedious duty. A woman passed by, the man glanced at her, then with a quick upward movement of his eyes seemed to strip her bare to examine buttocks and breasts, then returned to eating or whatever he was doing.

This was a phenomenon that I hadn't seen more than twice in my life up to this point. It reminded me of letters that Ann Landers used to print, once every year or two. They all read the same way: "My husband/boyfriend looks at women when we're out in public. I feel insulted/rejected, as though my company isn't enough for him, but when I complain he just says, 'I'm a man. That's the way men are.'" As I recalled, Ann Landers didn't go for that excuse. I wasn't minded to either. It was like witnessing an assault.

Truckers were assaulting women left, right and center and seemed to think nothing of it. Incredible! It made me long for a nice burlap bag (choir robe? nun's habit?) to cover myself with. Was this what men did? Had it been done to me? Undoubtedly. Arghh!!

It reminded me of a passage from Hemingway's *The Green Hills of Africa*, a memoir about a big game hunting trip he made in Tanzania in the 1930's. The trip took place at a time when not all Tanzanians had adopted the Western custom of wearing clothing. Hemingway recounts how his hunting party met an African man and his young, beautiful wife. She was stark naked. The phrase, "We all had her with our eyes," had stayed in my memory.

Well, but I didn't spend much time thinking about ogling after I worked out what I thought about it. I just tried to ignore what was going on and succeeded pretty well.

What I was really enjoying, though it didn't occur to me, was life as a team driver. Johnny was my security. He could get us out of anything that I could get us into, and bumping the dock was guaranteed with him around. If worst came to worst he could always do it himself. That had only happened once, on the difficult backing job in Phoenix, but it gave me a sense of security to know that, with Johnny around, everything would be all right.

Was I too dependent on him? Johnny brought this up once or twice. I thought not. For one thing, it was natural for me to be dependent when I was such a beginner. For another, I didn't see anything wrong with leaning on Johnny while he was around. I was used to both roles. For many years I had been a single mother, the one upon whom my children depended. I had also taught school. I didn't mind being in authority, but I also liked the position of being a student. I'd done a lot of that too.

That's what I told Johnny. Naturally I depended on him when

he was there. When he wasn't there anymore, I wouldn't be able to depend on him, but that wasn't his problem. In a similar way, I never killed a spider if there was a man within five miles who might do it for me, but if I had to I could deal with the situation myself.

But back to the frozen cookies from Utah. We were driving them to a Walmart distribution center in Moberly, Missouri. On this trip there came one of the times when I went to sleep while Johnny drove into the night. When I woke up, in the early dawn, we were parked at a rest area. I got out of the truck to use the restroom, remembering to leave my purse on the driver's seat in case Johnny woke up. After using the restroom, brushing my teeth and washing up, I came back to the truck. By now I had learned to be quiet with the door, so there was a chance that Johnny wouldn't wake up.

I prayed Morning Prayer, as usual, while lying on my stomach, trying to work the pain out of my hip. These days it often took two or three tries before I was more or less out of pain, but the pain always left in the end. It was definitely a morning phenomenon.

More ominous were the sensations I had been experiencing down my right leg: ankle pain, numbness and tingling in my foot, a feeling in my calf as though someone had grabbed my leg. These, too, always went away in the end. Later in the day I might have a slight feeling of weakness in my leg, almost a pleasurable feeling, partly because it brought to my attention that I wasn't in pain. I tried to savor it, but it was a reminder that all wasn't well just the same.

So far, I was ignoring these phenomena, having no idea what was causing them or what to do about it. I just worked the pain out in the morning.

On this particular morning in southern Illinois I thought carefully after praying. All the conditions were in place for me to drive off without waking Johnny up. I knew where we were going, knew the route, and we had talked about it the night before. Making certain that Johnny was actually in the truck was the next step. He was a quiet sleeper, so I needed to catch sight of some part of him and stood studying the heap of covers – quilt, sheets and pillows – until I spotted his left foot in its white sock. Now I was free to leave.

I started the truck and drove back out onto the Interstate. This morning I had decided to try listening to the satellite radio using one of Johnny's sets of headphones (he had two). They worked so well that I could forget my hearing problem when I had them on. Driving along in the quiet of the early morning, a gray, rainy day, was the most pleasant experience I had yet had as a trucker. And to think that I was getting paid for it! Maybe I would like this life...

I listened to Mass, then to some classical music, but took the headphones off when the route got challenging. There was a construction detour off onto a county road, an unusual phenomenon for Interstate highways – in fact, completely unprecedented in my admittedly limited experience.

I followed the signs carefully and had to make several turns. I wasn't surprised when I heard a thump, then saw a sleepy Johnny appear in the passenger's seat, looking around in a dazed sort of way. I quickly explained the detour and that it seemed to be going all right. He nodded but continued sitting there, helping me identify each turn. I was glad and we chatted as I drove. I mentioned how much I had enjoyed the headphones and listening to the radio earlier.

"That's illegal, you know," Johnny remarked. "The Highway Patrol will write you a big ticket for that."

I hadn't known and was appalled. "Illegal?!"

"Yep. That's why I only listen at night. That way they can't see if you have them on or not."

Upon reflection I thought that it was probably rather unsafe to drive with no hearing whatsoever, but it *had* been wonderful listening to the music.

We delivered the cookies to Moberly, then crossed the Mississippi to pick up a load of Dow chemicals going to the Chicago area, trip number fifteen. These we delivered the next morning, Johnny having done all the driving, then I drove to the Kraft plant in Romeoville, Illinois where we picked up a load of Nabisco crackers and cookies, set on 65 degrees, for the trip back East, which was finally going to happen, trip number sixteen, to Slatersville, Rhode Island.

CHAPTER 9

Going to Hooters
(May 8-18)

Freeway driving had become very comfortable for me by now, except for hip pain of course, but other kinds of driving hadn't. I admired Johnny's lack of anxiety. Shifting gears or getting on or off the freeway were things he did automatically, almost without thinking. Even backing up to loading docks didn't stress him. His attitude was one of anticipation of whatever challenge to his ingenuity a delivery or pickup might pose. He wondered *how* he would solve whatever difficulties presented themselves but didn't doubt that he'd be able to do so. He seemed to look forward to such breaks in the routine of driving.

With me it was far otherwise. Even getting off the freeway was still an ordeal, multitasking with a vengeance! When Johnny told me to take the next exit and go to a Pilot truck stop, it started a monologue going in my mind, preceded by a two-word plea to heaven, "Oh, help!"

"Ok, next exit ... Signal early to warn others ... Don't slow down too soon ... Ramp speed 40 ... Okay ... Down to ninth gear as soon as you're off ... that's it ... that's it ... now! (I performed the complicated downshift maneuver: clutch in, pull it into neutral, clutch out, rev the engine up about 300 RPM, clutch in, pull in into ninth, with or without a loud noise depending on how well the RPM's matched) ... Is the Pilot on the left or right? ... On the left ... Slow down ... High side the curve ... Should I downshift to eighth? ("Just coast," interjected Johnny) ... Which lane to turn left from?

129

There are two, so that means the outer one ... run up the *outside* of it ... Now stop ... Now look ... Wait for that car ... put it in fourth ... wait ... wait ... ("Go," said Johnny). Okay, let the clutch out slowly ... RPM's to 1500 ... straight ahead ... shift to fifth ... straight ahead ... *now* turn ... turn ... watch the back tires ... look ahead ... back tires ... *Where's the Pilot?!* ... Up on the right ... okay ... sixth gear ... Where's the turn-in? ... can't see it ... can't ... oh, there's a truck coming out – that must be it ... seventh gear or should I just stay at 20 miles an hour until I turn in? ("Grab a gear," put in Johnny. That meant, in this context, go to seventh. I shifted to seventh but that meant I'd have to downshift to fifth to turn in to the Pilot – you could conceivably corner in sixth, I thought, but seventh was impossible) ... Okay ... coming up on the turn ... slow down ... oh, signal! ... slow down to 15 ... 15 ... *15, darn it!* ... Okay, range lever down, yes (I downshifted to fifth) ... turn ... watch the back tires ... turn ... Which fuel island? ... that one? ... that one? ... no, *that* one."

I went way out beyond the chosen fuel island, then turned sharply back so the trailer would straighten out more quickly. This is where Johnny often said, "Watch it!" lest I take out the fuel island with the trailer, but this time I did it well enough, so he only said, "Yeah, that's it, now wiggle it." I did the series of small "s" turns that would line the trailer up exactly behind the tractor, then stopped once the fuel pump was even with the driver's door, remembering to set the tractor brake and put it in neutral before shutting the engine down.

"Whew!"

Two things distinguished the first part of the drive back East. First was spending most of the day driving on US-30 through Ohio, in order to skirt the toll roads. This was good practice for me, in that it was a different sort of driving from the more usual Interstates. Towns occurred about every 10 or 15 miles, always with a reduced speed limit, so I got lots of shifting practice. Then again, it was a very scenic route through Amish country. Over and over I came upon large farms with no wires running to them, clearly Amish farms being run without the benefit of electricity.

Johnny warned me, though, to be very careful of any horse-drawn buggies I might meet up with, not to make any loud noise with the truck, such as downshifting or hitting the brakes hard, that might frighten a horse.

I did see six or eight buggies. Happily, all but two were on the other side of the road. I was able to avoid any close encounters – and the Amish drivers were obviously working toward that end too, I thought, as up ahead I saw a horse canter (gallop even?) across a bridge, then turn right down a country lane before I arrived at the spot. I just "backed off," trucker parlance for slowing down, and let it all happen. The horse and buggy were well out of the way before I got there.

The second thing that distinguished the drive back East was a marathon backing practice at a Petro truck stop in Milton, Pennsylvania which had a back lot up on a hill behind the main parking lot, very suitable for practicing. I spent a couple of hours driving in circles and backing, or trying to back, in between two piles of trash that Johnny set up. He hopped around outside, critically analyzing each attempt, and chatting with other drivers as the opportunity arose.

I was making a little bit of progress with backing in a couple of respects. I was beginning to understand that the backing maneuver consisted of turning the steering wheel sharply to the right – to start the trailer going sharply left – followed by steering back to the left in order to get the tractor straight in front of the trailer again. This was called "getting under it." Secondly, I now understood that if the trailer went past the desired 90-degree angle, it was absolutely necessary to pull forward in order to put things right.

Right and left were still transposed in the mirror, but this was beginning to matter less. After all, the task was to back in between two other trailers: which one I thought was on which side was not of any real importance. I made many, many attempts during this long session, and nothing really occurred to make me happy about it, but equally, nothing went disastrously wrong either.

After resting, we went on, and that night I sat in the passenger seat watching as Johnny drove through New York City. He chose 3 AM as the best time for this. I was deeply interested, but it really was appallingly difficult driving. He kept needing to move a lane to the left to avoid being shunted off the highway. We also passed through several tunnels or underpasses so low that they made me want to duck.

Johnny avoided all the pitfalls and eventually we came out the other side into Connecticut. Even in the early morning hours, long before the time for a rush hour, traffic jammed once or twice going over bridges.

The delivery in Rhode Island was routine but left us with nothing to do afterwards. There had been no "preplan load" on the Qualcomm. We sent several messages to our dispatchers before finally getting one back to say that we were number 25 on a list of drivers waiting for loads.

I had pretty much taken over running the Qualcomm, both because I was a much better typist than Johnny (I had been a manuscript typist for 15 years) and because it frightened me to have him using the Qualcomm while he was driving. The Qualcomm itself was a rather odd device. It seemed to me to have elements of old and new technology about it. The idea that we could be in satellite communication with the company from anywhere (except the north sides of buildings) was modern. And the company always knew where its trucks were. This all depended on a satellite receiving unit, a white glass ball mounted on top of the tractor.

But the device itself looked primitive. Messages consisted of lines of capitalized letters. Since the company paid by the letter for messages in either direction, we all, dispatchers and drivers alike, were encouraged to use the shortest possible forms of words. "R U MT?" meant "Are you empty?" These were called free-form messages, where people just typed questions or answers.

Most communication took place with "macros," empty forms which only needed to have fields filled in before being sent. And only the characters in the fields actually were sent, or so I surmised. There were macros for all sorts of things: checking in each day, accepting or refusing a dispatch, arriving at or leaving a pickup or delivery, requesting home time, running early or late on appointment times — all these matters were normally handled by macro. You could also request directions to a pickup or delivery site or find out how many miles away you were by using macros. You could even find out how much your paycheck was for the week.

Being on a list of drivers waiting for a dispatch was a first for me, though of course not for Johnny. The trainers got better loads than other drivers under most circumstances and exercised a greater degree of control over where they went. Until now there had always been a pretty good preplan load sent to the truck before we went in to make a delivery.

We were now in a part of the country with very few truck stops. Johnny decided to go north to Massachusetts, not far away, to a truck stop he knew of, and wait there for the next load.

Once we were in Massachusetts though, Johnny was interested in finding a sports bar where he could watch a particular game from the NBA finals, scheduled for that day. His first choice was always Hooters. I had never in my life been into a Hooters until the basketball finals had started, some days before. Johnny told me several times that Hooters was a "family place," and I remembered seeing advertising to that effect, but one time in a Hooters was enough to convince me otherwise.

I was sorry for the young women, girls really, walking around only half dressed, and was glad to think that none of my three daughters had ever had such a job. Apart from that, given my hearing problem which was always much worse in a condition of high ambient noise, and my aversion to television, the restaurant was pretty close to my idea of hell. When we first walked through the door into a Hooters, I felt slapped in the face by an almost palpable wave of noise – the cocktail party atmosphere squared or cubed. Adding to the din were 25 or 30 television sets, mounted on the walls of the restaurant and tuned to various sports channels. Wall-to-wall TV's!

Yes, it was definitely a hellish vision, I thought. There was worse to come when Johnny drank a couple of glasses of beer with his chicken wings. It was absolutely against company policy to drink while "under a load," meaning that we had been dispatched. Well, we hadn't been dispatched, so technically Johnny had every right to drink. The problem was that he would not be able to wait six hours until he drove again but would have to drive the truck to a truck stop after the game.

He claimed to be able to drive perfectly well (better than me!) on one, or even two, beers. I believed him, but it was irrelevant. Some day he would be stopped, or get in an accident, even if it wasn't his fault, and be discovered to have been drinking. Then they would nail him. He wouldn't be able to drive commercially for years. Johnny was used to getting away with things. He took chances quite often. Once in a while the consequences were bound to land on him. It filled me with dread.

Additionally, I now had the power to get him fired, if I chose to exercise it. That was the last thing I wanted, my only worry being that I might inadvertently let it slip. I drank a beer too, partly out of loyalty, and partly with the feeling that if they fired him they might as well fire me too, if only for not trying to stop him.

This scenario had already been played out twice, so I heard the news that Johnny wanted to find a sports bar with something much less than joy. But I could never have guessed what would happen next.

We had reached Lowell, Massachusetts. Johnny got off I-495, the outer loop around the Boston area, thinking that he had seen a Hooters in this area, but we soon found ourselves on smaller and smaller roads. We were no longer on a truck route, and the streets were beginning to look decidedly residential when, turning left at a stop sign, we were suddenly confronted by an underpass, about a block away, marked with a sign saying "11'6"," or two feet lower than our truck. There was also a man, out walking his dog, coming toward us. This man immediately put up his hand to say "Stop" when he saw the truck. Johnny did stop, put the truck's flashers on, and got out to consult with the man. When he climbed back into the truck, he had decided what to do. There was no one behind us yet, so he backed the trailer leftwards, into the lane for oncoming traffic, then backed straight down the wrong lane for about a block, until he was able to turn left back down the same street we had come up before the turn that put us in such a dangerous situation.

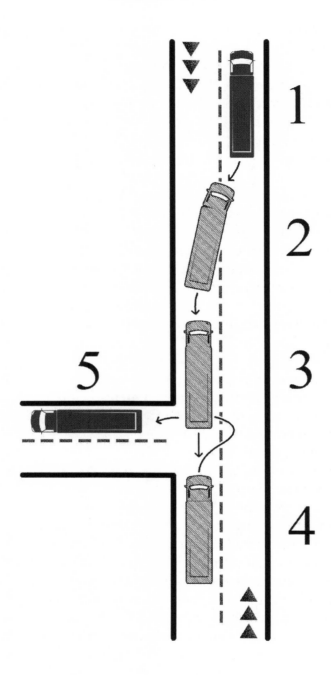

17. Diagram of how to back a semi in traffic

Once he had done this, and we were on our way again, he pointed out to me that by backing down the wrong side of the street he didn't have to worry about hitting anyone coming up behind him, as oncoming traffic would be visible from the front of the truck.

He found his way back to I-495 without any further trouble and located a Hooters in a different town, farther south. This time I had had enough of Hooters after only an hour or so. I went out and slept in the truck until Johnny came out, hours later, and drove the truck away.

The next day we were finally dispatched on a load. We were to pick up 41,319 lb. of Fruit$_2$O and drive it to Lansing, Michigan by early Monday morning, trip number seventeen. This gave us some extra time, so Johnny decided to visit Cedar Point, a huge amusement park near Sandusky, Ohio, on Sunday. He wasn't quite sure if it was open in the first half of May, so I got on the Internet at that night's truck stop in DuPont, Pennsylvania and found out that it was.

On Saturday we drove from DuPont to Youngstown, Ohio, then on Sunday morning went on in to Sandusky, where Johnny, after some frightening driving around tight residential streets in the small town, got permission to park the truck next to a convenience store within a few blocks of two Catholic churches, which I had also found on the Internet.

Johnny got on his bike and rode off to Cedar Point, while I walked to Mass.

When Johnny came back to the truck, some hours later, he was excited at having ridden a new, huge ride at Cedar Point. He had gotten into a bit of trouble with his bike, though, as it seemed that bicycles weren't allowed on the long causeway out to the island where the amusement park was located. A policeman had given him a ride across, but fortunately hadn't written him up, and he had been required to get a ride back with the park's security people.

It was now mid-afternoon. We spent the rest of the day driving to Lansing, Michigan, arriving at 8 PM for a 5 AM delivery the next morning. After delivering the load we drove 35 miles to a nearby town where we picked up a load for trip number eighteen, some tire-making chemicals which were to be delivered in Texarkana, Arkansas two days later.

I was now definitely doing all backing up to loading docks, but with lots of help from Johnny. The place where we picked up the chemicals was small, with only two loading docks. The job of backing up to either of them was rather different from anything I had yet attempted, easier if anything, but I didn't do it very well. The trailer wasn't quite straight when I bumped the dock. One side was touching the dock's rubber bumper, but the other side was at least three inches away. Johnny made me straighten it out of course.

When I was finally in, things began to move quickly. We were only picking up 18,000 lb. of chemicals, which were quickly loaded. This was, unusually, a place where we were invited onto the loading dock. I was interested to see the use of air bags to hold the load securely in place. A large paper bag, lined with plastic, was placed between the last two pallets on the trailer, then was inflated with an air hose until it filled all the space between the pallets. It was the last of a series of air bags, of varying sizes, to be applied to this load, which was now unlikely to shift under any reasonable circumstance short, perhaps, of an emergency stop.

Johnny explained that it was a superior sort of technology relative to the more usual load locks, metal bars with ratchets which were sometimes used in an attempt to brace loads. He had predicted that the load would be hazmat with placards needing to be affixed to all four sides of the trailer and was disappointed when the man in charge said that no, it wasn't hazmat – the chemicals weren't very dangerous. A hazmat load was one of the kinds of loads Johnny had hoped to encounter with me, so I would have a chance to see how they really worked. Both of us had the hazmat endorsement on our CDL's, one of the job requirements of working for Alan King Associates.

The drive to Texarkana was routine, except that we went through Indianapolis and stopped at Alan's terminal there, something Johnny would not ordinarily have done if he hadn't thought I should see it.

This particular terminal had quite a small yard. Johnny was eventually able to talk me through backing the trailer into an available spot, but it was tight. Everything about the yard was crowded.

As we arrived after business hours, I was not able to go into the office, nor could I buy any of the company logo T-shirts I was wanting to start acquiring, but Johnny was able to show me how to wash a tractor, and he talked a mechanic into changing the truck's fuel filter, something he probably couldn't have done at corporate headquarters where they would have insisted on doing a whole service, now overdue. Johnny didn't feel the need for a service and was unwilling to spend the hours that would have been required in order to get one.

Washing the tractor looked like fun, up to a point. Johnny got soaked doing it. The wash bay was equipped with a high-pressure hose, that sprayed hot water and even soap if you wanted it to. He worked hardest trying to get all the dead bugs off the grill and backs of the side mirrors of the truck. I was surprised when he opened up the hood and trained the high-pressure stream of water onto the engine itself. It seemed risky to me, but I suppose it wasn't as nothing bad seemed to come of it.

He also did a thorough job of cleaning the whole windshield. But, really, there was no part of that tractor that he didn't subject to the water. The truck came out looking very nice, especially after we used Windex on the insides of the windshield and windows. We sweet-talked someone into letting us use a Shopvac on the floor of the cab and were satisfied that things were pretty clean inside and out.

One disadvantage of the terminal was the scarcity of food, compared to a truck stop. Vending machines were all that was offered in the way of getting a drink or something to eat. On the whole, I was just as glad to leave after a few hours and go to sleep while Johnny drove to Tennessee. The world of truck stops was definitely better than the terminal world.

We arrived in Texarkana the next afternoon, early for our delivery, which wasn't supposed to be until the following morning. Johnny had some hopes of getting the trailer unloaded early, but it didn't happen. We were disappointed, when we arrived at the delivery site, to find that the dock workers weren't willing to do any such thing, even though they still had 20 minutes to work, and even though the load was so light and the pallets so few.

The whole setup at this company was very bad for semis. In the first place, there was an officiously worded sign about half a block before the security gates, warning drivers that they must slide their tandems *now* or not be admitted. The sign was followed by a very tight left turn into the yard, which would have been difficult to do with the truck stretched all the way out. But that was just the beginning of the nightmare. It was an old yard, designed for much shorter trailers than the 53-foot ones currently in use. Did they even design yards when this one was built? It looked more like a hodgepodge collection of buildings that had sprung up without benefit of any real planning. There were telephone poles, fire hydrants, various guy wires slanting down to the ground here and there – even railroad tracks.

This was one backing that Johnny did himself, both the afternoon of the attempted delivery and the next morning when we really did deliver the load. They were what is called "blind-side backing," that is, bending the trailer the other way from the usual. In a blind-side backing everything is opposite to a normal backing but seeing is much more difficult because you have to use the passenger-side mirror rather than the much closer driver's side one.

Nor did he slide the tandems when the sign said to. Rather, he argued with the security guards, demanding to talk with whoever had written the sign. He explained that they were asking him to, in effect, increase the turning radius of the truck, then drive it through a maze. And he prevailed. We threaded our way both times between and around all the obstacles. Johnny did the blindside backing required to get into the loading dock, *then* he slid the tandems. Once we were unloaded, he slid them back, and we left the yard, with me driving this time, and went 77 mi. to Pittsburg, Texas to pick up a load of frozen chicken for the start of trip number nineteen.

Later that day, when Johnny was driving again, I sent a Qualcomm message about the company where we had delivered the tire-making chemicals, reporting on their poor policies, giving them a bad rating and explaining as well as I could in the restricted space of a macro, limited to three lines of text in this case, what the problem was. It was a satisfying action, but I never found out if it produced any result.

18. Diagram of blind-side vs. normal articulation

The place where we picked up the chicken was nice and big, located outside of town, presumably on cheap land. Bumping the dock was relatively easy. Finding the place, too, was simplified by a huge statue of a Pilgrim's head, 30 or more feet high, placed prominently on the lawn in front of the plant.

We drove the frozen chicken to Rhinelander, Wisconsin, where we got lost as we drove into town. The directions to the plant which, as always, we had summoned up by macro from the Qualcomm, were unclear. Johnny was driving and made a wrong turn – as we soon realized. I was glad he was the driver, because we quickly found ourselves off any truck route in downtown Rhinelander. In the end, after asking a passerby, we got into the right part of town, only to be further stymied by the unclear directions. This time Johnny called the receiving company on his cell phone and was given good directions, which I later typed in a message to the dispatchers so that the next driver might have an easier time of it. A problem which we averted by calling was that the company had a different name on the building from what was on the dispatch or bills. This was not a common thing, but was also far from unheard-of. Companies were bought out and renamed, but it took time for new signage to be put up.

The Rhinelander company, once we got there, was very slow to unload the trailer, but eventually we were free to drive to Marathon, Wisconsin to pick up 35,592 lb. of cheese for the start of trip number twenty.

CHAPTER 10

Meltdown!
(May 18-21)

The climax of my problems with backing occurred at the Marathon pickup. Johnny had been talking to me on the way there about how short our time together was and how I would need to be more independent as I would be on my own before very long. In short, he was pushing me "out of the nest." He also predicted that I wouldn't be very happy for my first six months out on my own because "nobody is."

A large void was beginning to open in front of me as I contemplated life without a trainer. I already felt abandoned and aggrieved.

As we drove into the yard to make the pickup Johnny, for once, sized the situation up wrong. We were parked in other people's way and were told to move the truck to a place alongside a wrought-iron fence.

In his mood of making me be independent, Johnny told me to park the truck while he went in to do the paperwork for the load we were picking up. It was a relatively easy task but the problem was that I simply couldn't do it. I didn't set it up correctly, as I later realized, so I seesawed back and forth with the truck, trying to get the trailer parallel to the fence but unable to do so.

Finally Johnny came out from doing the paperwork and took a hand, directing me to pull much farther forward and get in front of the trailer, meaning that the tractor and trailer needed to be in a straight line relative to each other so that I could make the trailer move in the right direction as I backed it. Even with it set up properly I had a hard struggle to get parked. By the time I finally finished I was sure that the other drivers, and there were quite a few, were staring at me – whether with pity or contempt I didn't know.

Johnny unfastened his bicycle from the bottom of the trailer and rode around the yard in circles for ten minutes or so, while I went on sitting in the driver's seat, still smarting from having messed up a simple task so badly, waiting for a truck to leave our assigned loading dock so that we could back into it.

After a while Johnny got back in the truck. We sat together, watching the loading docks, while he gave me a talking-to that was evidently the result of his cogitations while riding around the lot on his bike. He said that I had better think about what I was doing, and whether or not I wanted to drive a semi. I was going to find it tough to be on my own. I pointed out that I was committed to Alan King Associates, having already spent six or seven weeks in the training program.

"You could be DOA," Johnny interjected.

"I could be *what*?!"

"You know what I mean." He struggled to express himself. "You could be dead on arrival when we get back to headquarters – just not take the test and leave. They couldn't stop you."

Well, yes, I guessed I did know what he meant now. If he didn't have confidence in me, maybe I needed to be even more worried than I already was. After all, he should know.

In the meantime, Johnny continued, I was going to do this next backing completely by myself. He wouldn't say a word. I could either set it up by driving in a big circle clockwise from where we were parked (being careful to miss a post which was very much in the way) or by sweeping a big circle counterclockwise. Of the two possibilities he recommended the first one, but it was up to me to choose. There was lots of room in front of the loading dock, so he was going to leave me to do it myself.

I sat there in the driver's seat, trying to decide which way to do the setup, and trying to summon up the courage to do this thing. As I watched, a truck came in from my right, swept a giant arc counterclockwise and backed up to an empty door. It was a beautiful display of competence, but it had a paradoxical effect on me. I suddenly found myself with tears in my eyes as I thought, "What a *stupid* thing to have to do!" The absurdity of the act, the outrageous nature of backing a 53-foot trailer so precisely, struck me forcibly. A trailer wasn't designed to be backed, as I had several times been told or read. The arcane skill which this driver practiced, and which he made look so easy, was an offense. The thing shouldn't be done, shouldn't *have* to be done.

At the other end of the building was a hydraulic lift which had seized, and up-ended, a somewhat different sort of trailer. Why shouldn't all trailers benefit from this more modern sort of technology? It would surely be within the realm of possibility, not even technically challenging, to design a system that would simply *put* a trailer wherever it was wanted – some sort of crane perhaps? Trailers could be made detachable from their chassis as intermodal containers already were. A driver could drive in under a machine which would lift the box of the trailer, place it somewhere to be unloaded, then return it to the chassis. No one would have to back anywhere.

The problem was a lack of respect for drivers, really. Nobody cared how hard it was to back a truck. Trucks often backed into things and did damage. The pylons at truck stops and shippers were usually bent at an angle and had paint scraped off them where they had been run into.

All these thoughts ran through my mind in much less time than it takes to tell – a matter of seconds, really. As I pondered and took in the nature of what I was being asked to do, having seen it from the outside as it were, enacted before my eyes, I felt completely overwhelmed. A wave of self-pity engulfed me, and I suddenly realized that I was about to cry – really cry. Rising abruptly from the driver's seat, I dived for my bunk, where I wrapped myself up in the quilt Johnny had loaned me, and which I loved. Then I built the pillows into a barricade and curled up into a fetal position while tears ran down my cheeks. I rocked back and forth, crying absolutely silently (30-plus years of motherhood having given me practice in this art). As I cried, I tried to think about my options.

The problem was that I didn't have any money, and nobody seemed eager to hire a 50-something woman with an inadequate work history. Without money I really didn't have the option of being "DOA," though I still thought staying home to raise the children had been a higher priority than having a career, closer to what God wanted of me. I was paying for it now, though. At least the kids had turned out well.

My thoughts ran in the familiar rut that had led me to the trucking industry in the first place: it was a "man's job," hence should pay more than the "women's professions" – standard advice from the 1970's – and truckers were needed so badly that almost anyone could get hired, and I couldn't/wouldn't teach because of my hearing, and I was too politically incorrect to get hired most places anyway, and I was damned if I'd go be a clerk at a 7-11 the way my CPA brother seemed to want me to.

The self-pity continued to wash over me as I thought of how cosmically unfair it all was. What was someone with a master's degree, who had graduated *magna cum laude* from college with a BA in Economics, who had made *Phi Beta Kappa*, what was such a person doing in this position? But what else could I do? I had no money ... The cycle went around again. I held onto Jesus in my mind and prayed over and over, "Help! Oh, help! Please help!" I began to think crazy thoughts as I rocked and cried. I was safe here in the corner of the truck, wrapped in Johnny's quilt and barricaded with pillows. What if I just stayed this way? What if I just never uncurled? If I went catatonic? They'd have to take me to a mental hospital, wouldn't they? And I'd be safe. Oh, help! And I could drop the responsibility of trying to earn my own living. I could just stay curled up. Please help! Safe behind my barricade of pillows. They would try to get me to respond, but I just wouldn't. I was pretty sure I could be strong enough to stay curled up, not responding no matter what anyone said. Oh, help! What if they held – ammonia, was it – to my nose? Only the truly catatonic didn't respond to that. But maybe I would *be* truly catatonic. Please, Jesus! Why was I in this position? Life in an institution would be boring, and they'd give me drugs that I didn't want. Oh, help! And they might even use electroshock therapy on me. Please help! Why did life have to be so hard? I'd be bored, though, and there was a stigma attached to those who had been in an institution. Help!

Johnny got out of the truck. I went on crying for a time, still silently. After a while I moved from my safe haven at the end of the bunk and looked out the window. Yes, he was riding his bike around the yard again. Did he even realize that I was upset? I had no idea. I went back to the bunk, cried a while longer, prayed some more, then got up.

Somehow the decision seemed made – I wasn't sure how or by whom. I would go on. I would try again.

When the time came, using Johnny's preferred option for setting up the backing, I pulled around clockwise, missed the post, and backed into the loading dock. It didn't go too badly.

I never found out if Johnny knew about my breakdown that day. He never brought up the subject and neither, of course, did I.

Though I didn't realize it, I had less than a week to go with Johnny. The cheese from Marathon, Wisconsin was supposed to go to some caves in Carthage, Missouri – huge, naturally cold caves where several companies leased space to store large quantities of cheese and other food.

We soon received a message, though, telling us to "swap out" our load for one going to Salt Lake City – again! Swapping out loads was a common practice. It generally happened either because a driver found he didn't have enough hours of driving left on his 70 hours in eight days to get the load delivered on time, or because a driver needed to go home and the company used this way of getting him there.

So I was not to see the caves of Carthage. We met the other driver in Des Moines at noon the next day, exchanged trailers and bills of lading (the man needed to get home to Missouri), and started for Salt Lake City with 24,165 lb. of non-temperature controlled "FAK" – Freight All Kinds – for Costco, trip number twenty-one. Again we had the pleasure of travelling more quietly, without the reefer running at all.

We drove through Grand Island, Nebraska, met up with Johnny's twin again for an hour or so, then pushed on toward

Wyoming. We were driving as a team by now, just taking turns driving.

Johnny went for a nap, leaving me to drive as far as I could. When I came to Wyoming's port of entry, rather late at night, I parked and went in to show them the truck's permit book. Almost as soon as I came back out and drove on down the road, I heard the thump of Johnny descending from the upper bunk. He jumped into the passenger seat and sat watching the road for a few minutes, then remarked that he had been sure I would bypass the port of entry, get pulled over by the Highway Patrol and collect a stiff ticket, in which case I would have flunked "the test." As it was, he continued, I had passed it.

I felt a chill. Flunk a test? Were there other tests? I inquired, as delicately as I could.

"Four or five others," came the reply. If I had flunked three or more, he would have been putting me on a bus. I very much wanted to know more about these other tests, how many I might already have undergone and how many remained, but Johnny had plainly said all he intended to on the subject.

Nevertheless, I continued to brood about it. A vivid mental image of being packed ignominiously onto a Greyhound bus obsessed me. Would he really have let me drive by the Wyoming port of entry? Clearly, yes. Not that I would have done such a thing. I understood from previous trips that the ports of entry in Wyoming were open all but two days of the year (today is almost never one of those days) and that it was always necessary to stop at them. Still...

And what were these other tests? The world, and Johnny, suddenly seemed less friendly.

I had already been doing more and more of the routine jobs as time passed. I was often the one to fuel the truck now, using Johnny's employee number and cards. I also dealt more and more with pickups and deliveries. I probably was almost ready to be on my own, if only it weren't for having to bump docks.

We delivered the load to Costco in Salt Lake City on Monday morning. Johnny told me that I was going to handle this delivery myself, exactly as if he weren't there.

It went well, but an amusing thing happened at the guard shack.

This load, a Proctor and Gamble one, was sealed with a large bolt seal. At the guard shack, I asked to borrow the largest bolt cutters, almost too heavy for me to carry, then walked to the back of the trailer, closely followed by one of the security guards.

I wasn't sure that I could cut a bolt seal by myself, but I intended to give it a good try. I managed to get the blades of the bolt cutter into the right position on the bolt then, bearing in mind that it was a leverage situation, I grabbed the very end of one of the bolt cutter's handles, pressing the other handle against the trailer door, and leaned as much of my weight against it as I could. Being overweight can sometimes substitute for strength!

There was a moment when I didn't think I was going to succeed. I saw the driver of the truck behind me, who wanted to get through the gate too, and who was being held up by me, climb down from his truck and start toward me, undoubtedly to offer his assistance.

I had only seconds in which to do this thing. I found a way to lean a little more weight onto the handle and snap! Half of the bolt seal fell to the ground, neatly severed.

I picked it up, plucked the other half from the latch, and handed them both to the guard, who took the bolt cutters as well. I opened the trailer doors.

Then I walked back up the length of the trailer to the guard shack, completed the check-in formalities and climbed back into the truck, where Johnny asked, "Did you do it?"

I nodded, grinning.

He grinned too. "You should have seen the look that other guard gave me," he remarked. "He thought I ought to be doing it instead of making a woman do such a difficult job."

"He didn't understand," I reassured him.

We both laughed.

The delivery went well. This Costco distribution center, like most of them, was very roomy, so I had no particular difficulty bumping the dock. It wasn't an alley dock backing situation.

After the delivery we drove up to Idaho to pick up a load of frozen potatoes going to the Chicago area. This was the start of trip twenty-two.

Johnny was good at finding parking places for semis, so he

sometimes didn't restrict himself to truck stops, as I undoubtedly would once I was on my own. We stopped at a nice Mexican restaurant on our way to the pickup. There was a large dirt lot next to the restaurant, so Johnny instructed me on how he wanted the truck parked – with an eye to being able to get out afterwards no matter who came and parked near to us. The meal itself was a welcome relief from the uniformity of truck stop restaurants.

Johnny mentioned that if we had enough time he was hoping to stop at a place called Lava Hot Springs on our way eastward. This, it appeared, was a natural hot springs in Idaho off of US-30 and not yet discovered by very many people. It had three pools of varying temperatures, all with round pebbles on the bottom that massaged the bather's feet. It was an interesting feeling, said Johnny.

We went on to the pickup after lunch. There were two sister plants for the potato company. They were right together, side by side. Inevitably we went to the wrong one first but were told how to get over to the one we wanted, then had to wait for a door to open up before we could back in to be loaded.

While we were waiting, a truck from another company pulled up to join the three or four miscellaneous trucks which were waiting for doors or were in a later stage of the process, getting ready to leave.

A large, rather coarse man climbed down from the driver's seat and walked over to speak to me where I sat waiting in the driver's seat. The questions he asked were quite ordinary – where was the shipping office? where should he wait? and so on and so forth. What was extraordinary, I thought, were his fulsome smile and his manner of speech, intonation and body language. He reminded me of nothing more than a grandfather making a total fool of himself over a small grandchild. He was simultaneously flirting with me and talking down to me After he finally left, I turned to Johnny, who had been sitting all this time in the passenger seat, apparently unobserved by the strange trucker.

Giving Johnny a look, I said just one word, "Jerk!!" But I put a lot of feeling into it. Johnny roared with laughter. When he managed to stop laughing quite so hard, he exclaimed, "Welcome to the world of trucking," to which I shook my head in disgust.

The same trucker came back over a little while later, to try again I suppose, but this time he noticed Johnny and soon left, for which I was profoundly grateful.

I thought about how happy I was to be out with a man, in spite of the unconventionality of it and various looks I got from time to time, before people remembered that this was the 21st century and decided to be "tolerant." One woman behind a fuel desk had asked if Johnny was my "husband or team driver or something." I replied, "Definitely 'or something'," and we had both laughed.

I had heard of different coping strategies for a woman driving alone. I might get a man's coat and drape it on the passenger seat. Some women had a large dog on the truck, but Alan drivers weren't allowed to have animals, so that was out, besides which, I thought a dog would be more trouble than it was worth. Of course, I could get a mannequin to sit in the front seat. It might deter the casual eye – much as my cello, placed on the front seat, had often been taken for a passenger by people who weren't looking closely.

CHAPTER 11

CDL School Flashback

Thinking about the flirtatious trucker, though, took my memory further back. At the CDL school I attended in North Carolina, recruiters had been, if not a daily feature of life, at least a twice-a-week phenomenon, usually two of them back-to-back. Most of them had been nice, several of them very nice indeed, though I had sometimes felt compelled to take what they said with a rather large grain of salt. But one or two of the recruiters hadn't managed to be nice even during what was basically a sales talk.

Most of the recruiters asked us why we were getting into trucking, as a way of breaking the ice I suppose. There were only seven of us students, so this didn't take a lot of time. Dennis, a NASCAR employee, was taking the course for insurance purposes, and already knew how to drive, in addition to his being a diesel mechanic. Of the other six students, most of us had worked out a rather stock response to the question – since we were asked it an average of perhaps four times a week. Dean had hurt his back working as a carpenter. Mary had gone to CDL school the year before but then needed surgery and lost too much time recuperating, so she had to repeat the course. Scott had been downsized from his previous job. Patrick — I couldn't remember Patrick's answer.

The seventh student was a large, affable young man, upon whom the responsibilities of life seemed to weigh rather lightly, and who carried several felonies on his record, something he seemed to regard more as a personal misfortune than as an occasion for shame. He had recently married for the second time and thus had eight children, four of them his own and four belonging to his new wife.

When this student was asked why he was getting into trucking, his answer was always the same: "Eight children." We other students were used to hearing this response and gave it a perfunctory smile when the recruiter for a flatbed trucking company asked the question. But this recruiter's response was different from the usual polite concern that the seventh student's answer usually elicited.

"Have you figured out what's causing it?" he asked earnestly.

The seventh student nodded sheepishly, while the rest of the class laughed. It was genuinely funny, I thought, but also had a bit of an edge to it. The recruiter went on to demonstrate more of this "edge" as he blatantly ignored Mary and me, while pitching the advantages of flatbed trucks to the men.

Flatbeds require a lot more strength than dry vans or reefers. There are heavy tarps that might need to be lifted. Loads need to be fastened down with ropes or chains. It was not an area of trucking that Mary or I were considering, but being ignored so protractedly seemed to bother Mary, who sat up toward the end of the presentation and began to ask questions about whether any women drove flatbeds, how much strength was really required, were there ways around it, and so on.

The answers she got seemed to imply that sweet-talking a man into doing the tying down for her would be her best bet. The implication that she might do something a bit more than sweet-talk in return for the favor was there too.

I found myself studying the man, pitying his wife and being glad that I wasn't married to such an obvious jerk, with his polyester pants, too-wide tie and hair combed carefully over a bald spot.

But worse was to come the next day, when a recruiter for one of the larger companies stopped by with a captive student, a member of a former class at our school. This recruiter, who was also a trainer for his company, painted us a vivid picture of the hellish life his trainee was now undergoing. Apparently, it was fortunate for the trainee that he was a man, as the recruiter/trainer mentioned that his first goal in training women was to drive them to tears sometime during the first few days of being out on the road.

When I had told Johnny this story, early during our time together, he had looked thoughtful for a minute, then had remarked, "That wouldn't be very hard," a sentiment with which I was in entire accord.

That was bad enough, I had thought at the time, but now this man, having excoriated his present student by talking about how much harder it was to drive a loaded trailer than the empties on which we students were currently practicing, and telling us how much trouble the poor fellow was having with gears and various other aspects of driving, now proceeded to tell a story of his brutality to his own wife. It seemed that she had ridden on the truck with him for a while, early in their marriage. At some point he had taught her how to run up the gears from second to tenth, going from a standstill to full speed, then made her drive down the freeway. That limited process can be taught quickly. But the wife was soon faced with a situation that was too much for her and, according to her husband, simply "bailed out," diving over the back of the driver's seat and into the bunk, leaving this particular man of little sense and no judgment to jump into the driver's seat and deal with the situation. The recruiter seemed to think he was making a point about the ditziness of women by telling this story. I thought it was much more about his abusive nature and irresponsibility in browbeating the woman into doing something for which she had not really been trained. I made a mental note not *ever* to sign up with this company, lest I be saddled with this creep for a trainer.

CDL school had started with a day of studying North Carolina's CDL manual in preparation for taking the test for a CDL learner's permit. Some students had to take the test twice, but by the third day of class we had all cleared that hurdle.

The classroom teacher, Jimmy Fields, was a big man in his sixties, who had been driving trucks since he was in his twenties. He had also spent 25 years in law enforcement. He had sticking-out ears, always wore overalls and was massive – 370 pounds he told the class – a smoker who periodically coughed until he choked, and even a little beyond, leading me to think about Chronic Obstructive Pulmonary Disease. Teaching the class seemed to be a sort of retirement job for him.

He was a real "down-home boy" as they are called in North Carolina. I was not from that part of the country, though I was living temporarily in North Carolina with Hungarian friends, so it took me the better part of three classroom days of intense concentration before I could understand more than half of what he said.

The man clearly knew a lot about driving, but he was not a teacher. He showed us videos and told stories. The stories were interesting, when I could understand them, but not strictly relevant to the material at hand.

After each video we took a multiple-choice test, then our scores were recorded in a grade book. Out of seven students all but a few were smokers so, what with Jimmy being a smoker too, we were guaranteed a break every hour or so. Partway through the course one of the other students and I each ordered a book on truck driving from the Internet. The other student was the only other person in the class with a BA. Clearly, he, too, was used to taking in information from the printed page. Both of us wanted more than we were getting from the videos. I worked my way through the book and had finished it by the end of the course.

Besides classroom instruction we also had labs and private driving lessons, both held a few miles away at what was called the driving range, a large oval track with a semi and two trailers parked on it. It had cones set up here and there so that we could practice parking and backing.

At the first lab Jimmy took the students two or three at a time and drove us around the range, demonstrating various aspects of shifting. He also lit cigarette after cigarette as he drove, in complete disregard of what the owner of the school had told the class in her welcoming speech to us, namely that smoking in the truck was absolutely forbidden.

After that first day, most of the lab time was devoted to practicing pre-trip inspections, as they were called. Part of the CDL exam was a test of our ability to do pre-trip inspections. The inspection involved naming over a hundred parts on the truck. I always wondered how much of it a real trucker did every day. It didn't seem very realistic to me to do the whole thing. Nevertheless, along with the rest of the class, I tried hard to memorize the whole list.

The procedure was to walk up on the truck from the front, looking first to make sure that the cab wasn't leaning one way or the other and that there weren't any puddles of oil, water or antifreeze underneath. Most of the rest – of the test anyway – was a question of naming things. We all learned lots of new words, except for Dennis, the diesel mechanic, who already knew it all and more. But for me at least, such things as slack adjusters, spring mounts, torsion bars and U-bolts were foreign territory.

Checking fluid levels was part of a pre-trip inspection, though it wasn't part of the test we would take. For the test we just had to point to the various parts of the truck and trailer and make sure that the part named was "present and not damaged." But it was a huge list [see Appendix. Pre-Trip Inspection Sheets, p. 271].

Driving lessons were good or not so good, depending on which instructor a student drew for a session. Each lesson was four hours long. We were to have 11 lessons. Several of the instructors were old men; one was 84 years old. He was an interesting character – had flown, driven trucks, operated heavy equipment, and had instructed in all these areas, but at this time of life he was more interested in going for coffee than he was in teaching truck driving. He, too, like Jimmy Fields, told endless stories, but his were unrelated to trucking. He wore a hat that had been chewed on repeatedly by a horse he had once owned – and showed it! He was a sweet old man, but after my second lesson with him I went to Jimmy and asked not to be assigned to him again, only to be told that I was the sixth of the seven students to make that same request.

After a few lessons restricted to the small driving range, we progressed to driving back and forth on an almost unused stretch of road with an empty warehouse at one end and a cul-de-sac at the other. We could get up to eighth or ninth gear, out of the ten, and also practice turning around in the cul-de-sac, turning corners and starting out on an uphill, all on this stretch of road.

Later still, we went for long drives on the local highways. We went to a small truck stop, more of a gas station really, to get a snack partway through a lesson, and also practiced backing between cones on the driving range. My later lessons usually included at least an hour and a half of such practice. Sometimes the instructor just went to his car and left me to wrestle with it myself, which I did, trying over and over to get the trailer into the right position.

At one of the labs, when we were again practicing the pre-trip inspection, looking at and naming brake drums, pads, slack adjusters, cotter keys, leaf springs and other such items, I was invited to lean way over a tire so that I could really see the brake pads. I did so and made a discovery.

"It's *filthy!!*" I exclaimed, as I inspected the layer of mud that coated everything on the back side of the tire. All the other students burst out laughing – and so did I when I realized what I had said.

The last two driving lessons consisted of driving a few hundred miles on the Interstate freeway and State routes. I was sorry for the long line of cars which trailed me up a State route for 25 miles or more, but couldn't think of anything to do about it, so I just suffered as I imagined the complaints and anger of the frustrated car drivers.

We also practiced driving over the test route for the CDL. I drove it three times before I was tested on it. There were various difficulties – a more-than-ninety-degree turn, some residential driving, Christmas ornaments on lamp posts, which were hanging down far enough for a semi to knock into them.

Every once in a while, I almost got into big trouble. Once when we were up in the mountains I turned out in front of a car and nearly took out a stop sign, all within 30 seconds. Mistakes tended to accumulate quickly in those early days. Failing to slow down enough for a turn would leave me flying around a corner in neutral, and I would forget to watch the trailer's back tires in my panic over trying to find a gear, for example.

The final written test for the CDL school was just a massive open-book exercise in looking things up in the FMCSR (Federal Motor Carrier Safety Regulations) book, with a few other questions thrown in. Most of the students seemed quite worried about the test. The seventh student, the felon, was not among them. He spent an hour or so at it, then turned it in first of all. All seven of us passed, but his was the lowest mark: 80-something percent.

I was the next to turn my test in. I missed one question, something about tires. I was annoyed as I had hoped for a perfect score and went in search of the right answer to the tire question. The owner of the school told me that I had the highest score the school had ever experienced, at 99.5 percent. The other students had also done extremely well. Scores ranged from 95-98 percent.

Jimmy Fields, when he came into the office and heard that I wanted the answer to the question I had missed, slapped me on the back and said, "Now don't you go chasin' that answer, girl. You just let it go. Ninety-nine ain't enough for you?" Well, no, it wasn't. I wanted to know the right answer and did eventually get it out of them.

The driving part of the test went well. I didn't make any real blunders. The more-than-ninety-degree turn went okay. I didn't knock down any of the Christmas decorations from the lamp posts. In fact, I felt quite good about the test. The examiner complimented me.

I was thinking about CDL school as Johnny drove across Idaho, heading for Lava Hot Springs. The CDL school had definitely given me nothing more than a bare-bones minimum. Mueller's school had helped get me ready for the kind of apprenticeship I was now finishing with Johnny. Almost everything I knew about trucking I had learned from him.

CHAPTER 12

The End of Training
(May 21-24)

The turnoff for Lava Hot Springs, from either direction, was down a very steep hill. We approached it from the west, which meant making several tight turns, then driving down Main Street right through the middle of downtown Lava Hot Springs (pop. 526).

It was possible to park the truck just off the street and parallel to it in a parking lot across the street from the hot springs. The parking lot belonged to a city park, and was marked with lines for car parking, but it was empty so Johnny just took up the whole thing; the truck occupied seven or so places and the other three or four provided some room in front of and behind the truck.

I walked downtown and got a small non-truck stop meal of a grilled cheese sandwich and some soup, not wanting to eat a large supper after the wonderful Mexican lunch, while Johnny spent an hour or so at the hot springs. I had been invited too, of course, but I didn't have a swimsuit on the truck and wasn't inclined to rent one and expose my fat middle-aged body to the view of someone I knew. I made a mental note to come back by myself if I ever got the chance.

The next day I drove 500 miles. Johnny had driven to Wamsutter, Wyoming after we left Lava Hot Springs. I started at 7 AM and drove the rest of the way across Wyoming, then halfway across Nebraska.

Johnny had been up much of the day, but the load was in danger of being late after he had sent in a macro to move the appointment time a day earlier, so he took over driving at 7 PM. I went to sleep. When I woke up the next morning, Johnny had apparently driven the rest of the way across Nebraska, all the way across Iowa and halfway across Illinois. We were now nearing the Chicago area and the delivery site.

I was amazed. Johnny, for once, seemed to be exhausted. He was bleary-eyed and looked about ten years older than usual. When I exclaimed about him having driven so far he responded that it was "just another 630-mile trucker's day." But he had done it without resting beforehand – or very nearly.

I did the backing at the Belvidere, Illinois delivery and managed to cover myself with glory – much to my surprise. The job of backing up to this particular loading dock was made very difficult by some construction that was being done in the yard, and which limited how far past the loading dock I could drive. Construction materials were piled here and there and were very much in the way. The result was that I had to do a blind-side backing. To my surprise, I didn't find all that much difference between the two sorts of backing. Johnny got me set up to his satisfaction, then I turned the steering wheel to the left instead of the right to start the trailer angling back into the space, and had to turn the steering wheel back to the right to get back under the trailer. Amazingly, it worked on the first try, illustrating the fact that set-up is ninety-eight percent of the job. I was in the hole and only had to straighten out – a relatively simple matter.

Johnny seemed to be enormously impressed. He immediately called our dispatcher and told the woman, "I'm not worried about her anymore. She just did a blind-side backing."

I didn't find what I had done all that impressive. And I wasn't sure he did either. After all, Johnny had basically talked me through it. Then again, I didn't see much difference between a blind-side backing and a normal one. Except for the greater difficulty in seeing – which I had coped with by getting out of the truck and looking – the two things were just mirror images, one of the other.

But suddenly I found that Johnny was now satisfied that I had finished training – on the basis of this, or on some other basis, I didn't know. Or had he just had enough?

The plan, as communicated to me, was to pick up the next load, some coffee creamer going to Minnesota, then to pass through corporate headquarters in Wisconsin and drop me off there. I would be tested and given a truck of my own if I passed everything. Johnny would help me move onto my truck then would drive on, by himself, to Minnesota where he would deliver the coffee creamer and go back to his life as a solo driver until Alan had another student for him.

It was brutally quick, I thought. I had known this was coming, but it was happening three or four days earlier than I had imagined. The more I thought about it, the more I realized that my whole security in this trucking life came from being with Johnny. I had hardly even started mourning the loss of him – somehow, I'd thought there was still time left. The fact that he seemed perfectly cheerful as he looked ahead to life without me made it a good deal worse. It was true, as Johnny had said in his welcoming speech two months before, that this had been "closer than marriage." How could I just go away and never see him again?

I was pretty certain that I wouldn't have much contact with Johnny once I was off his truck. After all, I had been watching his life for nearly two months – he was in almost daily contact with his brother when they were both "out," meaning "on the road," was in perhaps twice-a-week contact with some of his children, his soon-to-be ex-wife and his girlfriend. Most of his life took place wherever he was. Any person who happened to be around received a good welcome, and was well treated, but an absent person wasn't much missed. At least that was the way I analyzed the situation. I would quickly become someone to call every few weeks or months, like his other former students. Even that would depend on my acquiring a cell phone, something I had not yet done.

As we picked up the coffee creamer in De Kalb, Illinois for the start of trip number twenty-three, our last, I began to feel as though I was on a conveyor belt. Everything kept moving along even though I was in a state of shock.

And I lost my temper when trying to back the empty trailer into place in the shipper's drop lot. I set up for the backing and started it, only to find that I had overshot the hole. Johnny was dancing around, gesturing with both arms to point out where the back of the trailer should be. I wondered crossly how I was supposed to move the back of the trailer over. Rent a crane? I just hated being so incompetent. And Johnny clearly wasn't going to help either. He just kept pointing to where I should put the trailer.

Well, if that's how it was, I'd just go around and try it again. I had no idea how to accomplish what Johnny seemed to be calling for. I pulled forward, ignoring Johnny's surprised yell and frantic arm motions, and drove back toward the entrance to the yard, where I made a U-turn with some difficulty, drove back to the other end of the yard and made another U-turn, then started my setup over again.

I noticed a security guard, a little old lady driving a golf cart, who now pulled up beside the truck. I stopped, climbed down and talked with the woman, who expressed surprise at what I had done. Trucks weren't allowed to go back out the entrance. It was a one-way yard. I apologized, explaining that I had no intention of going back out, that I was just very bad at backing and needed a fresh start at setting it up. After I said this three times the woman seemed to accept it.

I got back in the truck and drove forward down the row, setting up the backing again. When I reached Johnny, he told me that he hadn't expected me to do what I had just done, which I already knew. He had only wanted me to move the back of the trailer over.

"I had no idea how to do that, so I thought I'd just try again," I said.

He shook his head and remarked that I had made a mistake. I should just have pulled forward a little and backed up again. Well, ... somehow, I got the trailer backed in, dropped it, and drove over to the loaded trailer, still sitting in a dock. We weren't allowed to pick it up yet, as loading was still going on, so I just backed up to it, shut the engine off and joined Johnny, who was waiting at a table in the shipping department's drivers lounge.

We sat for a while, waiting for someone to call us to the shipping window to say that the trailer was ready. The same security guard walked by while we were sitting there and stopped at our table. I found myself apologizing all over again, as apparently the subject of my turning around had to be discussed in great detail. I assured the woman several more times that I hadn't intended to go out the entrance.

After this I went back out to the truck to wait. Quite a while later a "spotter" or "yard dog," a man employed by the company for the sole purpose of moving trailers around within a yard, came by and told me that his computer said the trailer was now loaded. I could hook up to it.

There were signs in the shipping department saying that drivers must never hook up to a trailer until told to do so by someone in shipping. Did this spotter count as someone in shipping, I wondered? And wasn't sure. I hooked up to the trailer, but did the gentlest possible tug tests, then went inside to consult with Johnny. I found, to my horror, that the trailer was not yet finished. I shouldn't have hooked up to it. The spotter was wrong.

Nothing bad came of it. Nobody seemed to notice what I had done, but I resolved not to listen to spotters on such a subject ever again. Eventually we were told that the trailer was loaded. We signed the bills and were ready to go.

As we walked back out to the truck, we again crossed paths with the little old lady security guard. Again, we had to talk about what I had done in driving the wrong way in the one-way yard. I apologized yet again, realizing that you really don't get away with much in this life. I had paid dearly for my temper tantrum.

The feeling of being on a conveyor belt continued as I drove north from De Kalb and passed by Madison, Wisconsin. And the weather began to deteriorate. The rain pouring down from a leaden sky matched my mood. After a while, though, I found the driving on wet roads too nerve-racking. Johnny drove the rest of the way. We stopped for dinner but were nevertheless at corporate headquarters around 10 PM.

In the morning we met with Chip Walsh, the Driver Trainer Coordinator, who talked to the two of us together for a bit. I had to take a driving test and two written tests – one multiple choice and one for figuring out routings on eight different trips.

I took the driving test first, with a very nice older man. It went well. I had passed the same driving test at orientation, but it seemed easier now. It was about a half-hour test which consisted of driving through the small town that was home to Alan King Associates, then heading out into the surrounding countryside, where a bridge was used to simulate railroad tracks, apparently nonexistent in that part of Wisconsin, for the hazmat part of the test. When hauling hazmat a trucker is required to stop 15-50 feet from any railroad tracks, put on the truck's flashers, turn off the radio, open both windows, look up and down the tracks twice, then proceed across the tracks, staying in one gear from the moment the steer tires hit the tracks until after the back tires clear them.

The way back through town was more varied, taking in some left and right turns, a traffic light and several stop signs, and including a small excursion into a residential neighborhood. I enjoyed chatting with the examiner as I drove. I managed not to run over the curb on the sharp right-hand turn into the yard at the end of the test, unlike the first time I was tested when I had lost points for doing just that.

That left only the backing part of the test, and even that went reasonably well. I didn't set it up perfectly, but the examiner told me to pull forward and leftwards, farther than I would ever have done on my own, and the second try worked.

When we went back into the building, the examiner was smiling. He reported to Chip that he couldn't give me a perfect score because I hadn't gotten out to look before I backed up, but that was the only place he had found to deduct points.

Now Chip handed me the multiple-choice test, which was really a rather annoying one because a number of the questions were either ambiguous or else covered areas about which I knew nothing. I did my best with it, then went to get it marked and to talk with Chip about what I had put. It turned out that one of the questions didn't even *have* a correct answer. Chip had put it in there to give himself an opportunity to talk about oil pressure – its importance and the necessity of looking at the gauge when starting the engine. If the oil pressure didn't come up right away, something was badly wrong and it would be better not to move the truck.

After this, I took the routing test. This was rather fun, figuring out how to get from one city to another on eight runs. This test, when I discussed it with Chip, led to me learning quite a lot. His 30 years as a trucker really showed. He pointed out something very interesting too, namely that because of the way map projections are done, a northern route – all things being equal – is shorter than a southern route. In other words, on a map, a distance of two inches on I-90 is shorter than that same two inches on I-40, which is shorter than two inches on I-10. This surprised me, but once I thought about non-Euclidean geometry, and envisioned a sphere with pairs of pins at two different longitudes and string running horizontally, as if east to west, between them, I could see that this must be so. It all came from trying to represent a sphere on a flat piece of paper.

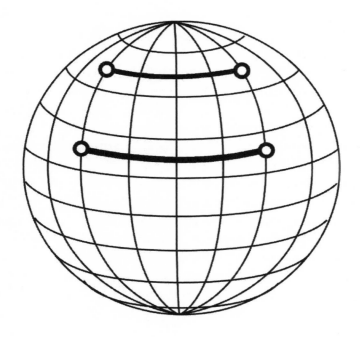

19. Diagram of a sphere with string

Chip also explained that the high mountain passes of Colorado were considered to be too dangerous, especially in the winter, and that a trip to California was the one acceptable reason for going "out of route," by running I-80 instead of I-70, then taking I-15 south. It added a hundred-some miles to the trip but was much safer.

After the tests, Chip and I went to the drivers lounge, met up with Johnny and talked about some of what had gone on in training. There was a lot of joking. A couple of other drivers came and sat in on the session.

Chip asked me a few more questions, such as what you shouldn't put on an upper bunk. I answered conservatively that you shouldn't put anything on the upper bunk that you didn't want to see projected through the windshield. It was then that Chip added some surprising information: sleeping on the upper bunk while the truck was in motion was considered highly unsafe and was absolutely forbidden. And Johnny had been doing it the whole seven and a half weeks! I gulped and tried to avoid looking at Johnny.

There was a quick trip through the headquarters building, so that I could be introduced to my new dispatcher, Kevin, who seemed like a nice young man. Then Johnny took me out to the shop to demonstrate the use of load locks to me. This was something he had forgotten to practice while we were out on the road. We had only had one load out of the 23 that called for load locks and either they had already been on or Johnny had put them on without me being there somehow.

Then we drove over to my assigned truck. It was a decrepit Freightliner, number 5431, a Columbia like Johnny's much newer truck but with only one bunk bed – and it had 329,574 miles on it, against truck 7373's current 55,000 miles.

As we climbed onto 5431 and looked around, I began to feel depressed. Even Johnny seemed a little subdued. The finish was peeling off the dashboard and other interior surfaces; it looked much like skin peeling off a sunburn victim. Apparently, someone had tried to clean the inside of the truck, probably trying to get cigarette smoke residue off, with something that attacked plastic. There were various other problems with the truck. For one thing, it was missing the nets that held things in place in the cubby holes. For another it only had a tape deck and radio, and I didn't have any tapes. We made a list of damaged and missing parts, working on a pre-printed Alan form. Then we moved my belongings from

Johnny's truck to mine. Johnny reminded me to get two load bars and also extra oil, antifreeze and windshield washer fluid to carry in the truck's side box, these things all being free at terminals. He shook hands with me and was gone, just like that.

PART II

On My Own

Map 3

CHAPTER 13

How to Give Away 1,800 Pounds of Cinnamon Rolls
(May 24-June 4)

Rain was again falling after Johnny left. I got mud all over the floor of the truck as I kept getting off it to get the things I needed, or to speak with someone in the shop about nets and the truck's other problems. The shop was able to install some of the missing nets. Others of them had to be special ordered, so I was told that I would need to get routed through headquarters once they arrived.

Around 6 PM my Qualcomm beeped with a dispatch. It was a load of frozen food to be picked up near Minneapolis and taken all the way to Utah. What a good trip for my first one alone! One problem, though, was that there were two deliveries to be made on this one trip. Part of the load was to be delivered north of Salt Lake City, the other, smaller part in Salt Lake City itself.

I dropped the task of getting my things stowed away in the truck and prepared to go make the 9 PM pickup. It took me much, much longer than it would have taken Johnny to get ready. I had to write the trip into my trip notebook, as Johnny had taught me, then acknowledge the dispatch with a macro, send a macro to ask for directions to the pickup site, write those directions into a spiral notebook with a marker – so I could read them easily – and look up the trip to Minneapolis in my atlas. At least I felt compelled to do all these things and most were truly necessary.

Then I had to hook up to the empty trailer that my new dispatcher, Kevin, had told me to take. Even this took me quite a while. By the time I started out I was in danger of being late for the pickup, so I felt stressed all the way to Minneapolis. Somehow, I had missed the fact that it was impossible to be late for a pickup involving a drop and hook, where a trailer was already loaded and waiting.

I found the place but wasn't sure where to park while I went in to make enquiries. I drove up a sort of alley beside the company's building. It was lined with parked trailers on each side and luckily there was room at the end of it to do a U-turn, though only barely. I made the U-turn, then drove back down to the loading dock area which was almost empty at 9 PM. By this time, I was ten minutes late. I walked in nervously, explaining to the woman at the shipping window that this was my first trip on my own. The woman looked at me rather sharply, then her expression softened and she evidently decided to be nice about the whole thing and wrote 9 PM as the arrival time even though the clock stood at ten minutes after the hour, and anyway, she probably knew that being late was impossible on a drop and hook.

I was told to drop the empty trailer in any empty space on one side of the double alley where I had just been and where I had made the U-turn. The loaded trailer would then be found on the other side. And the woman gave me the trailer's number, having gotten from me the number of the empty trailer I was going to drop.

I signed the bills, was given a copy, and walked out knowing that I was blessed in my first trip. I had the easiest possible task – a drop and hook – as well as a lot of miles. Now if I could just do it…. With a prayer I gritted my teeth, drove up the alley again, noticing three empty spaces as I went, and made the same U-turn as before. Coming back down the alley I set up to back into what I hoped would be the easiest of the empty places. I had to get out and look twice, but somehow managed to jockey the empty trailer into place. Then I dropped it, using the LAP acronym (Landing gear, Airlines, Pin).

The hard part of the task was done. I drove across to the trailer I was to pick up, getting turned around and lined up to it with some difficulty. Johnny could do a drop and hook in fifteen minutes. I took an hour and fifteen minutes, but in the end, I was ready to leave.

By now it was very late, after 10:30 PM, and I had been up all day, so I only went as far as Elko, Minnesota, a little over an hour down the road, where I managed to park in a rest area. The real parking places were full by this late at night, but there was room to park on the ramp leading off the freeway. I got a place behind another semi, leaving what I hoped would be enough room in front of the truck to pull out in the morning without scraping him with the trailer, just in case he didn't leave first. I hiked in to use the restroom, then walked back out to the truck, noticing that there had been room for only one more truck to park behind me and that someone had done it. The rest area was now full.

I put enough order into the cab of the truck that I could lie down on the bed, then brought my logbook up to date, doing as I had been taught, that day even, by Chip Walsh, and logging the drop and hook as fifteen minutes, even though it had taken me an hour longer than that. Then I put the hour drive to Elko as coming directly after the 15 minutes. My logbook now read as though I had arrived at the Elko rest area at 10:30 instead of 11:30. This meant that, on paper, I would have finished my ten-hour break at 8:30 the next morning and would be free to start a new 14-hour day at that time.

I wanted to get eight hours of sleep out of a 10-hour break. That left two hours in which to get a meal and a shower. In practice, though, these two hours tended to get eaten up by other things. For example, logs didn't have to be accurate to any more than fifteen minutes, so if I pulled off the road at, say 10:07, I would probably log it as happening at 10:00. And I never logged whatever time it took me to get parked, up to fifteen minutes in some cases. Then there was the logbook to do. On this particular occasion I found that half an hour of my two extra hours had already been spent. As I had arrived, on paper, an hour earlier than in reality, I would only need to wait half an hour after eight hours of sleep – just about right for washing up and getting some coffee out of the rest area's vending machine. That was all that could be done at a rest area anyway. They had no showers or restaurants.

In the meantime, though, sleep was the thing. Exhausted by all the events of this momentous day, I was soon fast asleep.

The next day, a Friday, I drove from 8:30 AM until 8:15 PM, for a total of nine and a half driving hours, but only made 475 miles, that is, an average speed of 50 mph. This came about because I was trying to follow the route that Johnny and I had taken when he had picked me up at the motel two months before. I remembered that we had gone through Fremont, Nebraska on US-30, but had trouble reconstructing how we had gotten there.

After a lot of map reading, I took I-35 south to Ames, Iowa, then picked up US-30, which ran parallel to I-80 about 40 miles north of it. I drove west on US-30 for the rest of the seemingly endless day. Every 15 or 20 miles there would be a town for which I would have to drop my speed to 45 mph or less for a few miles.

Months later, I discovered that I should have cut west at Minneapolis onto US-212 and taken an incredibly complex series of State routes to get to US-75/77 and thus to Fremont, Nebraska. Only there would I have picked up US-30 westbound. As it was, I had wasted almost the whole day with relatively little to show for it.

About 8:15 PM, I finally arrived at the Grand Island truck stop, where I had come with Johnny at the beginning of training, the first real truck stop I had encountered, and still my favorite. I fueled there; then, with its 400 parking places, I managed to find a parking place into which I could drive forward with no possibility of anyone blocking me the next morning when I would need to back out of it.

I took a shower, using the shower credit I had just put on my card by fueling, ate dinner and went to bed.

The next morning, I started at 6 AM. By noon I had driven 356 miles and, for some reason, felt exhausted. After consulting with Kevin by phone at the Wyoming port of entry, I stopped in Cheyenne where I napped for two and a half hours, then got up and had a meal and used the Internet to try to find a church for the next morning. The only thing that looked at all likely was an 8 AM Mass in Rock Springs, Wyoming, 258 miles away. The church was located along the Business Route for I-80, which told me that I could, at the very least, drive by it without getting off truck routes.

Rising at 4 AM, I was on the road by 4:30 and arrived in Rock Springs just before 8 AM, having used the fact that Wyoming was on Mountain time, an hour earlier than the Central time in which I logged. I had cut it very close, only stopping once, and that only for five minutes, at a rest area. As I drove along the business route, my questing gaze found what I knew was the church up on the right.

Then, looking quickly around, I found a parking place where a solid white line ran along a sort of bridge (but it didn't seem to be crossing anything much). I put the steering gear lock on, then walked a block and a half to the church where I arrived after the music had started but before the priest had processed in, as I was happy to notice. I was exhausted, but grateful to have been able to park the rig.

Just to make things even better, the priest was an African. When I introduced myself after Mass it turned out that he was a Kenyan and spoke Swahili. Hearing this, I gave him the usual greeting to priests in Swahili, which so moved him that he made a strangled sort of squeak of surprise, then hugged me tight! We enjoyed speaking Swahili for ten minutes or so, then I went on my way, rejoicing in the providence of God, who had gotten me to Mass in the nick of time and made two people so happy. And, there was no parking ticket on the truck when I got back to it.

It was Sunday afternoon before I first felt any need for air conditioning in this truck. When I tried to turn it on, I found that there wasn't any. Air conditioning became more important as the temperature rose going down into the Salt Lake Valley on my way to the Ogden drop yard – the only place I figured I could park. Even the drop yard was almost impossible for me – though I had practiced backing there two times. The yard was almost full, so I asked the advice of a couple of black men who were just going home – regional drivers for Alan. They helped me get into a space.

The temperature was in the high 80's. I slept with the truck's windows open, but I hadn't felt so sweaty since Africa. It reminded me a lot of Africa, actually. Lying in bed sweating until I fell asleep had been a nightly occurrence in Tanzania.

The next morning, Memorial Day, I started to the delivery at 4 AM and was the first truck to arrive at the delivery site. In fact, I was clearly too early, a case where Johnny's rule of being an hour early didn't work. Having guessed desperately at what place might be out of other people's way, yet leave it possible for me to set up for backing into whatever door they eventually assigned me, I parked and climbed out of the truck, then walked around the deserted buildings trying to find a receiving office.

After ten minutes or so, a security guard showed up and told me I'd be number one on the list when the warehouse opened at 5 AM. Eventually I was assigned a door. I was very unclear in my mind about how to set up for it from my actual position. It took me quite a while to get backed up correctly and by the time I had done it sweat was dripping off my nose and a collection of workers on break were clearly watching me, shaking their heads at each failed attempt. There came a time, though, when I was where I needed to be, with the doors open, and the trailer being unloaded.

Once they had finished and handed the bills back to me, I started for Salt Lake City. It was almost 8 AM, and I was struck by the good fortune which had dictated that this delivery would fall on Memorial Day, a day when there was no rush hour. It was a weekly delivery from Minnesota, which made me wonder what usually happened to whatever poor driver had to deliver it. He must have been late every week, I guessed.

I arrived at the second part of the delivery in good time and parked on the street across from a very difficult little yard, bounded by a wrought iron fence which was far too close to the loading docks. Signs told drivers to enter by one gate for doors 1-5 and by the other gate for doors 6-8. There seemed to be fewer than the normal number of workers present on this Memorial Day. Only one young woman was working in receiving, so everyone was having to wait. When my turn came, I found the woman to be very nice, though harried. I mentioned that this was my first trip without a trainer and begged the woman to give me an easy door, whatever that might be.

I was assigned to door five and did my best with it, but my first attempt put me in door six instead of door five, so I "wiggled" the truck over about 12 feet through successive iterations of moving forward to the right, then backwards. It took close to half an hour and left some strange tire marks on the asphalt.

Once I was finally in the correct position, I spent some time talking with a nice older man, an owner operator who had only five years of experience. He and his wife and a cute little dog had taken to the road after he had lost an engineering job. I introduced myself as a beginner, at which the man smiled and said he knew that already – he had watched me bump the dock.

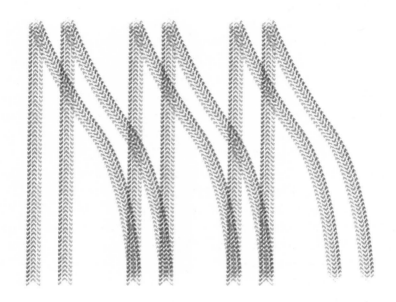

20. Diagram of tire marks from "wiggling"

After several hours the skeleton staff had unloaded the trailer. The woman in receiving told me that they were short two pallets of pizza crusts. I immediately called the OS&D (Overage, Shortage and Damage) department at Alan King Associates, as procedure dictated. I was asked for the product code number, which I found with some difficulty. Alan got started on the work that a shortage made, and I was free to go – or so I thought. When I pulled away from the dock to close the trailer doors, I found that there were still three pallets of "product," as it is called, on the truck.

Sighing, I went back inside, had to wait ten or more minutes to get the harried woman's attention again – she had been somewhere else in the building – and pointed out that the trailer wasn't empty.

"Yes, but those aren't ours," was the reply.

The woman was very helpful, though. She walked out to the trailer with me and was nice enough to be the one to climb in and investigate the situation. Lo and behold, two of the pallets were the missing pizza crust. It was less clear what the third pallet was.

I was told to back up to the door again – not a sinecure as I had had to pull out at an angle because of the shortness of the space in front of the dock. However, I managed it fairly quickly. Then I called OS&D again to report that the shortage issue was now resolved but an overage issue had been raised.

Eventually, after another hour and a half, it was determined that: a) the third pallet was cinnamon rolls which probably should have gone to the first delivery, b) the place where they should have been delivered didn't care about them, having already signed the bills to certify that they had received everything (and the cinnamon rolls might, in fact, have been "extra" – put in the trailer by mistake – I never knew the whole story) and c) I should donate them to any charitable organization that would give me a letterhead receipt.

This was hard to arrange on Memorial Day but the woman in Alan's OS&D department actually had a list of potential recipients in Salt Lake City so, after lots of phone calls, I was able to arrange for an organization called "Rescue Mission," which served the homeless, to come and get them. There were 60 cases, so it needed someone with a large freezer capacity. Several groups turned me down because they didn't have a way of keeping all 60 cases frozen.

By now I was parked in Salt Lake City at the truck stop where Johnny and I had stopped several times. I had the coveted end-of-the-row IdleAir space, where minimal backing would enable me to get out, so I was totally unwilling to leave, either to take the cinnamon rolls anywhere or to get my truck's air conditioning fixed. I was having a day off in Salt Lake City to visit my daughter and mother, so I explained to Kevin that I had a good parking place and the air conditioning would have to wait until I was nearer in time to being back on duty.

As for the cinnamon rolls, though, the Rescue Mission people were willing to come get them at the truck stop, so I told them exactly where I was and waited an hour or so until a van with three men in it pulled up. They were, I surmised, the shelter manager and two homeless men. They hadn't really grasped the nature of the job they had to do, as they were dressed in T-shirts and shorts, appropriate for the day's weather, with its 89-degree high.

I climbed down from the truck and turned the reefer off. The gauge temperature inside the trailer stood at -9° F. When I opened the back doors of the trailer clouds of vapor rolled out as the minus nine-degree air hit the almost 90-degree outside air.

I looked inside the trailer where the pallet of cinnamon rolls was sitting 53 feet away at the very front of the trailer, just behind the reefer unit. The men would have to walk 53 feet up the metal grooves that formed the floor of the trailer, then 53 feet back with each box they picked up. Sixty boxes meant thirty trips for each man.

I looked at them and shook my head.

"Don't you have any warmer clothes?" I asked. They didn't. "You'll have to take them for hot chocolate afterwards," I remarked to the boss, who shook *his* head and smiled in reply.

We used a fire brigade technique. Each of the two homeless men walked back and forth, bringing one box each trip to the back of the trailer. I grabbed each box as it was set down, lifted it and turned around to hand it to the manager, who then loaded it into the back of the van, which had been backed up to the end of the trailer.

This technique worked quite well; we emptied the trailer in 15 or 20 minutes. The van was very full with 60 boxes of cinnamon rolls, but they did all fit in. Each box held 115 tubes of the ready-to-bake rolls and each tube had a dozen pastries in it. I didn't actually do the math, but it was clear that the homeless people of Salt Lake City were going to be well supplied with 1,800 lbs. of cinnamon rolls. Might they even get tired of them?

I thanked the men for their hard work. They thanked me and gave me the necessary letterhead receipt, and even helped me get rid of the shrink wrap that had held the cases onto the pallet and the pallet itself, which they took away.

I used my day off to scavenge my mother's house for things I needed on the truck. A few of my own things were still there, so I was able to get a really good down comforter which I had bought for my son years before. Mother had made the switch to CD's, so it was fine for me to walk off with a shoebox full of cassette tapes, mostly of classical music. Those were the major items. I also grabbed a pillow and some empty plastic grocery bags to use as trash bags. My daughter and I made a grocery store trip to stock me up on water, peanuts and protein bars, the only food I envisioned carrying on the truck.

I had thought about having a cooler, a microwave oven – even a coffee maker? – but had decided that, for the time being at least, I wouldn't try to afford these things, even if they might pay for themselves quite quickly, but would do what Johnny and I had done, eating one restaurant meal a day and possibly one fast food meal. Then I would see how it went.

The next day I drove westward to Lake Station in the middle of the afternoon. There was a TA truck stop there which was an authorized service center for Freightliners. They were going to fix the air conditioning. The truck stop was nice and roomy. I was able to park the truck without backing it, then was asked to drop the trailer and bobtail into the shop. This wasn't difficult.

While the shop fixed my truck, I sat outside alternately reading and watching a man and woman feed pieces of white bread to a flock of seagulls. Was white bread good for them, I wondered? It didn't seem likely, but the seagulls were enthusiastic about it.

With the air conditioning fixed, and having hooked back up to the trailer, I was soon on my way, driving through Ogden at rush hour, then heading north to Idaho. Dispatch had me picking up 43,344 pounds of french fries the next afternoon and driving them to Frankfurt, Kentucky, trip number two on my own. I went in as early as I thought I could get away with. There was nothing memorable about the pickup but it did take place early enough that I could think of going to Lava Hot Springs if I routed the trip over US-30 to join up with I-80 just west of Little America.

The hill down to the Lava Hot Springs was just as steep as I remembered it, the turns through downtown just as tight. I negotiated all of it with great care, and successfully (that is, without taking anything out with the trailer), then found that the same parking place Johnny had used was again available.

I rented a bathing suit and enjoyed the hot springs very much. They were almost too hot; the third of the three pools *was* too hot as far as I was concerned. I stayed out of it after testing it with a toe. I walked through the pools to the coolest spot I could find. The sensation of the round stones on the soles of my feet was indeed unusual. Even the coolest end of the coldest pool was pretty hot. Half an hour was enough for me, though I had enjoyed floating around and also chatting with the few other visitors. I climbed out and went to shower feeling deeply relaxed and hoping that the hot water had done my hip some good.

The hard part turned out to be getting up the even steeper hill on the eastern edge of Lava Hot Springs. I started out in second gear and found, to my surprise, that I couldn't shift to third because the truck came to a halt more quickly than I could shift! I had heard of such a thing with a heavily-loaded trailer, but this was my first time of experiencing it. After another failed try at shifting from second to third I simply crept up the hill in second gear, making lots of noise. It was a relief to reach the stop sign at the top and turn right onto level ground where I could run up the gears normally.

I drove US-30 into Wyoming, where I had to stop at the port of entry, as always, to show the truck's permits to a Wyoming State official. By now I was dead tired and had more than half a mind to park the truck at the port of entry so I could sleep. Little America drew me, though; it wasn't far away now and would have amenities that the port of entry lacked – food, in particular. Also, Kentucky was far away. I felt under pressure to get there as quickly as possible. I was pretty sure I could do it if I drove as hard as I could but wasn't sure that I had any time to waste.

Johnny was better at figuring that sort of thing out. He had taught me to add ten percent to whatever figure the dispatch named for total loaded miles, in this case 1,803 + 180, which came out to 1,983 miles. Then I divided that figure by 50 as a loose estimate of driving time, in this case 39, say 40, hours. Then for every 10 hours of driving time I needed 10 hours of rest. I made a diagram:

10 hrs drive	May 31	7
10 hrs rest		
10 hrs drive	June 1	24
10 hrs rest		
10 hrs drive	June 2	24
10 hrs rest		
10 hrs drive	June 3	24
	June 4	1
total hrs 70	total hrs	80

I had left Lava Hot Springs at 5 PM CDT on May 31, so I had 80 hours before the June 4 delivery which had a 2 AM appointment time in the Eastern time zone. There appeared to be enough time, and ten hours to spare, but I didn't feel secure about it. And what were the consequences of only driving seven hours before I shut down at Little America? I hadn't come on duty for the day until 1 PM, so in principle I could drive until 3 AM but was too tired to do so. Little America was so vast that I was gambling on being able to park there even at midnight, but it was exceptional to be able to park anywhere at midnight, much less 3 AM. More often, stopping that late would mean parking on an on-ramp or off-ramp, as even the rest areas would be full.

My gamble paid off. When I eventually arrived, exhausted and having trouble keeping my eyes open and focused, the parking lot at Little America was not at all full. I was able to park near the back of the lot without even having to back up.

The next day was routine. I drove 524 miles, reaching Brady, Nebraska, about halfway across that state.

An upsetting incident occurred during the early afternoon somewhere in Wyoming, when I passed another truck. With Alan trucks governed to 65 mph, passing was a relatively rare occurrence, often happening only once or twice in ten hours of driving. I had much more practice at being passed and using my headlights to flash the other driver over afterwards, something that happened very frequently, say thirty or more times a day, depending on traffic.

In this case, though, I had actually caught up with a truck and needed to pass it. I signalled and pulled into the left lane, battling a feeling that I shouldn't be passing this truck, that I'd be sorry – but what else could I do? I had caught up with him, so of course I had to pass him. I inched up alongside the other trailer until our two rigs were running side by side at 65 mph, occupying both lanes of I-80.

Then it happened. To my horror, I saw a brown mother duck, followed by five or six fuzzy little ducklings, step off the side of the Interstate and start across. The mother duck seemed full of quiet confidence and pride of motherhood as she led her brood of ducklings onto the asphalt of the shoulder.

I was spared the view of what happened next. It was my truck that hit the mother, I thought, projecting the courses of trucks and the mother duck forward and taking speed into consideration. I bitterly regretted the incident. True, the mother duck had been as good as dead from the moment she started across the highway – no action on the part of either of us drivers could have saved her. Swerving would have threatened the lives of various people, especially if one of us had lost control and hit the neighboring truck or gone off the highway, but the ducks were dead almost before I could have moved the steering wheel.

One or two of the ducklings might have survived, I thought in a shocked way, as I continued down the Interstate, but it didn't really matter; they wouldn't live long at such a young age without a mother to protect them and teach them whatever it was that ducks needed to know.

Their deaths saddened me considerably. I knew that I wasn't to blame but I still felt guilty. My truck had only been the instrument of their slaughter. I hadn't had anything to do with it, volitionally at least. Seared into my memory, though, was the image of that proud, happy mother duck and all the cute little ducklings. It stayed with me for days, weeks even, and made me sad whenever I thought of it. If only I had heeded that still, small voice within that had told me not to pass the truck!

It was true that the highways of this country are slaughter-houses for animals both wild and domestic. I had already seen hundreds of carcasses: opossums, raccoons, skunks, deer, dogs and cats. I had managed to miss a deer early one morning. It was hesitating on the grass verge of the highway when I first saw it, wanting to cross but undecided. Then it stepped out onto the pavement. I wasn't very near to it so I backed off on the accelerator and watched it cross, knowing that if it paused or turned back I would have to hit it as squarely as I could, remembering Chip Walsh's talk on the subject.

Fortunately, on this occasion the deer kept going and made it safely across the highway with room to spare, stepping sedately into the grass on the other side. I thought later that I had done well not to blow the air horn at it. If there was anything more fearful and prone to panic than a deer, I reasoned, it would be a deer that had just had an air horn blown at it.

The only other thing I had killed so far was a beautiful bright-red bird, not a cardinal, a bird of a more scarlet red color, which splatted against my windshield one day, then blew off, leaving a splotch of blood that grieved me every time I saw it and which stayed on the windshield until the next rain.

I killed bugs by the thousands, of course. In fact, it was turning into quite a problem the way there were bugs all over the windshield and the backs of the side view mirrors. Nothing seemed able to remove them from the mirror backs; they were impervious, even, to the high-speed jet of hot water available at terminals. Or at least I couldn't get them off. I thought that Johnny had managed it.

The windshield was easier. I had worked out a method that I called the "short person's windshield washing technique" for cleaning windshields without climbing up on the tires the way Johnny did. I was unwilling to do this and knew that company rules forbade it as being too dangerous. I didn't think it was so dangerous for anyone young and active but was convinced that I personally would fall and break a bone, or worse, if I made a practice of climbing on tires. I had to do it occasionally to add oil; I wasn't going to do it multiple times per day for cleaning the windshield.

The short person's windshield washing technique consisted of using the long-handled squeegee to presoak the windshield, spreading washer fluid all over it with the sponge side of the squeegee then letting it sit while I went inside to use the restroom, buy a drink and/or a newspaper. Step two was the main washing, using the squeegee again to scrub hard at any bugs I could see. As a last step I ran the windshield wipers as I pulled forward from the fuel island, including pressing the button that made washer fluid spray all over the windshield. This didn't deal with the area of windshield not covered by the wipers but was as good a job as I could do. Rain was the real answer, always a blessing if it wasn't too heavy. Even a moderate rain would clean the windshield completely.

After the duck massacre, and after reaching Brady, Nebraska, where I lay over for ten hours, I ran into trouble the next day, a Saturday, through being a beginner. The best way to get from I-80 to I-29 involves skirting Lincoln, Nebraska and cutting a corner, using a State route, NE-2, to do so. As I drove through a suburb of Lincoln on that State route, the trailer ABS warning light suddenly lit up on the dashboard. What did it mean? I wasn't sure. Was the trailer dragging somewhat? I imagined that it was. The brakes didn't feel normal. Were the trailer brakes perhaps locked up? Maybe I should pull over! I looked feverishly around. After a few minutes I found myself driving on a long straight road, though still city driving, with a shoulder just about wide enough for a semi. The ABS light was still on. I started the emergency flashers going and pulled off the road, running long enough to get the trailer off too.

Once the back of the trailer crossed the white line and was truly off the road, I stopped the truck, never giving even a thought to the triangles I was supposed to set within ten minutes of stopping, one in front of and two behind the truck. I sent an emergency macro to road service, then waited.

Other trucks went by. It was a popular shortcut. Another Alan driver hailed me on the CB, and I explained the problem. He told me I was okay to run with the trailer ABS light on and asked if I needed him to stop. I answered that I didn't, as I was in communication with road service. A few minutes later I received much the same information in a Qualcomm message from road service.

I started the engine, put the truck in gear, released the tractor brake ... and found that the truck wouldn't move. Darn it! The trailer brakes *must* be locked. I sent a frantic message to road service which resulted, after an hour or so and several supplemental requests for my exact location, in the appearance of a mechanic in a van.

He was a nice man, a Christian to judge by the bumper sticker on his van, proclaiming that his boss was a Jewish carpenter. He checked everything out thoroughly but couldn't find a problem with the brakes and eventually suggested that I might not be able to move because all the tires on the right-hand side of the tractor and the trailer were in soft dirt, the shoulder not being quite wide enough for the whole rig.

I felt like a total fool. Had I wasted three hours and the price of a service call for nothing whatsoever? The man was very nice, and never lost his respectful tone of voice, but it appeared that this was indeed the case. On his advice, I engaged the differential lock and was able to move the truck.

The mechanic, being very careful, followed me to a small truck stop five or six miles down the road in order to check the brakes one more time and make sure they weren't heating up. They weren't, so after getting him an authorization number for the call, more than a hundred dollars (!), I was on my way again.

The delay, while frustrating and embarrassing, made it a reasonable thing to go to Mass in Columbia, Missouri the next morning. I even knew where to park the truck, having been there when I was out with Johnny. The problem was how to log such a thing. I couldn't think of any legal way to do it. I couldn't stop in a McDonald's parking lot for ten hours. But if I stopped well short of Columbia, and there weren't a lot of places to choose from, I would have to "slide hours" – that is, lie about when I had driven – either that or run out of drive time. Lying on a logbook in order to go to church didn't seem like a very good way to honor God. It was the only way I could think of though.

I hadn't talked with Johnny since getting off his truck. Now I tried to call him from the public phone at a rest area and made the discovery that I couldn't reach him. The connection just didn't seem to work. I drove on to a truck stop and tried the phones there with the same result. I was sure that Johnny would be able to advise me about how to log what I was doing, but I simply couldn't reach him to find out. Eventually I just did my best with it, sliding the driving time about three hours, pretending that I had stayed in Columbia overnight. I went to Mass.

It seemed highly ironic to me, though, that the first time I had lied on a logbook came about through wanting to go to church.

I arrived in Kentucky later that same day, early for the delivery which wasn't until 2 AM. It was only 10 PM, and I wasn't sure how to proceed. Should I go in four hours early and try to deliver the load? I got off the freeway and parked along a street, not very busy at that time on a Sunday night. I sent a Qualcomm to the night dispatchers, but they didn't have anything helpful to say. After sitting on the street for half an hour or 45 minutes I decided to take a chance and go to the delivery site.

The dispatch directions were a bit vague. I found myself on a small dark street with a yard containing some trailers and loading docks on the right and railroad tracks up ahead. The place on the right was dark – no signs of activity there. I couldn't see any kind of sign with the name of a business. On the other hand, I wasn't sure there was anything much beyond the railroad tracks. I didn't want to get stuck in a dead-end situation, so I drove into the deserted yard, parked, and got out to explore.

It didn't feel at all safe to be walking around in a deserted industrial area so late at night, but I couldn't think of an alternative, so I walked down the road past the railroad tracks and found what I was looking for, the company where the french fries were to be delivered.

Knowing now that I could drive farther without getting stuck, I went back to the truck, climbed in and started the engine. Getting out of the yard wasn't very simple. I went forward, started a left turn, but realized that I would inevitably sideswipe one of the trailers parked crosswise in the yard if I persisted in this course of action.

So, I stopped, climbed out of the truck and walked back the length of the trailer to study the situation. Backing up and going back out the entrance I had come in looked like the answer. I would need to back the trailer up beside an empty flatbed trailer that had been on my right when I pulled into the yard.

I got back in the truck and began to back. It was difficult to see where I was going in the dark – the mirrors always gave me trouble at night. I suddenly had the feeling that I had better stop. Climbing out once again ("Get Out And Look" or, if you don't, "Get Out And Look Stupid" after you hit something, as Mueller had put it), I found that my trailer was within an inch of hitting the parked flatbed trailer! Well, I worked it out eventually and, driving over the railroad tracks, turned left into the yard of the place where I was supposed to be.

Here there was lots of activity and many bright lights, a scene of organized confusion, with trucks backed up to loading docks, trailers stored on one side of the lot, cars parked here and there.

Leaving the truck in what I hoped was an out-of-the-way place near the beginning of the yard, I took the bill of lading, trip notebook, my CDL and a pen and found the shipping/receiving office. Two middle-aged men were standing in the office, one black and one white. The black man looked more dignified and impressed me as probably being the boss, but this turned out not to be the case. As the two men finished their business, it was the black man who walked out. I was left alone with the white man, who put on a rather different air when dealing with a woman and became simultan-eously patronizing and flirtatious – a bit like the obnoxious Idaho driver of a few weeks before, but thankfully, to a much lesser degree.

This worked to my advantage up to a point, as he decided to indulge me by letting me back up to door number 10, even though I was so early. Going back outside, I saw that door 10 was on the far end of the docks. There would be no possibility of doing the conventional setup for backing up to a loading dock. On the other hand, there was a lot of room in front of the dock and I theorized that I could probably sweep a giant counterclockwise arc, then just back straight up to the dock. Or I could have done so if it wasn't for the small red sports car parked four-square in the middle of where I would have to drive to set up this backing.

Sighing, I walked back into the building, where I had to wait a few minutes to get the man's attention as he was now dealing with someone else. Once he finished, I spoke to him, saying that I wasn't sure whether or not I could back up to door number 10, but that I was sure that I could *not* back up to it unless the red car got moved.

"What red car?" asked the man.

"The one that's in my way," I replied.

Sighing heavily and rolling his eyes, the man said, "Let's go see," and led the way back out to the yard. He rolled his eyes again as he saw the car, which now had two men standing by it. I demonstrated the way I hoped to set up the backing to him, using my hand to sweep an imaginary path. He concurred with the plan, saying "That's how it's done." I was glad to have this corroborating evidence of having analyzed the situation correctly.

In the meantime, the man went to speak to the sports car people while I walked back to my truck and climbed in, praying that I could do this thing. I couldn't hear what the boss said to the men, but could imagine all too well that he was asking them to move so that "the woman" could back up to the loading dock, undoubtedly with more rolling of eyes as he asked them to play along with my unreasonableness.

Once the car was out of the way, I made the large arc and then, to my great surprise, backed up to the loading dock with no trouble whatsoever, apart from starting to go the wrong way as I always did. But I was able to pull forward a little and correct what I had done.

Then I had to borrow some wire cutters from another driver to cut the braided-wire seal before I could open the trailer doors and finish bumping the dock. It all went very well. The office man seemed much less patronizing when I went in again to get my signed bills.

Once the french fries were unloaded, I was free to go. The problem was that I was out of hours but had nowhere to park the truck. I drove about five miles to the nearest rest area where I was fortunate to find a parking place along the shoulder of the off-ramp leading to it. I logged it as still being in Frankfurt, though I doubted that it really was.

CHAPTER 14

Numbers
(June 4-11)

Trip number three on my own started the next day (well, technically the same day but at the other end of it) with a 10 PM pickup in Cincinnati, Ohio of a load of Smuckers products going to Stevens Point, Wisconsin. That left me with a lot of time on my hands and hearing that the trailer might be ready early, I arrived at the plant before dark. I was told that the trailer was stuck in the loading dock and they needed me to back up under it, hook up to it and then push it backwards toward the dock in hopes that the hook holding the trailer to the loading dock could then be released.

I found that the loading dock was on a slope. This made it look as though the trailer was much too low to hook up to, but another driver pointed out that it wouldn't look so bad once the tractor got onto the downhill slope too.

With a good deal of difficulty, and working with a dock employee, I managed to get the trailer unstuck from the loading dock. I pulled it up the slope, then stopped to close the trailer doors, noticing as I did so that the trailer was loaded to within a foot or so of the back doors – well behind the line painted five feet forward of the doors on the inside of all Alan trailers next to a stenciled sign which warned,

"IF MORE THAN
38,000 LBS
LOAD AHEAD
OF THIS LINE"

193

As the load weighed 40,986 lbs. according to the dispatch, this worried me a lot. The question was, should I make a big fuss right at the end of the working day? To question the load would probably delay me by five or six hours while the trailer was reloaded, if I could even make anyone pay attention to me. I wasn't sure, and I hated confrontation. Besides, I only had about 24 hours to drive 524 miles or more and didn't want to lose the time it might take.

I had to "scale" (weigh) the load on my way out of the yard. The man running the scales refused to weigh the axles separately. All he was interested in was making sure that my total weight was under 80,000 lb. He told me that there was another set of scales a few blocks away where I could get the axles weighed separately if I wanted to. I would have preferred to drive across these scales in steps, finding out the steer axle weight, then the steer axle plus drive axles' weights together and finally the weight of all the axles. With a bit of arithmetic, it was then possible to figure out exactly how much weight was on each set of axles. But again, I couldn't bring myself to be that confrontational and wasn't sure enough of my ground to make a stand. Someone else was waiting to weigh, so I left, but rather unhappily.

I had never used the other type of scales, the truck stop ones, and wasn't willing to venture into unknown territory, where turns might be too tight to negotiate. And I hadn't really understood where those other scales were, anyway, so I simply hoped for the best and drove away.

I made it as far as Illinois that night, to a place called Farmer City. The next morning when I woke up I found a message waiting on the Qualcomm. Kevin wanted to know why I was out of route. It was nicely phrased. Kevin always had a light touch with Qualcomm messages. Oddly, it was almost always possible to read tone of voice in Qualcomm messages, even with only a few words.

The message shocked me. I studied the road atlas and realized what had happened. I had avoided Chicago and thus had failed to cut a corner. It had hardly even been a conscious decision. I had just thought, "Oh, that's Chicago!" then had skirted it, taking I-74 west to Bloomington, where I could pick up I-39 northbound.

It hadn't even occurred to me that I ought to go through

Chicago. What a horrible thought! Even with Johnny, Chicago had been awful at 10:30 AM. What would it have been like at night, I wondered? Well, I had gotten away with not going through it once. I hoped I wouldn't get routed that way very soon again because I really didn't want to go through Chicago.

Later that day, in Wisconsin, I found that a weigh station was open, so I had to drive across its scales. No red light came on; I proceeded on my way, thinking that the load must, after all, be legal.

But when I delivered it at Stevens Point, Wisconsin, there were some damaged items. The receiving company refused a case of jam which had a couple of broken jars in it, and also a sack of flour which had somehow gotten split open. I talked with OS&D at corporate headquarters and was told to bring the items in. I was on my way there anyway, as my truck's missing nets had arrived. It would be pleasant not to have cassette tapes falling on my head anymore, as they had done several times.

At headquarters the next day I had the opportunity to speak with Chip Walsh. I mentioned the Smuckers trailer to him and he told me that with such a heavy load, loaded so far back in the trailer, the back axles had undoubtedly been very overweight indeed. He seemed astonished that I had made it through the Wisconsin weigh station, which had a reputation for being strict, but decided that whoever read the scale simply hadn't believed their own eyes when they saw that the back axles were 4,000 lb. overweight or whatever it was.

According to Chip, it was also the trailer being loaded so far back that had caused the damage to jam and flour. They had been bounced around too vigorously. I made a resolution not to be fooled this way again. Weighing really was necessary for such heavy loads. Normally, the driver would have picked up the load already sealed and waiting, without getting to see how it was loaded. Only the mischance of the trailer being stuck at the dock had given me the opportunity of knowing that it was loaded much too far back before I started driving it.

I also apologized to Chip for costing the company money with the spurious service call in Nebraska, when nothing whatsoever was wrong with my brakes. He dismissed this as "beginner stuff," something the company understood.

The next day, nets installed, I picked up a loaded trailer from the corporate drop yard and headed for the Chicago area, trip number four. Oh well! At least I wasn't driving through it. On my way down I stopped at the Walmart on the Wisconsin-Illinois border. I wanted to buy a CB radio. They were always supplied by the driver rather than the trucking company. Until now I hadn't found time to buy one. Companies where we picked up or delivered sometimes monitored a CB channel to take questions from drivers or tell them when and where to dock, so it really was necessary that I get one.

The Walmart parking lot had a sign posted forbidding large trucks to park, but there were at least a dozen semis already parked there. I decided to ignore the sign. I quickly got into trouble when I tried to park next to one of the yellow trucks with the huge archangel painted on each side. I hoped to see the driver and have a chance to ask him if the company was a good one to drive for. The trouble came because I didn't go out far enough before cutting back to line up beside him. Again, as in Kentucky, I suddenly had the feeling that I had better stop. Sure enough, I was only an inch away from his trailer, about to scrape it with my trailer. I got out to look. I would only have one chance to turn the steering wheel in the correct direction. If I made the wrong decision, I'd be up against the other trailer for sure.

From outside of the truck I could see which direction I needed to turn the tires as I backed up. Fortunately, the other driver seemed not to be around. I climbed back into my truck, put the flashers on and backed until I was clear, then went to a different part of the lot to park, deciding that I didn't want to talk with someone I had almost hit, even after the fact.

Now I got into more trouble. The parking lot, designed for cars, not trucks, had various little curb-lined triangular islands marking the ends of rows, with grass and bushes planted in the middle of them. Trying to turn back into a different part of the lot, I saw that I was running the trailer tires over the curb and grass of one of these islands. I had spared the bush.

I parked, making an inner vow never to do this again, at least not until I wasn't such a beginner. I went into the store and bought a CB radio. When I came back out I discovered that a car had parked too near to me while I was in the store. I asked advice from a trucker about how to get out of the lot. He suggested a possible pathway, and seemed to think that I wouldn't have any trouble. I made it out without any more problems, drove the rest of the way down to the Chicago area, dropped the trailer off, then went to the nearby Kraft plant to pick up a load going to Ft. Worth, Texas.

Johnny and I had been to the Kraft plant in Ft. Worth where I would need to deliver this load – it was the place with the not-so-sweet grandma where we had been so held up. I felt relatively happy about the load, in spite of the grandma. For once, I didn't need to dread going into a totally unknown situation and having to size it up.

Backing up to the loading docks, both at the Chicago delivery and the subsequent Kraft pickup, went outrageously badly. I was rescued both times though – something that hadn't happened before. At the first place, I set up badly for where the trailer had to be put. The whole situation was tight. I seesawed backwards and forwards over and over, not making any progress. Finally, I bailed out on the attempt, went to the end of the yard and did a U-turn, came back to the other end, did another U-turn, set it up again – and it still wasn't any good.

At this point a yard dog came by in his little vehicle-for-moving-trailers (the right equipment for the job!) and offered to put the trailer into the place for me if I would drop it. I quickly accepted his offer, thanked him from the bottom of my heart, dropped the trailer right where it was, picked up an empty and drove it over to the next pickup, in the same town but at a Kraft plant, the start of trip number five on my own.

And it happened again! The load was a live load. I had to back the empty up to a loading dock so the warehouse workers could load it up. It just seemed to be a day when I couldn't back at all. After I had struggled with it for a while, again a yard dog came along and offered to do it for me if I would drop the trailer. He was a 50-something man, not very attractive, balding and dressed in a dirty, sleeveless undershirt which left the tattoos on his upper arms uncovered. Some of his teeth were missing and what hair he had was gray and looked as though it had been combed with an eggbeater. But he looked like an angel to me at that moment and I told him so a little later, after he had put the trailer into the loading dock and I had hooked back up to it again. I saw him going by in his little trailer-moving vehicle, stopped him and thanked him profusely, telling him that he was an angel and an answer to a prayer I hadn't even prayed. He looked abashed, as though being called an angel might be a rarity in his life.

So twice in one day I had been bailed out. I felt relieved, of course, and grateful, but also humiliated. Would I *never* learn to back?

The rest of the day I drove southward through Illinois, enjoying the 55 mph truck speed limit, which most truckers hated but which I liked because the cab of the truck was so much quieter at 55, or the 58 I was actually going, when the engine wasn't pushed right up against the governor that kept it from going faster than 65.

Only a few states had the invariable 55 mph speed limit for trucks, but some of them were big. California, Illinois, Ohio and Oregon were the ones I knew of. The speed limit was most strictly enforced in Ohio, or so I had been told. Truckers had been ticketed for going as little as three mph over the speed limit. My last speeding ticket, which I had gotten in 1981, had been given to me by an Ohio Highway Patrolman, so I kept strictly to the speed limit in Ohio.

This business of having what was called split speed limits, one for cars and another for trucks, was disliked by truckers. It made semis into obstacles for cars, much like rocks in a riverbed. All car traffic had to flow around us. Passing another truck was even worse, as four-wheelers stacked up behind us. While I was convinced that it was dangerous to have one speed limit for trucks and another for cars, the lower speed limit was quieter for me and enabled me to listen to music better.

By now I had received a couple of paychecks for driving on my own. They were disappointing. As a trainee I had been making $300/week for the first half of training, then $500/week as a more advanced student. Now I was getting paid the beginner rate of 28 cents per mile. This would go up half a cent per mile every three or six months. If I made it through my first year it might rise quite a bit. I was hazy about the details of this; it seemed a long way off.

The bottom line was that I was paid $205 for my first week on my own and $238 for the second week. What a disappointment! A fairly simple calculation showed that I would have to drive 1,785 miles/week to equal my pay as a student. I had driven just under 1,300 miles the first week. Also, the advances I took to buy meals and make the occasional Walmart trip, for protein bars, water, peanuts and miscellany such as napkins and paper towels, were cutting into my pay.

The idea that I was working 14 hours a day, seven days a week for $205 in my checking account was so outrageous that I could hardly take it in. The job was totally demanding. The irregular hours off, when a pickup was scheduled a long time after a delivery for example, took place randomly and not in places of my choosing.

It was true that as a beginner I didn't always manage things as well as I might, but the fundamental fact remained that I was away from any place I might call home. Lots of work was required: picking up and delivering loads, filling out paperwork, planning trips, sending Qualcomm messages, and driving. Of the above list, only the driving was paid, along with, occasionally, what was called detention pay, hourly pay for time spent at a shipper or receiver outside of certain parameters to do with appointment times. It wasn't very generous to say the least.

I recalled a message that had come across the Qualcomm when I was still out with Johnny, announcing that he would receive four dollars detention pay on his next paycheck. As this represented, in reality, something like six hours out of our lives, I was quite incensed for Johnny's sake and felt like saying to them that they should just give it to the Missionaries of Charity or someone who would want it – not insult Johnny by calling it pay as though his time was only worth 67 cents an hour. And Johnny, who felt much the same way, told me that he had received detention pay in as small an amount as $1.80.

So, no, it was really just the driving that was paid, and not very well in my case as I was now finding out. This was referred to by truckers as "paying your dues" for the first year. I sometimes wondered what percentage of new drivers actually made it through the first year. It wasn't a high percentage I was sure, certainly under fifty percent and probably much lower.

Only the big companies even took beginners, apparently because it changed their insurance rate structure very much for the worse. And they had a tendency to fire beginners over things which would get a more experienced trucker a reprimand at most. Did thirty percent of beginners make it? I wondered. Ten percent? Even fewer?

There were two sorts of days, I was discovering – driving days and days with a pickup and delivery. Sometimes a delivery happened one day and the next pickup not until the following day, creating yet other sorts of days, but that wasn't the generality.

Driving days fell into a pattern for me quite early on. When possible, when I could arrange things that way, I drove from 4 AM until 6 PM (the 14 hours). The main advantage of this was that it was usually pretty easy to find parking in a truck stop at 6 PM – and I was always seeking the sort of parking that could be done without backing up. I had made a rule for myself that I only backed up when it was necessary, that is, at shipping and receiving docks. The rest of the time I didn't care to take the risk of hitting something, nor did I care for the prospect of making a total fool of myself in front of who-knew-how-many watching eyes, eyes of (mostly) men, virtually all of whom could do it better than I.

Leaving at 4 AM also had the advantage of putting the difficult pre-dawn driving at the front of the day when I was relatively fresh. A disadvantage was that rest areas were full when I started driving. They didn't reliably start to clear out, and so weren't really usable, until seven or eight in the morning. This was easily dealt with, though, by pulling through a truck stop fuel island. I could take enough time to use the restroom and buy more coffee, all that I needed to do in the first hours of a driving day.

The method that I eventually heard about from a more experienced trucker, was to try to drive 250 or even 300 miles before taking any more than five-minute restroom breaks. Driving that far then entitled you to a meal and a 40-minute nap (but not a shower) for a total break of no more than two hours. Then you tried to do it again, drive another 300 miles, before running up against the 14-hour time limit. In this way, it was possible to drive more than 600 miles a day.

But that was later. In the early days of being on my own I didn't know of this method and was pretty much constantly exhausted, "not keeping the driver's side door closed enough" as was sometimes said. I would use up all my energy driving 400 miles, stopping every 150 miles or so, then be too tired to drive any farther. Things went much better after I learned to try to drive 300 miles at the beginning of a shift, then take a real rest.

It was only after the close of a 14-hour shift that I normally thought about showering. I couldn't eat, take a shower and sleep for eight hours in the time that was available to me once I had gotten off the freeway and parked (and allowing half an hour for getting started in the morning). It was sleeping time that got cut into, every other day at least. Either that or the shower got postponed, sometimes beyond what was reasonable. Laundry had to wait for one of the random waiting-around times that sometimes got thrown at me.

Days with a delivery and a pickup were very different from driving days. Pickups and deliveries used up two or three hours each, and sometimes much more, of the 14 hours that I could work before being required to take a 10-hour break. Even a drop and hook took me an hour or more, as against Johnny's 15 minutes. When I was out with Johnny, I had tried for a while, as a matter of conscience, to log the real hours involved. He had laughed at me but let me do it. The result, I quickly found, was that I ran out of hours on the 70 hours in 8 days part of the log in very short order. Doing my own logging had been part of an abortive attempt on Johnny's part to have me practice that aspect of trucking. At the time, I solved the conscience difficulty, if you could call it solving, by having Johnny take the logging back over.

Chip Walsh had talked to me about how to log deliveries and pickups on the day I was tested, pointing out that unless I was actually on the dock, I wasn't required to show it as being on duty. After all, I might be lying in the sleeper berth the whole time.

And apparently it was perfectly legal to "slide" hours in this case, showing the whole process taking place either immediately after I arrived or immediately before I left. That had possibilities as far as being able to get a 10-hour break in those cases where I was held up for outrageously long periods of time. The catch was needing to anticipate the possibility of using the time as a break. If I didn't spend most of it sleeping it didn't do me any real good because I'd be too tired to drive even if I could do it legally. That was probably why Johnny so often napped at pickups and deliveries.

Anyway, if a delivery or a pickup occurred on the same day, as they usually did, it used up six or eight hours of the 14 hours. Even if I had slid one of them to minimize the effect, I found it hard to drive much more than 400 miles on such a day. Sometimes I couldn't even drive that far.

The trip down to Ft. Worth was made pleasant by the discovery of an interesting independent truck stop south of Little Rock. It was preceded by an unpleasant episode, though. My original plan had been to stop at the one of the North Little Rock truck stops which had IdleAir. I had been there with Johnny but hadn't grasped how early the place filled up. Arriving at 8 PM or so, I found a conga line of trucks circling the IdleAir places, hoping for one of them to open up – which occasionally one did. I spent 20 minutes or so at this profitless pastime before deciding to try the much smaller truck stop across the street.

Now things took a real turn for the worse. The small truck stop was laid out on a pattern that required pulling through the fuel island in order to be oriented correctly for attempting to park in any of its parking places. I didn't notice this interesting fact until I had already messed up by driving into the exit. This left me needing to do a U-turn on the other side of the fuel islands, in a place where there was nowhere near enough room for a U-turn. Worse, I found myself facing all the trucks as they sat in the fuel islands. One truck in particular, which had already pulled forward after fueling, was very much in my way.

I began the arduous process of trying to turn the truck around through a long iterative process of pulling as far around to my left as I could, alternating with backing up as far as I could with the steering wheel turned the other way. I was making progress inches at a time – with no assurance that this way of doing it would ever work – when a nice driver, a black man, decided to help out by directing me. I was grateful and, as always, felt that I had "come home" in seeing a friendly black face. It reminded me of Africa days.

I was making some progress with his help when someone yelled and I saw that a driver had backed out of a fuel island so that I could drive through it the wrong way and escape. Quickly thanking the black driver for his help, I did just that.

I had now wasted at least 45 minutes and was in danger of overrunning my 14 hours. I went back to the IdleAir truck stop across the street, where I pulled through a fuel island and studied my truck stop directory. There was a truck stop listed – an extra-large one at that – off of I-30 in a place called Glen Rose. It was only about 30 miles away. I headed for it.

When I arrived, exhausted, but just barely within my 14 hours, I found, to my delight, that not only was it a huge truck stop, with lots of parking available at any time of day or night (much of it not paved but that was of little importance), but also it had IdleAir and most of the IdleAir spots were unoccupied.

I drove straight into one of them, shut the truck down, then chatted with a friendly IdleAir employee who showed up at my window within seconds and helped me get the template into place in the passenger's side window, then handed me up the IdleAir control unit.

Afterwards, I went to the truck stop's restaurant where different food was available from the run-of-the-mill truck stop restaurant food, and had a bowl of genuine Campbell's tomato soup before bed.

The next day I had a funny experience with a weigh station due to my hearing problem. Johnny had taught me to turn off the radio and open a window when I went through an open weigh station. The first thing was to decide whether or not the weigh station was open. Most were closed. If it was open, though, it was necessary to pull in, unless the off-ramp was overflowing. Often there were arrows pointing to two lanes at the entry to a weigh station. One lane led to the official scales, the other bypassed the scales and led back to the freeway. The driver had to follow whichever arrow lit up green after the truck was weighed in motion by scales set into the concrete of the off-ramp.

Even if a weigh station was open, it was at least even money that a given truck would be pointed to the bypass lane. Only once had I pulled into a weigh station and had to show my logbook. That was always a possibility, though, and I had seen drivers sitting on the shoulder of the freeway near weigh stations, presumably catching their logbooks up, just in case.

Sometimes we did have to weigh, of course. Johnny had taught me to slow down to three mph for this, then follow whatever directions flashed on signs or were given by loudspeaker. And I was to be very careful not to step hard on the brakes while the truck was on the scales. Scales had been broken that way. Weigh station scales were enormously costly. In the worst case, the driver's company was charged if a driver ruined a scales through ignorance or stupidity. The company would probably decide I was too expensive to have around if I broke even one set of scales, Johnny said. So, I was careful not to make sudden moves or go too fast through weigh stations.

And I did always turn off the radio and open the window at least a crack when I went through a weigh station, but I had almost forgotten the reason why, as it was so unusual a thing to be spoken to by loudspeaker.

On this occasion I hadn't even noticed the loudspeaker and only gradually became aware that a voice from it was saying, "stop... Stop!... *Stop!*... STOP!"

I stopped.

"Now back up," said the voice. "Back up... back up... keep backing up... back up ... " Once I had backed almost a whole truck length, the voice said, "That's enough."

With a Texas drawl, he continued, "Now, let's try it again, driver."

I drove forward slowly, stopping on command, then was given

permission to proceed on my way, amused, but also rueful about my hearing.

The rest of the trip to Ft. Worth was routine, except for the delivery, which was a drop and hook with a yard check. I recognized the yard where the grandmother-type had made Johnny's and my lives so unpleasant. This security guard was a different woman, but equally unpleasant in her own way as she answered "no" to my request to use the restroom.

"No?!" I was stunned. What was I supposed to do?

"It's against the rules," explained the guard. "I can't let you."

It took me two solid hours to do the drop and hook with the yard check. There were more than 20 Alan trailers there. Writing down all the information about them (trailer number, loaded status, and reefer fuel tank level) took quite a while, as did typing it into the Qualcomm macro. And I still wasn't all that fast at drop and hooks either. Finally, I was free to go.

The next day, Sunday, I drove into Arlington, Texas early so I could go to Mass. The church was only a mile or so away from my next pickup, for trip number six, at US Cold Storage in Arlington, a load going to Houma, Louisiana. I had already been to the Arlington church the day that Johnny had spent at the Six Flags amusement park, but then I had been bobtailing, which had made everything much easier.

Even so, I had had trouble with some overhanging tree branches, had scraped the roof of the truck quite badly, when I drove away from the church and got into a residential neighborhood by mistake. I would be careful to avoid that route.

It was early enough on Sunday morning that there was almost no traffic. This was all to the good, I thought, as I circled the church on the nearest main streets, looking for a possible parking place. I was fortunate enough to find a high school on the very street I would take to the next pickup, and only six blocks away from the church. On a Sunday morning in summertime there seemed to be no danger of blocking school buses, so I parked alongside the school, in the long bay used by the buses to pick up or drop off students.

I put the steering gear lock on and left a note taped to the driver's side window, explaining where I was and when I would return, in case the police took an interest, then walked the six blocks to Mass through the warm, muggy air of an early summer morning.

After Mass, one of the ushers was nice enough to give me a ride back to the truck. Then I proceeded to the pickup, just down the road, where I missed the entrance. I knew what I had done almost as soon as I passed the turn-in, and began looking frantically for a way back. It was especially nerve-racking as the street, once I was beyond the plant, looked more and more residential.

There was a four-way stop intersection just ahead which looked big enough for a U-turn if I used "all the available space," as Johnny's voice inside my head pointed out. It was now considerably later than when I had arrived for church, with a lot more traffic around, but I waited my turn at the four-way stop, then cut sharply to the right while signaling a left and proceeded, very definitely using all the available space, to pull a U-turn. It worked!

It was a sad thing, I mused, that there really wasn't much cars could do if a semi chose to pull such a trick. I had noticed this once or twice before, but from the point of view of a car driver. Now I was seeing it from the other side.

The delivery in Louisiana was the next morning, after a night spent at a rest area, and involved a lot of driving on small country highways. It was pleasant, I thought, driving along an almost empty roadway out in the country in the early morning hours. If I had not been worrying about the next loading dock it would even have been relaxing.

The dispatch directions worked, and I found myself in Houma, Louisiana, a place I had never been. The delivery went well enough. I was disappointed that nobody seemed to be speaking French, or Cajun more accurately, as I had hoped to hear some.

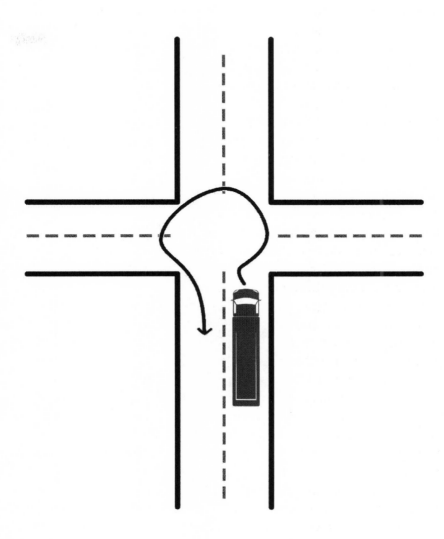

21. Diagram of pulling a U-turn at a four-way stop intersection

CHAPTER 15

Spider Bites
(June 11-20)

My next dispatch was to Plaquemine, Louisiana, near Baton Rouge, to pick up a load of plastic from a Dow Chemical plant there for trip number seven, going to Hebron, Ohio. A prolonged scrutiny of the relevant atlas page, plus talking with another driver, convinced me that Route 1, a State route, would be the most direct way to get to Plaquemine from Houma. But the trick was to find Route 1.

I started up Route 20, as I had been advised to do, and watched for signs. It was a tricky route, with construction going on and detours which led me all around a small town, full of tight turns, with occasional signs promising Route 1.

Construction driving was something that all drivers did often, especially in the summer. From the beginning of my time out with Johnny, I had had to accustom myself to driving the narrow lanes of construction zones. They often had a concrete barrier down one side. Once in a while there were concrete barriers down *both* sides of a lane. This still had the power to make my toes curl.

More commonly, construction zones had a line of orange and white striped barrels. Some states had warning signs proclaiming that hitting a barrel would be treated the same way that hitting a worker would. Johnny had made rather a point of giving me the same warning.

This had led to a little fantasy scenario which sometimes played in my mind when I saw the distinctive barrels: a few lines pirated from "Alice's Restaurant," of going to jail and being asked by another prisoner,

> "What were you arrested for, Kid?"
> "Hitting a barrel in a construction zone."
> ["and they all moved away from me on the bench there... "]

Eventually, after at least eight different signs, I was actually on Route 1. But after fifteen or twenty minutes I began to question which way I was going on Route 1. Direction hadn't been mentioned on any of the signs. Nor had there ever been a choice of Route 1 one direction to the left and Route 1 the other direction to the right, for example. Now mention was being made of a town some miles ahead, and it seemed to me that I might be going the wrong way.

Pulling off the road on the shoulder-less State route was no simple matter. After a long five or more minutes I found a roomy enough, solid-looking enough dirt shoulder and pulled off to study my atlas. Sure enough, I was headed the wrong way. More than that, I was almost to US-90, but 20 miles the wrong direction of where I had crossed it before.

What should I do? I could undoubtedly turn around at US-90 and head back up Route 1 in the other direction. But what were my chances of being able to stay on the route through all the road construction of that small town?

The alternative was to go way around on US-90 until it connected up with the Interstate. I had already questioned Kevin, my dispatcher, on this point via Qualcomm. His reply had been that it was my call to make. I didn't like either option, but decided to play it safe, even though it would take me the rest of the day.

The appointment was on a first-come-first-serve basis, represented by the numbers 11:11 on the dispatch for appointment time. Also, the load was a drop and hook, so I needed to fuel the reefer, which was well below the ¾ of a tank which was required when leaving a trailer at a shipper's yard.

Hours later, at 5:10 PM, I was at Breaux Bridge, Louisiana putting fuel in the reefer, when the Qualcomm beeped. It was a change in appointment time to 5:30 PM. I was 50 miles away from Plaquemine, so I immediately send a macro to say that I would be late, and pointed out in the comments section of it that it had been 11:11 and I was 50 miles away, a distance I could not cover in the less than 20 minutes before the new appointment time.

When I eventually arrived at Plaquemine they considered me to be late and also denied that the load was a drop and hook. They wanted to load my trailer. I was given a dock number, had a lot of trouble backing up to it as there was not very much space in front and there was deep mud off the edge of the asphalt. After half an hour of wrestling with the trailer I was finally lined up and ready to back the last few feet to the dock, only to realize that I didn't have room to open its doors. There wasn't enough room to pull straight forward far enough to clear the trailers on each side of me, and they were too close to my trailer to permit opening the doors from my current position.

Just then a black driver came along and asked if he could help. He seemed friendly and had already diagnosed my problem.

"You'll just have to do it again," he told me, then laughed as my face fell.

Another driver came by at this point, another black man, and the first man explained to him what the problem was, ending with, "You should have seen her face!"

Then he told me to back up some more – it might be possible to open the doors if I got nearer to the dock. I didn't understand this, though I had heard of it. It worked! I backed up some more, the two men opened the doors and I was all set, door-wise.

The next problem was that I was within a few hours of the end of my 14 hours. If they didn't load the trailer pretty quickly I wouldn't be able to leave. And they didn't load the trailer quickly. They didn't even start loading it. I went in and talked with the woman at the shipping desk and was given permission to stay on the lot if necessary. This would enable me to start my ten hours off when I had arrived at the shippers, i.e., at 6:30 PM. In other words, I would be free to leave at 4:30 AM the next morning.

I probably made things worse by going into the employee lounge for a while and doing a crossword puzzle I found in a newspaper there. Although I felt at home among black people, it was apparent that the black men who wandered into the lounge didn't feel any equivalent way about me. When, in the interests of being friendly, I commented on how good one man's dinner looked, he offered me some of it, but in a way that seemed to indicate I had broken a rule of etiquette. I refused the food, of course, and left soon after, but the hours went by and no loading started.

I went to sleep as soon as I could. I was awakened by someone banging on my door around 10:30 PM. It was one of the black workers, to say that the trailer was now loaded. His attitude struck me as odd – he seemed both defiant and apologetic, as if he had mistreated me somehow.

I got up and went into the building to sign the bills. The same young white woman was working at the shipping/receiving counter. I wondered idly, while I signed my name, if the workers were reacting against me or against this woman in keeping me so long. But it really didn't matter.

I went back out to the truck, drove to the front end of the lot, where I had been told that I would be out of the way, and which put me far, far away from any restroom, and, after shutting the trailer doors, went back to sleep with the windows open. The outside temperature was in the mid- to high eighties. For some reason I had never succeeded in getting the truck to idle without stalling out after five minutes, so no air conditioning was available.

When the alarm clock woke me at 4:15 AM I realized that I had basically been parked next to a Louisiana swamp. The load weighed 44,299 lb. so I thought I had better weigh it to make sure it was balanced and not overweight on either axle. I had heard that a ticket for being overweight could be very expensive. There was a certified CAT scale just a few miles away in Baton Rouge, so I headed there and got onto the scales with some difficulty. Then I had to lean out of the door and press the scale's call button with a broomstick handle – one more disadvantage to being short.

The load was not overweight. It weighed less than 80,000 lbs., but the back axle was too heavy. After some deep thought, and sketching out of the situation, I did the calculation for balancing the load, slid the tandems four holes and weighed the truck again. This time, to my relief, the two axles were within 100 lbs. of each other and both were under the 34,000 lb. legal limit. I had calculated correctly!

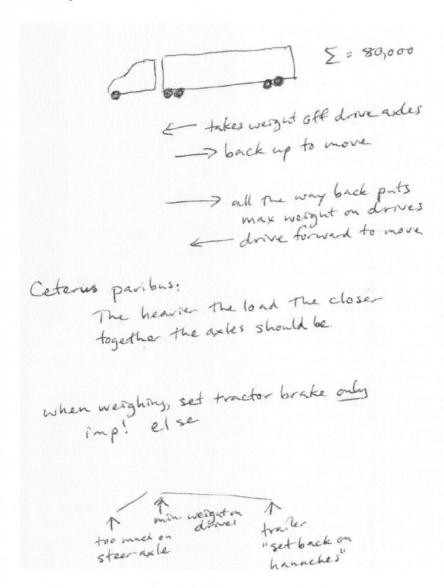

$\Sigma = 80,000$

← takes weight off drive axles

→ back up to move

→ all the way back puts max weight on drives

← drive forward to move

Ceterus paribus:
The heavier the load the closer together the axles should be.

when weighing, set tractor brake *only* imp! else

min weight on drives

too much on steer axle

trailer "set back on haunches"

22. Tandem sketches from my spiral notebook

Ever since I got up, I had been absentmindedly scratching what I at first assumed to be mosquito bites. The itching was so bad that it finally caught my attention after I had slid the tandems. I turned on a light and examined myself, finding that I had about twenty of what were probably *not* mosquito bites. Spider bites was my tentative diagnosis. There were eight on the sole of my left foot, five on the side of my right foot, also one on that foot's instep, one on my thigh, three on my right arm and two on the index finger of my right hand. They were the sort of bite that itched more when you scratched them. In the end, I just had to decide not to scratch at all; the torment produced by scratching was worse than the torment of the bite itself.

A worse aspect of the situation presented itself as I drove northward. I began to think that I was still being bitten. Could the spider still be in the truck?! In the middle of the afternoon I found out when I pulled through a fuel island in Mississippi. As I climbed down from the cab I felt a tickle on my left arm. When I moved my hand to scratch it there was something there! It was a small, brown spider. I crushed it between my thumb and forefinger, wincing at the crunch, then examined it closely before dropping it on the ground. That was the end of being bitten, so clearly it had been the spider, but the itching went on for several weeks, only gradually tapering off.

I reached Hurricane Mills, Tennessee at the end of the day. It was lovely to be farther north where it was cooler, and nicer yet to be at a truck stop with IdleAir. I would have air conditioning that night! Having driven 537 miles I was exhausted. But I was also faced with a dilemma. The next day's delivery was still 478 miles away, to be followed by a pickup, 35 miles from the delivery site, at 4 PM. I was pretty sure I would be late. I couldn't start until 4:15 AM and it would take me most of the day to drive 478 miles.

Having had an upsetting conversation with the night dispatcher [see Prologue], and after crying myself to sleep, I started at 4:15 the next morning, drove until 8 AM, when my usual dispatcher would be at work, then called him from Kentucky.

Kevin was his usual sympathetic self and straightened everything out in short order. Yes, it was unfortunate that I had been held up so long at the pickup and gotten lost in the first place. The load I was on was to be delivered on a first-come-first-serve basis, but the delivery window of the company, when they accepted shipments, was 7 AM until 2 PM. He doubted I could make that and would move the delivery to the following morning. Could I be there at 7 AM sharp on the 14th? Yes, I was sure I could.

The next load was on a preloaded trailer, so Kevin didn't foresee any difficulties about it. Preloaded trailers could be picked up at any time. I would then have a day and a half to drive 529 miles, as the load didn't deliver until 4 PM on the 15th.

Unlike the phone call of the evening before, this one left me feeling comforted and reassured. Things weren't so bad after all. The rest of the trip went routinely. I arrived in Hebron, Ohio about an hour after the close of the delivery window, spent the night at a truck stop, got some extra rest, and made it to the delivery site right at 7 AM on the morning after. I had a hard time with backing, as always, but got it in the end. It reminded me of the chemical plant in Michigan where the setup was unusual in that you came in almost parallel to the dock, rather than at right angles to it – easier really, but nothing about backing was ever easy for me.

The man doing the unloading also seemed to be the supervisor, an unusual occurrence. He was fairly cross and spoke about how busy he was. I had apparently held him up, both by being a day late and by taking such a long time to bump the dock.

He unloaded the trailer in no time flat and I was soon on my way to the next pickup, 34 miles away, for the start of trip number eight. This was a huge Kraft plant, very well organized but with a horrific bureaucracy. There was no personal contact with anyone, and no chance at a restroom. The drop and hook was accomplished without any interaction other than talking on the CB radio to women in guard shacks.

I spent a frustrating hour dropping the empty trailer in one lot and picking up a loaded trailer from a different lot, then headed for Atlanta, Georgia. There appeared to be plenty of time on this load, so I took it pretty easy, shutting down for the night after only a few hundred miles, then starting off again at 5 AM. I was worried about being early, so I took the time to go to a Walmart in Cartersville,

Georgia, north of Atlanta.

It had a convenient setup, with a truck stop just up the hill from the store. Truckers had worn a path in the grass, walking up and down the hill to and from the Walmart. I was able to drive straight into a place, then made the walk myself, buying water, a new pair of jeans and some food.

I spent an hour and a half in Cartersville, including eating lunch and fueling the truck. The result was that I was late on the delivery, in part because of a traffic accident which brought freeway traffic to a halt.

This inevitably made me late on the next pickup in an Atlanta suburb, the start of trip number nine on my own. The pickup had been scheduled for only an hour after the delivery time, which had seemed too close even without being late on the delivery. I arrived at the shipper well after the stated hour to find myself one of five or six Alan drivers picking up from the same place.

By the time I had picked up this load and gone to the company's terminal, in another suburb of Atlanta, I had been working for 16 and a half hours, which put me in the invidious position of having to lie on my log book. There was simply nothing else to be done.

Worse yet was the knowledge that it was all caused by my ignorance, as I found out by talking with another Alan driver at the terminal. The load I had been late with was a Kraft load, which meant that I could have delivered it any time. Being early was impossible with Kraft loads. I could have come in three hours early and have been on time, or even early, for the next pickup. They would have loaded me a lot sooner if I had been on time. Being late put you to the end of the line and meant that the company would load you after everyone else, at their convenience. So, I could have done it all within 14 hours if only I had known that Kraft loads could always be delivered early.

I explored the terminal, which was new to me. The drivers lounge reminded me inexorably of the Third World, of places I had seen in Africa. There were sofas and easy chairs made of upholstered cushions on wooden frames. The cushions were frayed, the frames lacked most of their original varnish and were dented where they had been kicked or bashed against harder objects.

Everything was in poor condition. Nothing matched. The linoleum on the floor was damaged. The paint on the walls was scarred. The lounge might or might not have been dirty, but it looked dirty. There were the usual vending machines, one for coffee, one with cold drinks, one with sandwiches and other small food items. There was a laundry room with handwritten signs posted on the walls proclaiming that trying to use all three washers at the same time would blow a fuse.

The next morning, I left for Pennsylvania with three days in which to drive 750 miles. This meant I could stop by the friends' house in North Carolina where, on paper, I lived. This would be my first time home since I had started with Alan. It wasn't exactly home time, as I didn't even have enough time to spend a whole day there, but was more commonly referred to as "going through the house."

It was a short day's drive, only 310 miles. A tanker had evidently burned during the night, somewhere near the South Carolina border. There was still a big traffic jam, right after a merge from one highway to another. I had my CB on, as I always did when traffic jammed or when going through a big city. As I crept up the on-ramp, packed solid with four-wheelers and the occasional semi, I heard a voice on the CB say, "Come on over, Alan." Looking to my left, I saw a white semi holding back to let me merge. I picked up the CB mike and replied, "Thank you, driver," as I merged, hearing in reply, "Any time!"

It was nice to be home in North Carolina, though it really wasn't home any longer. I was able to have lunch with the local priest, as well as going to Mass and confession. I also, finally, bought a cell phone – my first.

I left the next day, after lunch, had an easy drive up to Virginia, then hit it pretty hard on Monday, leaving at 4:15 AM and arriving early for the 5 PM delivery. I was there by 2:15 but it didn't do me any good, as I was just made to wait until the appointment time.

My next trip, number ten on my own, started with a pickup in Ohio, 146 miles from the previous day's delivery. I had a day and a half in which to drive 950 miles to Tulsa, Oklahoma, and I couldn't do it.

I was trying, and might have made it, though I was already in a daze, "driving without awareness" as Mueller put it, when a light must have flashed red on my dispatcher's board – as I had heard that they did when a truck was too far away from a delivery site for it to be likely to deliver on time.

I received a Qualcomm enquiry: was I okay for an on-time delivery?

I answered that I wasn't sure. Eight o'clock the next morning was seeming awfully soon and I still had a lot of miles to drive.

What had gone wrong? I didn't know. I had driven as hard as I could. It was true that I had taken ten and a half hours off, rather than exactly ten hours, but that couldn't have made much difference – or could it?

Anyway, I was bone-tired, so when Kevin sent me a message to drive back to I-57 and take it south to Mt. Vernon, Illinois, where I would be swapped out, I was relieved.

The transfer happened routinely, except that I did an exceptionally bad job, even for me, of parking at the truck stop. I nearly ran into several things. It was necessary that I put the trailer into a position where I could drop it and the other driver could back up to it, so diving into a parking place was not an option.

The next driver of the load was an older man, very nice. He pointed out that one of the trailer's hubs had an oil seal problem. I was ashamed. I had noticed the liquid which had accumulated in the hub but had theorized that it was from the previous night's rain, though I had wondered why only one wheel was affected. Now I knew better. I seemed never to come to the end of mistakes I could make; I was always finding new ones.

The other driver helped me with which macros I needed to send in order to split from the trip and pick up the new trip, number eleven. Once I was hooked up to the new trailer, I took a three-hour nap and felt a lot better.

CHAPTER 16

Peanuts and Monteagle
(June 20-24)

This new load had a lot of time on it; it didn't need to be in the Atlanta area for two days. Two days was more than enough time to drive 503 miles. I started for Atlanta and the Alan terminal. My plan was to stop at a truck stop in Nashville, Tennessee, which had IdleAir.

"Man proposes but God disposes," wrote Thomas à Kempis.

This particular plan was brought to ruin in two ways. It was almost 9 PM when I reached the Nashville area. I immediately found myself in a massive traffic jam caused by construction. Nashville was doing bridge work and had shut down all but one lane of the main Interstate through town.

Where I-24 and I-65 converged, traffic was backed up for miles. There was a lot of talk on the CB about whether or not it was possible to skirt this mess, but for me, at least, it wasn't. I couldn't do the map work well enough while driving in the dark and I had already passed the exit I would have needed to take. So there I was, literally for two hours, while traffic crawled through Nashville.

Eventually, and just as traffic was starting to clear, I came to the truck stop exit. The truck stop was in downtown Nashville! I lacked the courage to mess around with a semi in a downtown area unless I had directions telling me exactly where to go. It also occurred to me that with traffic the way it had been, and with it now being after 10:30 PM, the chances of finding parking at that truck stop were very nearly zero. The moment for taking the exit came, and went. I was still on the freeway.

219

Now I had trouble. For one thing, I had finished my 14 hours at 10:30, so I was running illegally. For another thing, I was deadly tired. For a third, there weren't any truck stops or rest areas nearby, and any truck stop was likely to be completely full at this hour.

I pulled through the fuel island of a small Pilot truck stop 16 miles down the road. There was no prospect of parking there, but at least I was able to go in and use their restroom. Back in the truck, I headed on down the Interstate, hoping now for an off-ramp, knowing that there was a weigh station where I might be able to take refuge, but that it was too far away. Everything was too far away, and I was so tired.

If I got pulled over now, they would write me a big ticket in addition to shutting me down for ten hours. But what could I do? There was no place to stop. Finally, 25 miles after the truck stop where I had pulled through the fuel island, I saw a couple of semis parked on an off-ramp. This indicated to me that, unlike most on- or off-ramps, it was possible to park there. I signalled and pulled off the freeway, eased off the road and pulled up behind the second semi, as always leaving enough room to pull around him in the morning if I left before he did. I popped the tractor brake and shut down the engine, then rose from my seat, dizzy with fatigue, to find ... peanuts everywhere!

What on earth?! I had been hearing some small sounds and had caught a glimpse out of the corner of my eye of something when I was at the truck stop but had been too tired to pursue the matter. The lid of the peanut jar had apparently vibrated loose, then had fallen off. As the jar was on the top shelf of a cabinet, peanuts had gone everywhere, shaking with the motion of the truck. There were peanuts on the shelf in front of the now-open jar, peanuts on the shelf below that one, on top of the lower cabinet, on the floor, on the bed. I picked the jar up off the top shelf. It was still about half full. That meant there could be no more than half of a jar of peanuts scattered around, but it was absolutely amazing how many peanuts are in half a jar.

I was too tired to cope. I confined myself to ridding the bed of peanuts, then fell into it, head spinning, and was asleep in less than a minute. It was 12:30 midnight, so I had worked two hours longer than I should have – 16 hours instead of 14.

I awoke, refreshed, to the quiet and the clean air of early morning in Tennessee. It was about 7:30 local time, 6:30 on the time that I logged. The trucks in front of me were gone. Needing a restroom, I started the truck and drove up to the top of the off-ramp, where I had to wait for rush hour traffic to give me an opportunity to turn left. After several minutes another truck came along from my right and flashed his lights at me as he hit the brakes, meaning that he would block traffic while I turned. Carefully pulling away from the stop sign, I turned left and saw up ahead the sign for a Love's truck stop. I pulled through a fuel island, but there was a parking place I could drive forward into, so I simply parked instead.

Having bought a very welcome cup of coffee, I cleaned all the peanuts I could find out of the truck – though I continued to find stray ones among my possessions for months: in my clothes, in boxes, in my briefcase, shoes, bedding, everywhere! It was Christmastime before I saw the last one.

Then I did the best I could to make my logbook look as though I had driven legally. Pretending that I had stopped at 10:30 PM was not unreasonable for the number of miles I had driven that day – 503. Anyway, it was the best I could do and left me free to start at 8:30, a time that was now fast approaching.

As I drove on through Tennessee, I had the most frightening experience I had yet had as a trucker. About 30 miles west of Chattanooga is Monteagle, a mountain with a long, steep down-grade. The downhill part is so dangerous that there is an inspection station at the top of the mountain for eastbound trucks. All semis are required to exit, then go through one of two traffic lights. Does someone inspect them? I wasn't sure. I hadn't driven this hill before, though I had heard of it from Johnny.

A large map of the upcoming descent was suspended beside each traffic light, along with a list of recommended speeds based on the truck's gross weight. I chose 35 mph as the appropriate speed for my truck, so I started over the top of the hill in eighth gear. As the truck began to pick up speed, I reached over and flipped the switch to turn on the engine brake. A couple of times in the preceding week I had thought to myself that the engine brake sounded very quiet and had wondered idly whether or not it was really doing anything much to slow the vehicle's speed, but it hadn't occurred to me that it might be broken.

It occurred to me forcibly now, as the truck continued to pick up speed and I didn't hear any sound of the engine brake coming on. Using the technique called snub braking, I kept braking the truck down to 35 whenever it got up to 40 mph, but I found that I had my foot on the brake much more than half of the time. It was taking only a second or two for the truck's speed to jump from 35 back to 40 whenever I let up on the brake.

I was beginning to feel desperate and to wonder what I should do, having come somewhere between half a mile and a mile down the four-mile downgrade, when suddenly the engine brake kicked in with a roar. Immediately the truck's speed began to rise much more slowly. I found myself using the brake only occasionally on the rest of the descent and realized that things were now okay. As soon as I stopped, though, I sent in a macro to request that the terminal near Atlanta, where I was heading, fix the engine brake.

As I drove the rest of the way to Atlanta, I now kept noticing that the engine brake wasn't coming on reliably. It always came on eventually, but not when I first flipped the switch.

In spite of stopping for a meal at the TA in Cartersville, Georgia I arrived at the Alan terminal at 2:30 PM, where the men in charge of the shop, two of them, both very kind-looking older men with gray hair and friendly smiles gave me a big welcome, telling me that they had been tracking me all the way in because apparently the satellite unit on my truck was malfunctioning. They proposed to replace it.

I explained the engine brake problem, telling them about that morning's frightening experience on Monteagle and could tell that they took me seriously. They would look into it. I also gave them the wish list that every trucker accumulates, of little problems that would be nice to have set right: the panel that kept popping open, maybe a CD player instead of the tape deck, the windshield wiper switch which didn't always turn the wipers off, etc., etc.

Of these smaller items the most important one to me was that I had never once succeeded in opening the storage compartment, a space reached from the outside of the truck behind the driver's side door. This had been true from the beginning with truck 5431.

On the day I picked up the truck, Johnny had tried to open the compartment to see if any of the extra oil, antifreeze or windshield washer fluid that I should carry was already inside it. Standing on the ground outside the truck, but with the driver's door open, he had reached in and pulled the release handle, located behind the driver's seat. It promptly came off in his hand. He reinserted the handle, pulled it without any result, then rapped sharply on the door of the compartment with the heel of his hand, pulled the release handle again, rapped the door twice more, pulled the handle... In the end, the door opened. The storage compartment was empty.

I wrote "storage compartment door latch" onto the list I was compiling of problems with the truck. Later, after Johnny had left, I went through the list with one of the mechanics at corporate headquarters. When I came to the storage compartment door latch entry the mechanic reached behind the driver's seat, pulled the release handle, which promptly came off in his hand, reinserted the handle, pulled it without result, rapped smartly on the door of the compartment with the heel of his hand, pulled the release handle again, rapped on the door again, and so on and so forth until, eventually, the door opened.

At this he announced triumphantly, "It works!" My opinion was that it didn't work, but I wasn't sure enough of myself to stand my ground. Later, when I tried to open the storage compartment to put in the spare gallons of oil and other fluids that I had garnered from a shelf in the shop, I tried this same technique. I pulled the handle, which came off in my hand as expected. I reinserted it, pulled it, rapped on the door, pulled the handle again, rapped the door again. The only variation in the program was that the door didn't open for me.

After exhausting my patience, I walked back into the shop to ask for help. Grumbling, the manager of the shop came out into the rain with me and went through the by-now-familiar procedure, complete with the handle coming off in his hand on the first try. But he got the door open. Giving me a look as if to say, "What's your problem?" he walked away, leaving me to stow the oil and other bottles in the compartment and to hope that I would never need them.

Now, at the Atlanta terminal, I brought up the subject of the door again. This time a mechanic lubricated the latch and was able to open the door without going through the whole of the usual act. But, lubed or unlubed, I never once succeeded in opening the door.

I knew that if it ever came right down to it I could get at the oil, etc. by lifting the bunk inside the cab, but this was very hard to do. It involved clearing everything out from around the edges of the bunk (purse, books, computer, briefcase, water bottles, suitcase), then releasing a latch on the side of the bunk and holding it with one knee while I put every bit of strength I had into lifting the bed, trying not to hurt my back. Sometimes I succeeded, other times I didn't. Well, maybe I wouldn't need the oil. So far, the engine seemed not to be burning any.

In Atlanta, waiting for the engine brake to be fixed, hoping they could fix it, I walked upstairs to the sordid drivers lounge. A small collection of drivers was present, as usual, a motley group of men and women, most of them overweight, looking completely unrelated – there was no common look to truckers as far as I could tell.

When the mechanics finished with my truck, they told me that they had fixed the engine brake problem. The switch had been bad. They had replaced it and didn't expect it to cause any more trouble. And the satellite unit had been replaced. To my surprise, this meant that I had lost all my sent and received Qualcomm messages. The unit normally stored the last 100 or so messages. I was now missing several key pieces of information. I had lost the dispatch for the job I was on, also my last payroll and some PO numbers that I would need in order to submit the paperwork for recent trips.

It was a real lesson in writing things down at the time, I thought. I had regarded Qualcomm messages as being one hundred percent safe and now they were all gone. I had to ask Kevin to send the crucial messages again.

I delivered my load the next day to a Walmart distribution

center. They were always well-designed, with easy backing. After the delivery, I returned to Alan's Atlanta terminal, only to be dispatched to a late-night pickup (a spotted trailer) at Unilever, inside Atlanta's loop, the start of trip number 12 on my own, going to Indianola, Mississippi.

One of Alan's regional drivers, a nice black man, told me exactly how to get to Unilever. I was grateful for his advice, especially when I saw that I would probably have missed the place if I had just gone by the dispatch instructions. There was a much-more-than 90 degree right turn as soon as I got off a freeway, of which I was particularly glad to have been warned.

When I reached the pickup site I parked, then went in to shipping to hear which trailer they wanted me to pick up. The man in the Shipping Department told me to drive "down the hill" and drop my empty anywhere I could find a place. "But," the man said, "don't double park it. I really hate it when drivers put trailers in front of other trailers. And be sure to slide the tandems all the way back." Then he told me which trailer to pick up. It was in a loading dock at the front of the building.

Once I headed down the hill, off the asphalt onto a dirt lot, to the part of the lot where empty trailers were stored, I began to understand why other drivers were likely to double park empty trailers. The lot was already full to overflowing. First I drove past a row of trailers on my left. They were parked all on a slant. There was a hole in this lineup, but a trailer was parked on the right in such a way as to make it difficult or impossible to set up a backing. For me, of course, it was impossible. I made one attempt but quickly bailed on it as I saw that I would inevitably be up against the crosswise trailer on my right.

Also on my right there were quite a few trailers parked in a hodgepodge – it reminded me of biology class in high school, and pictures of "Brownian motion" — absolute chaos. I began to think that this company ought not to be given any more empty trailers until they used up some of the ones they already had.

I went farther forward into the depths of this dirt lot, which ran down one side of the factory. I spent about half an hour making a serious attempt to, in effect, parallel park the trailer along an empty stretch of curb, but just couldn't do it. I worked up quite a sweat trying, though.

Finally, another truck driver came by, having previously passed me on his way in. He had squeezed his empty into the farthest away part of the lot, the part where I had been afraid to go for fear of being unable to turn around and getting trapped. On his way back to the loading docks he stopped to ask if I needed help. I told him what I was trying to do. He suggested a different place, farther along than I had yet been. It almost looked to me as though it was not really a place at all, but it was easier than what I was trying to do and probably wouldn't actually prevent anyone from getting by.

I dropped the trailer after only a bit of maneuvering, then bobtailed up to the front of the building, where I found that the trailer I was picking up was much too high at the front to hook up to. I had never had this problem before, but it was the reason for looking at height alignment. The height of this trailer was very much off, so I set to work to lower it, turning the landing gear around in the higher gear setting, the only possible way to turn the handle on a loaded trailer. Every three sets, or so, of 12 rotations, I would check the height again. After at least 120 turns (I lost track) it looked like a possible thing to hook up to the trailer. I had lowered the front edge of it more than four inches.

The sweat I had worked up earlier was as nothing compared to the way I was sweating now. Drops of perspiration were dripping off my nose and onto the lenses of my glasses, and I was sure that I could have wrung out my shirt.

When the thought occurred to me, about halfway through lowering the trailer, that I had forgotten to slide the tandems on the trailer I had dropped, I had a short, sharp battle with my conscience on the subject of going back, hooking up to the trailer again and sliding the tandems. I had already been at this yard for an hour and a half; it was nearly midnight. I lost the fight. I would leave the empty trailer's tandems "unslid" and hope that I wouldn't get reported and be in trouble.

With the tractor hooked up to the new trailer I was finally free to leave. I drove back to Alan's terminal, parked, and went to sleep. This was a load with a lot of time on it. I had more than 48 hours in which to drive 402 miles – much more than I needed. I wondered if I had been demoted to a B-list of drivers, if such a thing existed, who were only given short loads with lots of time on them. After the fiasco where I had had to be swapped out on my way to Tulsa it wouldn't have surprised me.

Kevin had told me that weekend loads often had a lot of time on them. I believed him, but still wondered. Would I ever get a nice long run again?

Having so much time on my hands, I decided to stop in Birmingham, Alabama, which was en route to this load's Monday delivery in Indianola, Mississippi, to visit EWTN headquarters (Eternal Word Television Network – the Catholic TV channel) and go to Mass.

Birmingham was less than three hours from Atlanta. I hung around the terminal until after 2 PM, taking 15 hours off instead of the usual ten, but was still in Birmingham by 5 PM. My truck stop directory had shown me a small truck stop not too far from the TV station's headquarters, so I tried it first, though I was extremely dubious about small truck stops – and, sure enough, it was nearly full (all seven spaces!), and I couldn't make the right kind of setup to get into the one remaining space.

After two tries, I gave up, drove over to I-65 and took it north a few miles to a nice big truck stop where, at that time of day, there was no trouble finding a space; I was able to drive forward into one. Then I went inside to consult a phone book and ordered a taxi for the next morning.

I had visited EWTN once before. When I arrived there the next morning, I found it to be all that I had remembered. Such an atmosphere of prayer! And the grounds were beautiful. The taxi pulled up in front of the main building. After I paid the driver and got out, I noticed an elderly woman who was looking at me rather quizzically – she seemed surprised that I had arrived in a taxi.

I explained that I was a trucker and had left my truck at a nearby truck stop. The idea of me being a trucker seemed to surprise the woman even more, but she offered me a ride back to the truck stop after Mass. I accepted gratefully. I really wasn't making enough money to be taking taxis here and there. The one-way ride from the truck stop had cost nearly 40 dollars.

After Mass, I found myself chatting with three other women, all of whom seemed appalled at the idea of me being a trucker, and to be quite certain that it was inappropriate. I pointed out that I had been seeking God's will all along and would be glad to be shown something else to do, but that, so far at least, He hadn't shown me anything else. They seemed convinced that He would.

CHAPTER 17

No Eng?
(June 24-27)

I would never have guessed that I was only four days away from quitting my job with Alan King Associates, although my hip was getting more and more painful, to the point that I was beginning to wonder what I should do. Once or twice I found myself driving down the road in the morning with tears running down my cheeks because I was in so much pain. But quitting, when it happened, had nothing to do with my hip.

After Mass, I treated the elderly woman who drove me back to my truck to lunch at the truck stop restaurant. Then I drove over US-82 toward Indianola, Mississippi. The adventure for that drive was going under a bridge marked 13'6" for height, exactly the same as the height of a semi. When I saw the height marking on the underpass I immediately pulled off the road to my right, and set the emergency flashers going while I consulted the front pages of my trucker's road atlas for the list of low clearances in Mississippi. I didn't find any on US-82. The route was also highlighted in orange, the atlas's method of designating a truck route.

I took a certain amount of comfort from the reflection that a few semis had passed me going in the other direction, semis which had presumably come through this underpass from the other direction. In the end, and after taking a deep breath and gritting my teeth, I drove under the exact center of the underpass – and didn't feel anything scrape. It was okay. A posted height of 13'6" was supposed to mean that a vehicle of that height could pass underneath, rather than that the underpass itself was exactly 13'6." I had never wanted to test that theory, but now I had.

By 3:30 I had reached the Pilot truck stop in Winona, Mississippi, where I-55 crossed US-82. I was a little more than an hour away from Indianola, but this seemed to be the nearest truck stop, other, perhaps, than small independent ones.

It was in the 80's here, and muggy. After using the restroom and buying a cold drink, I decided to make one more try at idling my truck so I could have air conditioning while I sat at the truck stop.

The following material is taken, with comments interspersed, from a summary of events that I wrote soon after they transpired, when everything was still very clear in my mind.

"June 24 (Sun) afternoon
Trk gauges go to zero (x4) when I try to idle at truck stop. Third time 'no eng' light comes on even though engine is running and I drive it around lot to get a better parking place in case a mechanic needs to look."

In fact, I was so rattled by this unexpected phenomenon that for the first time I forgot that I had put the steering gear lock on. I backed out, on my third try at starting the engine, tried to put a twist into the steering to get the back of the trailer headed to the right, and found that I couldn't move the steering wheel. Recollection suddenly came to me and I pulled forward again, stopped the engine, got out and took the steering gear lock off, then got back in and started it up again.

Again, in addition to having no speedometer, tachometer, or oil pressure, water temperature and transmission fluid temperature gauges, I also had no odometer reading or voltage reading, just the words "no eng." I thought I could hear the engine running though and, sure enough, the truck moved when I put it in gear and let the clutch in.

I drove one and a quarter times around the truck stop parking lot, looking for a place that would allow the truck to be reached from the front, but not wanting to back into any of the available places.

Finally finding a place I thought would be suitable, and that I could drive forward into, I parked the truck again.

> "[June 24 (Sun), afternoon, continued]
> I call Rd. Svc. twice, another Alan driver (Maureen) helps me. Rd. Svc. tells me to check alternator belt and release tractor brake to make it idle. After all that, gauges come back."

The other Alan driver wasn't staying long. She had pulled through a fuel island after fueling and was parked out in the middle of the asphalt, in the sort of parking place that truck stops occasionally have which is good only for a short time, certainly not for all night.

The driver was nice to me. She knew how to make a truck idle, so for the first time I could be sure that it really was the truck that had a problem, rather than it being just my ignorance that kept me from being able to make it idle. I knew there were things that had to be done with the cruise control switch and running the RPM's up, but didn't know exactly what.

Maureen was driving a nice new Peterbilt, but before it she had driven a Freightliner. It took her a few minutes to be sure that she was remembering the idle procedure correctly, but in the end we were sure – the truck really wouldn't idle.

Before this we had enlisted the help of a different company's driver, just to make absolutely very sure that all the belts the engine was supposed to have were there – and they were. Maureen also checked the fuses while I watched.

Maureen offered her cell phone to me and even called road service back for me when I had trouble hearing on the phone. The road service man pointed out that I was "in the middle of nowhere" and would have to drive a long way to find a Freightliner dealer. As the gauges were now working again, I agreed that the sensible thing was to make my delivery the next day, then head for Memphis, which had a Freightliner service center. My next pickup was in Rossville, Tennessee, a town not far east of Memphis.

Maureen was headed north but was willing to stay in Winona so

231

I could sleep in her truck. She seemed to regard lack of air conditioning as a terrible thing. I didn't wish to impose in this way and turned the offer down. It wasn't *that* hot – I would sleep with the windows open. I held a private theory that it was safer to have the windows all the way open than it was to open them halfway, because it was less obvious that way that they were open at all. A person just glancing at the truck, I reasoned, might take it for granted that the windows were shut (just very clean?) whereas a half-open window was hard to miss.

The night wasn't too unpleasant. My delivery was for 4 AM, so I was on the move again at a quarter after two in the morning. I drove westward for a little over an hour and found the place without any great trouble. It was a grocery store distribution center for a kind of grocery store I had never heard of.

> "June 25 (Mon)
> Gauges still working. I del. at Indianola, MS, then
> drive to Rossville, TN for p/u."

The day took a turn for the worse at the Indianola delivery site. I was blessed in my door assignment. I bumped the dock with the help of another company's driver, the driver whose truck I would hit if I messed up too badly. These drivers, the ones whose trucks were threatened, often volunteered to help – in self-defense I assumed – once I had made several tries at the thing and had demonstrated my incompetence pretty clearly. They almost always treated me like a man, though, by asking if I wanted help and pointing out that they weren't wanting to interfere with me doing my job. I didn't have that kind of pride, and was always grateful for help, so would accept gladly.

After I was backed up to the loading dock with the trailer's doors open, ready to be unloaded, I took the bills and walked over to receiving, where I found a long line of men standing in a rather squalid hallway. The walls of this hallway were painted gray up to a height of three and a half or four feet, then whitewashed the rest of the way up. It wasn't very neatly done though, as the line between gray paint and whitewash was wavy. The floor was covered in black rubber tiles, some of them with a chunk ripped out of a corner, others with parts that had come unglued and were sticking up, ready to trip the unwary.

There were two windows at the end of the hallway, but not much seemed to be happening at them. After a five- or ten-minute wait, someone leaned out of a window and called for the drivers in doors 50 through 55. I was in door 54, so I was one of the lucky few called to a window. It seemed grossly unfair to me, though. The others had been there longer than I.

I handed in my bills and was told that I could wait in the truck while it was unloaded, the normal procedure. I went back out to the truck and rested as well as I could with the whole truck bouncing up and down from time to time as someone drove a forklift in and out of the trailer. The light was red for my door, meaning that the trailer's bumper was hooked to the dock. Everything seemed normal.

It dragged on, though. No one came for me. Eventually, after the light had been green for a good while, I went back in. No one was there now. I noticed a pencil scrawl on the whitewashed part of the wall and leaned close to read it. It said, "If you've never been to jail this is what it's like." I could well believe it.

Eventually I was able to talk with a person, who said I should keep waiting: my papers would be out shortly. I went back out to the truck. Forty-five minutes later, nothing having happened in the interim, I went back in and asked again. This time it seemed to me that I was getting on the nerves of the employee. I went back out to the truck and called Kevin to complain. Could anything be done, I asked?

The bills were finally handed to me at 8:45 AM, five and a half hours after I had arrived and a good three hours after they had finished unloading the trailer. Jail indeed!

I drove back to the Winona truck stop, got something to eat and bought some more coffee. Then I headed for Rossville, Tennessee. The gauges were working, so I thought I had better deal with the next pickup before doing anything about them. Besides, my husband, an electrical engineer who could also fix cars, had always said that intermittent electrical problems were very difficult to diagnose and were usually too much for ordinary mechanics. What would happen if I showed up with all the gauges working and said that yesterday they hadn't worked for an hour? It didn't seem terribly likely that any mechanic would be able to fix the problem from this description.

I drove to the Memphis area for the pickup for trip number thirteen, my last though I didn't know it. I was early, but had been told that the trailer I was picking up might well be ready early. And so it proved. Having arrived at the pickup site just after 2 PM, I was back on the road a little after three.

I had started work at 2:15 AM; that meant I would be up against 14 hours at 4:15 PM, so I went only as far as West Memphis, Arkansas, a place with several large truck stops. I found a nice IdleAir place at the Petro truck stop there and shut down for the night.

There was enough time on this load to catch up on my sleep. Rather than taking only ten hours off I took 15. I left West Memphis at 6:45 AM, headed for San Antonio, Texas, and some time off with my second daughter, her husband and their baby, who was going to be baptized.

The issue of the gauges going dead was on my mind, though. I knew that the problem hadn't been addressed and might recur at any time. Shouldn't I at least try to get it fixed before it happened again?

When I first got on this truck, I had found old messages on the Qualcomm from the previous driver and had read them with interest. There were pleas, and finally demands, for a different truck. This one had been in the shop too many times and had broken down at awkward moments. I had sometimes had the sense that this truck might let me down at a crucial moment. The, fortunately temporary, failure of the engine brake on the hill west of Chattanooga had not been reassuring. Without wanting to anthropomorphize, I didn't trust truck 5431.

"June 26 (Tues)
At N. Little Rock (I think) I come upon a Freightliner center and send a Qualcomm to ask

permission for the gauge problem to be checked out. Permission is denied. They tell me the 'normal procedure' is to get routed through a terminal."

This angered me. I was being made to throw away a perfectly good opportunity for getting the truck fixed. I had plenty of time for it without risking being late on the load. I was 1,000 miles from the nearest terminal. I disagreed completely with what road service was saying and was afraid it would cause trouble later. On the other hand, though, the gauges had only malfunctioned once, two days before. Maybe they wouldn't do it again.

I didn't believe that. I knew it would happen again.

I entered Texas sometime in the early- to mid-afternoon. It had rained every time I'd been in Texas this summer and today was no exception. I drove up to, then in under, a dark gray, almost black bank of clouds. It was as though someone had turned off the lights.

The clouds were moving fast, roiling and sending out tendrils – truly a terrifying sight. Then the rain began. It poured! Visibility was restricted. Driving became a real challenge. There didn't seem to be anywhere to stop and it was never quite bad enough to force the issue. Also, the rain stopped from time to time, giving hope that it might be possible to get to the other side of the storm. This finally happened, though another bank of clouds, sitting on the horizon, gave promise of a storm later on.

> "June 26 (Tues) cont.
> At 16:10, mile 360,260.4, gauges fail again while I am driving toward Dallas. After a few seconds they recover for a few seconds, then go out for approx. 5 miles. I find a TA at Rockwall, TX and phone Rd. Svc. again. Rd. service says the TA shop won't be able to fix the problem 'unless it's just fuses' but gives authorization number for them to check it out."

The sudden zeroing of the gauges while I was driving had given me a real adrenaline rush. I had looked around wildly to consider whether I could pull off the road. I couldn't. Then I had spotted a billboard announcing a TA only 20 miles away. All TA's were Freightliner service centers, for simple problems anyway.

I prayed that I would be able to get as far as Rockwall. Then when the gauges started working again, and stayed on this time, I was enormously relieved. Of course, they might go out again any second... This kept me in a state of nervous tension for the best part of 20 miles.

I found the TA truck stop without too much trouble and, better yet, somehow managed to back into a place, never easy at what was only rated a "Large" truck stop. I usually confined myself to "XL's" if possible.

But here I was, actually parked, feeling relieved and very happy. The problem with the gauges would have to be addressed now. Moreover, the bank of clouds on the southwestern horizon looked extremely threatening. I could have driven several more hours, but I would call it a day here and be thankful.

When I called road service to get an authorization number the man laughed at me. "They won't be able to fix it unless it's just fuses," he said through his laughter. Was it possible that he found any aspect of this dangerous and lamentable situation funny? I didn't know if I was furious or just appalled. But he gave me an authorization number, so I went into the shop and was eventually able to talk with a mechanic about what had been going on.

He told me that he would hook a computer up to the truck's computers (four of them on every truck, or so I had been told) and see what codes they were displaying. I could pull into bay number three.

"Should I drop the trailer?" I asked, having in mind the Lake Station truck stop in Utah where they had asked me to drop the trailer before they worked on my air conditioning.

"Not necessary," replied the man.

I was taken aback. If I once left my nice parking place I would never find another.

"Let me rephrase that," I responded. "By practically a miracle of God I'm in an actual parking place and I'm planning to spend the night here. May I drop the trailer, so I won't have to try to find a place when you're done?"

By now the man was grinning broadly. "Sure," he answered, nodding.

Gratefully, I hurried to drop the trailer, then bobtailed over to bay three.

> "[June 26 (Tues) cont.]
>
> TA shop checks out engine and finds 5 codes, one of which is 'reserved.' They call Freightliner to ask what this means, but Freightliner won't tell them.
>
> "TA Shop advises me that I will have to go to a Freightliner Center as they can do nothing more.
>
> "I phone road service which tells me to do my del. the next day at 8 PM, then take the truck to the Freightliner Ctr. in San Antonio. They also give me the phone number so I phone for an appt but am told that it's first come first serve from 7 AM to 2 AM."

The mechanic was very kind, and somewhat mystified by the problem. I was discouraged by Alan's attitude. They weren't taking this thing seriously. What were the chances of me getting all the way to San Antonio, a distance of 300 miles, without the gauges going out again?

I couldn't possibly drive any distance if they went out and stayed out. For one thing, a truck was required by law to have a (working) speedometer. It was the lack of tachometer, though, that bothered me almost more than not having a speedometer. I did much of my shifting based on what the tachometer read, and the rest of it by looking at the speedometer. The combined effect of having both of them out, I had noticed, was to make me feel as though I had gone blind.

Then there was the oil pressure gauge being out. An engine could be destroyed quite quickly without adequate oil pressure. The water temperature and transmission fluid temperature gauges were out too. All of these seemed pretty important, but it was the lack of speedometer and tachometer that blinded me and made me think I ought not to drive the truck.

Well, the gauges were working again for the moment. I would

have to try doing it Alan's way.

I hooked back up to the trailer and went to sleep, being only half awakened later on by a terrific thunderstorm and pouring rain in the middle of the night.

> "[June 27 (Wed)]
> The gauges are working so I leave Rockwall at 04:15 am and drive to New Braunfels, where I arrive at 09:30."

By the time I got up at 4 AM the rain was over, at least for the time being. I drove to Waco, Texas, glad that I was going through the Dallas/Fort Worth "metroplex," as it is called, so early. It was bad enough at 5:30 AM. I didn't like to think about what it would have been like at rush hour. I stopped in Waco for a 15-minute break then drove on to New Braunfels, 37 miles from my San Antonio delivery, where I arrived at 9:30 AM. I went inside for a shower and breakfast.

> "[June 27 (Wed) cont.]
> After breakfast I go out to read Qualcomms (which necessitates turning the ignition key). The gauges come up showing 'no eng,' so I communicate w/my dispatcher, who forwards the message to Rd. Svc. Rd. Svc's response is that I should get routed through a terminal (nearest one is Atlanta, GA or Indianapolis, IN) to get 'dashboard light' repaired.
> "Sent another Qualcomm to point out that this wasn't a question of illumination. I turn the ignition 5 or 6 times during the next hours, always with the same result."

So it had happened. The nightmare had arrived. Even now, I didn't believe that Alan would try to make me drive the truck without gauges. It must be a question of a misunderstanding. I called Kevin on my new cell phone. He just didn't seem to understand that I couldn't drive a truck without gauges and that it was unfair to try to make me do so.

> "[June 27 (Wed) cont.]
> I then phoned and Qualcommed Chip Walsh."

So, I played my last card. I began trying to call Chip Walsh. I had always thought of him as being on the driver's side. He would help. I sent a Qualcomm message addressed to him, left a message on his voicemail, then sat back and waited for him to call.

In the meantime, I called my daughter, to bring her up to date on the situation.

> "[June 27 (Wed) cont.]
> He eventually called me and urged me to make the delivery w/out speedometer or tachometer. I categorically refused."

My faith in Chip Walsh was misplaced. I couldn't believe my ears when he told me I should drive the truck in its current condition. What, drive blind for almost forty miles?! I was terrified of doing such a thing. Nor was it legal to drive a truck without a speedometer. But Chip wouldn't back down. Desperate, and forced up against a wall, I said no. I wouldn't do it. I would quit if that was the only way to keep from having to drive the truck before it was fixed.

Even that didn't make him relent. So there it was. I was out of a job.

The knowledge that I could easily lose this job, with or without being at fault, if I had an accident – that knowledge had been close to me through the preceding months. But it hadn't occurred to me that I could lose my job because Alan King Associates would try to make me do something illegal.

God, as always, had been good. I was able to call my daughter back and arrange to be picked up, together with all my possessions. What if I had been in Indiana? or Tennessee? Or practically anywhere else in the country? What would I have done, lacking the money to rent a car?

Chip had told me to give him five minutes, then call Kevin. I did so and assured Kevin that I would stay on the truck until Alan determined what they wanted to do with it. Luckily there were still quite a few hours until the delivery time, although all this talking back and forth had taken a long time, and it was now afternoon.

Sick at heart, and in shock, I began to organize my things and pack. I scanned in my last trip, threw away some too-big clothes that weren't in good condition, was amazed at how many things I had on this truck.

All this time I was waiting to hear what would now happen to the load. There was another Alan driver, an owner operator, at the New Braunfels truck stop, a fact which I had pointed out to Kevin. But in the end I received another Qualcomm advising me that a tow truck would arrive within the next couple of hours.

This didn't surprise me. Short of being fixed on the spot, and an electrical problem of this sort probably *couldn't* be fixed on the spot, towing was the only legal thing that could be done with the truck.

I would need to back the truck out of the IdleAir parking place I had found that morning so the tow truck could get in front of it.

I sent a good-bye message to Kevin, thanking him for being my dispatcher and expressing my regrets at leaving the company, and received an equally nice message back from him.

In the meantime, my daughter arrived, accompanied by her six-month old baby and her father-in-law, who was visiting from California. We crammed everything into the car. The others went inside the truck stop to get a snack while I continued to wait for the tow truck, which finally arrived about half an hour later.

I was tormented by the knowledge that whatever I did with the steering gear lock and its accompanying padlock would probably be wrong. If I took them with me the load would be left unprotected. And, really, I already had far too many things in my daughter's car, and no particular use for these locks unless I was driving a truck.

But if I left the load padlocked and the steering gear lock on the truck, what were the chances of them giving back my 85-dollar deposit? The two locks would almost certainly disappear somewhere along the line.

After a lot of vacillation, I decided to make the sacrifice. I pointed out to the tow truck driver that the load was padlocked and showed him the key to it.

This was after I had started the engine for the last time and backed out of the IdleAir space, then pulled forward until tractor and trailer were in a straight line so that the tow truck could hitch up to the tractor.

When I started the engine, all the gauges were working again. I stared at them dully. It didn't seem to matter.

Having handed the keys to the man, I went inside the truck stop to find my family, ate a piece of blueberry pie that was offered but which I didn't really want, then climbed into the small car, now uncomfortably full holding, as it did, three adults, a baby and all my things. We headed for San Antonio, half an hour away.

CHAPTER 18

Off the Truck
(June 27 and Afterward)

When I woke up the next morning, I was in much worse pain than usual from my hip. And I couldn't seem to get the pain "worked out" as I usually did in the morning. It was true that the pain had gradually been getting worse, but this was a quantum leap into a whole new world of pain.

I took an anti-inflammatory pill that my son-in-law gave me. I spent my days sitting on a large blue ball that was supposed to help you sit correctly or draping myself over it. I made an appointment to see a chiropractor. I didn't attend my grandson's baptism.

In spite of all my efforts, for the next few weeks I was in unremitting pain. Riding in my daughter's car left me crying out in agony. I couldn't sit in the seat but had to crouch on the floor of the small vehicle, facing backwards, my head pillowed on my arms. This was the only position I could tolerate.

I remember my daughter asking desperately, tears in her voice, if there wasn't something she could do to help. We couldn't think of what it might be.

More bad news arrived when I realized that Alan hadn't paid me for my last week of work. Upon calling payroll I learned that I had been charged $700 for "abandoning" my truck. This came out of the blue. I didn't remember having heard any kind of warning about this. I was actually in the position of owing Alan money, several hundred dollars, rather than the other way around. And yes, they had charged me $85 for not returning the steering gear lock and padlock.

Abandoning the truck! When I had worked all day *not* to abandon it! My daughter's in-laws began to talk about hiring a lawyer. Her mother-in-law's brother was a District Attorney in Wisconsin, Alan King Associate's home state, and could be asked for advice.

In the meantime, though, I talked with my mother, who had a lawyer on retainer. This lawyer's advice, when he was asked about the problem, was that I should write a letter to Alan King Associates, explaining the circumstances and asking for a refund of the $700.

The chiropractor's appointment, when it came, was enlightening. An x-ray of my back showed that my lowest lumbar vertebra was not in the right position relative to my sacrum. The vertebra had somehow slid half an inch forward, a condition called spondylolisthesis. Half an inch of sliding represented "Grade 2," a category at which surgery was necessary about half of the time.

This rang a faint bell in my mind. I eventually remembered that I had been given this same information 25 years previously. At that time the condition wasn't causing me any pain. The doctor of a quarter of a century earlier had asked me two or three times, even five or six times, if I was *sure* I didn't have any pain, but in the end had said that, well, some people didn't have pain from such a condition and that it might, or might not, give me trouble later on when I was older.

Now I was older, and it was giving me trouble. Apparently back trouble was at the root of all that I had thought was hip pain. It was also responsible for the numbness and tingling in my foot, the sensation of the calf of my leg being grabbed and the slight weakness in my right leg after the day's pain was over.

Not that the day's pain was ever over these days. I spent most of my time sitting on the blue ball. My daughter and I made a trip to a back store where she bought me a book about back pain that had what looked like some useful exercises.

I read the book in very short order and started trying the exercises, though I made a mental note of the warning at the beginning of the book, which stated that these exercises were good for the most common causes of back pain but could be harmful for others.

In spite of pain, I composed a letter and a one-and-a-half-page summary of events and sent them off to Alan. I was pleased with the letter, which I wrote under the white-hot heat of inspiration.

July 11, 2007

Human Resources
Alan King Associates.
[1234 Main Street]
[Anytown], WI 00000

In Re: Annette Wilcox
Truck No. 5431
Termination of Employment
6/27/2007
New Braunfels, TX

To Whom It May Concern:

I am writing this letter to ask that Alan King Associates make an exception to its policy of charging drivers seven hundred dollars ($700) when they fail to return equipment to a terminal, noting that the possibility of an exception is an eventuality foreseen on page 141 of the current Alan Driver Manual. I wish to point out five relevant circumstances which I hope will convince you that this is a suitable case for an exception:

1) The truck was not in legal operating condition, lacking the functioning speedometer called for in FMCSR 393.82.

2) Alan's Code of Ethics/Conduct states that, "Obeying the letter and spirit of all laws, rules, regulations, and policies is the foundation of ethical business practices at Alan King Associates." Driving forty or more miles without a speedometer obeys neither the letter nor the spirit of the law. This same code of ethics also says, "If the law conflicts with this policy, you must comply with the law." I believe that statement should apply to this situation.

3) I was following the last of the Compliance Procedures in the Code of Ethics/Conduct, namely, "Always ask first, act later. If you are unsure of what to do in any situation, seek

guidance before you act." I spent an entire day making good-faith efforts to avoid leaving the truck but couldn't find any way out of the pressure being applied to me to commit an illegal act.

4) Returning the truck to a terminal that was many hundreds of miles away was not a possibility.

5) Short of being fixed on the spot, towing was the only legal course of action to take regarding Truck 5431. This state of affairs was not caused by me or by any action of mine but was caused rather by the condition of the truck itself. If only I had been allowed to get it fixed in Arkansas!

I very much regret having been pushed to the point of quitting Alan King Associates, which I still regard as, in general, a good company for which to work. Please live up to your reputation for fairness by righting this inequity.

Thanking you in advance for your consideration, I remain,

Yours very truly,

Annette F. Wilcox, MA

cc: Chip Walsh, Driver Trainer Coordinator
    Kevin, Dispatcher

I also made plans to get out of San Antonio, not wishing to impose on my daughter and son-in-law any longer. I flew to Salt Lake City, where I stayed with my mother.

The first task was to buy a blue ball, the second to make an urgent appointment with a physical therapist friend of my sister-in-law. He had an advanced degree.

The first night at Mother's house, a wonderful thing happened. I no sooner lay down on the guest room bed than I realized that it would be impossible for me to sleep on it. I went to get a camping pad, a two-inch thick block of foam covered with canvas, from the closet under the stairs, and put it on the guest room floor. I made myself as comfortable as I could on it and went to sleep.

When I woke up the next morning, I was in less pain than I had been in for several weeks. It was the first thing that helped.

When I saw the physical therapist, a few days later, he taught me a lot. He gave me an exercise to do and told me to throw the back book away as being totally wrong for my condition. I had actually been hurting myself, both by doing the exercises in the book and by doing the exercises that my physical therapist sister-in-law had told me about months previously and which I had called "working out the pain in the morning." This physical therapist was highly dubious about me ever driving a truck again, at least not without having back surgery first.

I was not to lie on my stomach. Lying on my stomach did harm. I was not to bend backwards at all. Bending backwards was a bad position for my condition. And, most important, I should take a hand towel, fold it in four, and place it at my waist in order to keep my spine straighter while I slept on my side with a good body pillow between my knees. This turned out to be the second thing that really helped.

It had always been at night that things got worse with my back. I had often thought that if only I didn't have to go to sleep I could have no pain at all. Impossible, of course, but the thought had recurred many times throughout the last months. Now that I slept on the camping pad with a hand towel at my waist, I began to feel better every day.

One day, while out on a drive with my twins, who also lived in Salt Lake City, we happened to pass a small truck stop with six or eight semis parked in its tiny lot. I craned around in my seat to keep the trucks in view as long as I could. To my surprise, I found that there was a broad grin on my face as I stated the obvious, "Oh, look! Semis!"

Although I had applied for several other jobs, this made me think that going back on the road might be what I wanted most to do. Driving a truck had proved to me the truth of the maxim (was it a maxim? it needed to be) that "God is close to the desperate." I missed the closeness to God that I had felt because of my desperation. It might be worth driving again just to regain that sense of closeness.

I had been frightened hundreds of times in my month as a solo driver. Many times, I had found that "courage came with doing." I had to start driving, scared as I was, before receiving the grace to continue. As I started off, I would remember that, oh yes, I *could* do this, at least up to a point.

A couple of weeks later I saw a doctor at the University Hospital. He sent me for an MRI. When I met with him a second time, he had evaluated it. His verdict was that I would probably need surgery eventually, but that I could take my time about it, as the surgery was very expensive. Better to wait until I "had all my ducks in a row" as he put it.

In the meantime, though, and differing from the opinion of the physical therapist, this doctor found it not unreasonable that I try trucking again, as sitting was the least stressful position for people with my condition.

Then Johnny phoned! He had heard that I had had trouble. He was coming through Salt Lake City. Would I meet him for breakfast and tell him all about it?

I was eager to get Johnny's opinion of all that had transpired. I wasn't yet driving a car, though I thought that it wouldn't be long before I could, so I asked the twins to come too.

The thought of a truck stop and truckers ogling my youngest daughter who, like all of my daughters, had a very nice figure, was intolerable. I spoke to this daughter before we went to meet Johnny and warned her to dress modestly, saying that some truckers were the sort of men who might ogle a woman and that she should dress with that in mind.

Never had a command been so thoroughly obeyed! I had forgotten about this daughter's theater background and acting major. I didn't know how she did it, other than that it involved a long skirt and a long-sleeved shirt belonging originally to a boyfriend, but she seemed to have no figure whatsoever. It was impossible even to surmise what might lie beneath her clothes.

I was highly amused, but even more so by a stray thought that, as so many things had passed down the line of my daughters without me needing to do anything more than teach the oldest one, so this might very well pass *up* the line. It seemed likely that any of my daughters who met me at truck stops in the future would dress like nuns. A bubble of merriment rose within me every time I thought about it.

We had a nice breakfast I think, but I hardly noticed the food in my eagerness to tell Johnny all about the events around quitting Alan. I also had a lot of questions for him on other trucking-related subjects. It was so good to see him!

The twins seemed frightened of walking between the huge semis as we looked for Johnny's truck. This surprised me, as I felt at home among the trucks, but there was a time, not so long before, when I wouldn't have.

Once we found Johnny, and were seated in the truck stop's restaurant, I poured out the whole story, using the "summary of events" as an aide-mémoire and giving him a copy of the letter I had written to Alan King Associates. He took it away to read at his leisure but gave his opinion that Alan shouldn't have asked me to drive the truck without a working speedometer and tachometer. I wasn't quite pleased with his reasoning – he seemed to think it was a beginner issue. *He* would have driven the truck, he said, but it wasn't right that they had asked me to.

I was convinced that it was wrong to drive a truck that wasn't in a legal operating condition. A sentence had been floating in my mind for weeks, something about "how can you get permission to do an illegal thing?" which I had finally realized was from "Star Trek." This meant I could ask my son, a walking "Star Trek" compendium, for the whole quote. He gave it to me without difficulty. It was from "Star Trek III" where Dr. McCoy had said, "There's not going to be any permit. How can you get a permit to do a damned illegal thing?" Yes, that was exactly what I thought.

Johnny couldn't seem to understand my point of view. He said, however, that he would talk to a friend of his in the human resources department and would tell her that I shouldn't have been asked to drive the truck, so I had to be satisfied with that.

We also talked about what was basically a system defect in Alan's road service department. I had assumed some sort of continuity with road service. In my mind, the mechanics with whom I talked would pull up a computer screen on truck 5431 which would tell them all about the history of the problem. Dispatch did an equivalent sort of thing whenever a driver called in.

There was evidence to suggest, though, that this wasn't the way it was with road service. It had always seemed like starting over from scratch to talk with them. Maybe things would have been different if I had summarized the problem every time I called, saying something like, "Three days ago I called because ... and yesterday this happened ... " and so on and so forth.

Alan's dispatchers did such sophisticated things with computers that it was hard to realize that road service might be just "winging it," without any information whatsoever on my truck. It fitted what had happened though. They had even seemed to think that a dashboard light bulb just wasn't working at one point.

Alan needed to work out some better way of dealing with truck problems. Road service should routinely pull up a history of calls. If only I had realized...

Johnny advised me not to take too much time off from driving or I would have to start over.

"I believe in you," he added.

This remark warmed my heart and stayed with me for weeks. It was the answer to what had happened toward the end of training. He did believe in me, after all.

In his opinion, based on what I told him of some of my adventures on the road, I had been doing all right – "making it." He said he had wondered if I might work something out with backing, come to terms with it somehow. He seemed to think that I had. I wasn't so sure.

Now that we were back in contact, Johnny called me every week or so. He offered to drive me anywhere I wanted to go – North Carolina, perhaps, back to the friends with whom I had been living when I turned to trucking. It was a gratifying offer, I thought. I said I would keep it in mind.

Then came a phone call where Johnny reported that he had talked with his friend in human resources on the very day that my case was being decided and thought the matter would be resolved in my favor. Sure enough, I received a check for $700 in the mail soon after that conversation.

Also, Johnny was deeply impressed with the letter I had written to Alan, as he told me the next time he passed through Salt Lake City, when we met up again. He even told me a story about being an employee representative on the hiring board of the community college where he had worked for many years. When they had reviewed the letters of people applying to be the new president of the community college, Johnny said, none of the letters had been as well written as my letter to Alan. Well!

We got caught up on his news as well. He was still planning to build a new strip mall for his friend, but the date had gotten pushed out while they waited for various financing and permit issues to be resolved. He had only had one student since me, Alan having cut way back on the student part of their recruitment program. This student was a man who *had* managed to stall the truck on an uphill grade. I shuddered.

The next time Johnny called, he asked me what I was planning to do. The only job I had been offered was a dead end one, using my knowledge of French to be a customer service representative. I told Johnny that I'd like to be driving again but hadn't really started looking.

"I've been thinking that I should check on your hiring status with Alan," Johnny remarked, "and see if they've cleared your record now that they gave you the money back."

My spirits rose. I suddenly realized what I wanted to do, even though I hadn't thought of it before. I'd go back to Alan if I could. Alan was the only trucking company I had worked for. I hadn't wanted to quit in the first place, hadn't planned to quit.

"Oh, yes!" I exclaimed. "Please do check."

We made plans. If Alan rehired me, Johnny could give me a ride across the country to corporate headquarters in Wisconsin. That way I could take more of the things I needed on a truck with me than if I travelled by plane, and I could have a refresher course in driving, too.

Johnny would probably even let me drive, I thought wryly, though he wouldn't have any business to do such a thing and it would be taking an enormous risk. If I were to have an accident! But even just watching Johnny drive was educational and would be a refresher course all by itself. Would I drive if he let me? Or would I insist on keeping the rules, I wondered. Well, I didn't have to decide right now. It hadn't happened yet.

We finished our conversation, Johnny promising to get back to me in a day or two with whatever he found out from human resources. He called the next day. My record had been cleared. I should call a recruiter.

A week later Alan rehired me.

CHAPTER 19

Twelve Years Later

Twelve years later I've driven more than a million miles in a semi. I've trucked in all 48 contiguous states, as they are called. I've crossed the border into and out of Canada at least 200 times, with a record of three times in one day: out at Port Huron, Michigan, back in at the same place and out again at Buffalo, New York at the other end of the day.

Around the time that I finished training I felt as though the Lord was saying to me, "You're going to love trucking." My mental reply was, more or less, "I'm going to *what?!* Have You lost Your mind?"

But it must really have been the Lord because He was right. I do love trucking. Most of all I love the sense of closeness to God that comes from needing His help so often. I miss Him when I'm off the road. At such times I find myself seeming to function almost without God, living life by routines, only sometimes remembering to pray and having to set aside time to do it.

I love all the time I have on the road for prayer and listening to Catholic talk shows and homilies. "This keeps sounding like a retreat to me," a priest friend once said when I had described my life of praying a Rosary and several Chaplets of Divine Mercy daily plus other prayers, listening to Mass, Catholic shows on EWTN, CD's on Catholic topics.

I like not being in an office, the independence of being left alone to do my job, only interacting with the company when I need to. I love seeing my children and friends, scattered as they are across the

253

country, more often than I otherwise would.

The ever-changing landscape is a perpetual delight. I have seen so much beauty:

- Three moose: papa, mama and baby, standing up to their knees in an icy stream. The image is burned into my memory, though I saw it only for a few seconds as I swept around a curve of I-94 in Montana
- A vast field blooming golden in Canada, backed by a grove of trees just leafing out pale green ("Nature's first green is gold, her hardest hue to hold," wrote Robert Frost), with just a few trees whose new leaves are a dark red hue scattered among them
- Autumn leaves of every imaginable color, orange, yellow, red, dark red, with occasional lakes of deep teal seen while driving south from Buffalo, New York on US-219
- The waters of Lake Huron, seen from the Blue Water Bridge which arches high over the meeting of Lake Huron and the St. Clair River. The lake is sometimes a breathtaking navy blue and the river ranges through various shades of aqua, turquoise and teal. Once there was an enormous freighter, 700 feet long, making its slow way under the bridge as I idled over the arch of the bridge with the truck in second gear, going about two miles per hour
- The seasonal progression of the corn, starting when the fields are newly planted, just sprouting, looking as though someone had raked the whole field with a comb dipped in green, then growing week by week until the corn is six feet tall, and all the fields tasseling out within a few weeks of each other — one of the mysteries of life.

Glorious!

Twelve years later I can tell a story of the continual mercies of God "tempering the wind to the shorn lamb" [Psalm 6:2] repeatedly, in fact constantly. I depend on the Lord every day. My times of dryness with the Lord come and go, that "well of darkness" where the Lord seems to withdraw to show you if you want Him or just the gifts He brings. But in His most hidden times, He never stops giving me answers and practical help with trucking:

- Parking places without number; someone pulls out just as I pull in, and it's a place I can get into
- Timing on backing jobs; someone blocks my path, then just as they move someone else moves too, making the hole double-wide and much easier
- An idea of where I might stop that night floats through my mind in the morning, and sure enough, that's exactly how far I can get
- I feel constrained to push on and it turns out to be necessary ("I have no desire to press hardly upon you" from "HMS Pinafore," but I feel His regret)
- Being woken up sometimes, and always a different way ("God who cannot even make two snowflakes alike," as Fr. Terry Fullam once remarked); His timing makes the load come out better than my alarm clock setting would have
- Keeping me safe — always, always safe — on the New Jersey Turnpike at 2 AM, in snowy, slippery conditions, in downtown Cleveland, on lonely industrial streets in the middle of the night
- "Stop here" and it turns out that the next place wouldn't have worked, *when* I heed, sadly not always.

Did I ride off into the sunset with Johnny and live happily ever after? Well, no. The company decided that if Johnny hadn't succeeded with me the first time, there was no reason to think that he would on a second or subsequent attempt.

I flew to company headquarters, then waited several days for another trainer, one Bobby Shafer. He proved to be a very kind man, and knowledgeable, a former Hell's Angel type and jailbird who had turned his life around after a car accident involving a drunk driver caused him to have a leg amputated.

"That's what it took for the Lord to get my attention," as he put it.

We drove together for only a week or ten days, as Bobby soon decided that lack of self-confidence was my biggest problem. He made himself available to be consulted on technical issues, though. As he's a trained diesel mechanic he has often helped me with advice in all the years since.

It was with Bobby that I got to the caves of Carthage, Missouri after all, the delivery site that Johnny and I had been diverted from. You drive into the side of a mountain and find yourself among big stone pillars. You can imagine how scared I was. Happily, Bobby did that backing himself, while I got out and watched with admiration.

And we saw the fox that came in the early mornings for the food that employees set out. Quite an experience!

After my time with Bobby, Alan King Associates turned me loose in my own truck. I drove for them for nine months but was eventually fired for damaging a man's truck when I turned too soon pulling out of a very tight spot. I just barely nicked his mirror and fender, but I had previously done $220 worth of damage to a trailer in an incident in a West Virginia rest area. That made two incidents in less than a year and Alan King Associates doubled points on beginners, so I was fired.

A friend I'd made at the company, Janet Medlock, who has been on the road since the early 1970's and has driven many millions of miles and seen everything, commented later, "What you did don't amount to a hill of beans." In fact, she did much the same thing herself about a year later, but not being a beginner, she wasn't fired. I was horribly upset but started looking for another job and eventually found one, in spite of having been fired, doing team driving. I did that for a year, then went to another big company for a number of years, one of which I spent as a Canada Regional driver.

In the end I went to a small Omaha-based company, W. N. Morehouse Truck Line, Inc., where I've been ever since. It was founded in 1932 by the great-grandfather of the brothers who currently run it. There are only a dozen or so office employees. They know all of us by our first names, and even the owners greet me in a friendly way when I walk in. The chief dispatcher found out in my first weeks with the company how I preferred to run, and pretty much caters to my preferences. That's why I've stayed with

Morehouse for five years. I like to start early and end early, though not as early as I described in my first month on my own. Middle-of-the-night deliveries tend to leave me feeling shell-shocked and ill, but seldom happen, probably once a year or less.

From constant stress and near panic, the job has evolved into something like a tour of the country, going from one familiar place to another.

Did I ever learn to back? Sort of. Up to a point. With reservations. But that setup that used to throw me still does. What happened was that the emotions went out of the situation. I got used to coping with my limitations. Having made lots of mistakes, and having had more than a few near misses, I now know what I can do easily, what I can do only under duress, and what I'd better not attempt. Some hard backings go really well, almost miraculously so. I set it up and back right in with no corrections. Then the next easy job might go badly.

Very, very gradually I have ratcheted my backing level up, over a period of twelve years, from "spectacularly awful" to my present level of "fairly competent." I'll never go to the world backing competitions, unless as a spectator, but I get along. It doesn't take much to get fired in this industry, so the fact that I'm still employed after twelve years speaks for itself.

I called Johnny one day and told him I had finished learning to back. I was at a recycling center in Michigan where I had to back in off the street, miss a pickup truck on one side and a dumpster on the other then back under a building with a wall six inches from one side of the trailer and a pillar six inches from the other. What pleased me was feeling only disgust at the existence of such a place rather than the panic that it would formerly have inspired.

There were three stages, emotionally speaking, to my first years as a trucker. The first year or so was permeated with desperate cries for help, "O Lord, *please!*" I was on the verge of panic many times a day and just had to force myself, in fear and trembling, to do whatever was required.

Eventually I began to feel the still, small voice of the Lord laughing at me sometimes.

"O Lord, *please* help!" [with this rest area I'm about to pull into].

"[A chuckle] You can do rest areas."

"Okay, yes, that's probably true, but-You'll-help-if-I-need-it, right?" [said very fast, with passion].

A second stage was reached when I realized that I only needed to worry when I needed to worry. I could poison my whole life worrying about the next difficult thing, a cramped backing job or a big city at rush hour, say, but I didn't have to. The hard parts might be awful but they lasted only an hour or two and then I'd be back on the open road which was how I spent the great majority of my time and where I was okay.

I reached the third stage after a good couple of years of driving. My friend Janet, the trucker with so much experience, and I were talking. She made the observation, "You know, it should be getting easier by now."

It hadn't, but five or six weeks later it did. It occurred to me one day that nothing seemed to be bothering me much and my emotions were staying on a pretty even keel. I thought, "Janet's right! It *is* getting easier." Even today, though, I'm nervous going to an unfamiliar pick up or delivery site. I don't call anybody or listen to music or do any distracting thing until I've negotiated my way there and bumped the dock.

There's no denying that this is a dangerous job, one of the ten most dangerous in the US, according to the statistics. Another time I was talking with Janet about a well-known woman trucker, Darren Baird, the first woman to pass the UPS driving test back in the 1970's. I had met up with her once at a terminal in the Atlanta area and we had talked for an hour or more, both of us being at loose ends. She gave me some backing advice which I use to this day. Darren Baird had been featured on television when Jane Pauley went out on the road with her for a week and every morning reported back on the experience to her colleagues on the "Today Show."

Janet and I were talking about Darren Baird's sudden death, which we'd just heard about. In spite of her forty-some years of experience, Darren had skidded off the highway on a rainy day in the Knoxville, Tennessee area. Her truck had plunged over a 50-foot cliff and Darren was dead by the time rescuers reached her, several hours later.

I tried to make the case to Janet that, with all Darren's years of experience, there must have been someone else at fault in the accident: a four-wheeler who had cut her off or some other mitigating circumstance.

Janet is a forthright woman. "Now that's where you're wrong," she said flatly. "It can happen to anyone, any time."

Two of the last twelve years I've been off the road, trying to make it in the clerical world of a middle-aged or older woman who has failed to make a career. As in the book *Nickel and Dimed*, by Barbara Ehrenreich, it doesn't seem possible for me to earn enough money that way, so I'm on the road for the time being.

Has anyone ever had more reason to trust God than I? To paraphrase St. Polycarp, "Forty-five years have I served Him, and He never did me any wrong." God always sends someone if I really need help. I cherish the closeness and am grateful, though I realize that I won't find out *all* the things He's done for me until eternity.

In the meantime, as it says in Psalm 63:7,
"In the shadow of Thy wings I sing for joy."

ACKNOWLEDGMENTS

Many thanks to Dr. Ronda Chervin for her constant encouragement regarding this book, and for her friendship. Thanks to my daughter Jean for reading the book in manuscript form and for her many valuable suggestions. Grateful thanks for their last-minute help to Roger and Ellen Thomas, without whom, even so, it would not have happened.

To pirate from the book *Night's Bright Darkness*, by Sally Read, though with suitable changes: "The reader will note that this is the story of my learning to be a trucker, not an entire life. Any people close to me who have not been mentioned should not feel this is indicative of their importance to me."

GLOSSARY

alley dock or "12/9" backing: a technique for backing up to a loading dock, starting from being at a right angle to it.

apron: the flat metal plate on the underside of a trailer which surrounds the kingpin.

articulated vehicle: a combination of vehicles having a pivot joint, such as a kingpin or ball hitch, which allows for a sharper turn than would otherwise be possible. Examples are a semi, a pickup truck pulling a camping trailer, or an RV pulling a car or boat.

Auxiliary Power Unit (APU): a small diesel engine attached to a truck that provides energy for functions other than propulsion, such as heating, air conditioning and AC electrical power.

backing off: slang for slowing down, usually just by taking one's foot off the accelerator without using the brake.

bill of lading: a document that lists goods being shipped and specifies the terms of their transport. Any load must be accompanied by a bill of lading or the driver risks being accused of theft.

Blind-side backing: backing with the tractor cocked the wrong way – which makes it much harder to see either side of the trailer [see 18. Diagram of blind-side vs. normal articulation].

bobtail: a term for a tractor driven without a trailer attached. Used as a noun, verb or adverb.

bottoming out a gear: reaching the highest speed that a particular gear permits.

bridge law: it specifies the maximum allowable distance between the kingpin and rear axles. California's bridge law is notoriously short and they enforce it more rigorously than other states.

bumping a dock: backing up to a loading dock, doors open, in such a way that the trailer can be loaded or unloaded.

buttonhook or jug handle turn: an extreme way of turning in tight situations [see 10. Diagram of a "button-hook" or "jug handle" turn].

CDL: Commercial Driver's License.

coming through the house: trucker parlance for being on a run that has your home somewhere along the route. You stop off but only for a few hours.

company drivers: employees of a company who don't own the truck they drive, hence carrying no responsibility for paying for fueling, repairs or maintenance of equipment.

contiguous: being in actual contact; touching along a boundary or at a point. "The 48 contiguous states."

coupling/uncoupling: the act of connecting to or disconnecting from a trailer.

crotch, of a fifth wheel: the center of the fifth wheel, the part which contacts the kingpin.

deadheading: operating a commercial vehicle without a load, to return home or to pick up the next load.

delivery window: the time slot during which a receiver accepts deliveries.

differential lock or switch: a device which disables the differential of a motor vehicle. Throwing the switch makes the drive wheels on both sides of the tractor act together, which can be useful in situations of questionable traction.

dispatching: the scheduling and control of truck pickups and deliveries.

DOT: Department of Transportation.

DOT physical: the physical exam mandated by the DOT for truck drivers.

drop: disconnect a tractor from a trailer, uncouple.

drop and hook (as opposed to live load/unload): either dropping an empty trailer and picking up a preloaded one, or dropping a full trailer and picking up an empty one.

drop lot or yard: a storage place for trailers, usually without facilities, where you drop a trailer and perhaps pick up another one.

engine or Jake brake: an air-compression inhibitor that turns the engine into the primary braking system. Its right use is to slow a heavily loaded truck on a downhill slope.

FAK: Freight All Kinds. A common abbreviation which doesn't specify much about the load. It could be anything from fish sticks to insulation.

fifth wheel: a horseshoe-shaped coupling device for connecting a tractor to a semitrailer. It consists of a circular lower half with a locking bar, mounted and attached to a tractor and made to attach to the kingpin mounted on the underside of the semitrailer [see 13. A fifth wheel hitch].

flipping (or doing a flip): turning around on a freeway by getting off at an exit, then getting back on the same freeway, but going in the opposite direction.

floating gears: shifting without using the clutch pedal, by finding the right RPM's for the gear you're shifting to.

FMCSR: Federal Motor Carrier Safety Regulations.

four-wheeler: trucker parlance meaning "car," especially one driven rudely or incompetently. A term of derision.

gelling (of diesel fuel): the tendency of diesel fuel to solidify if it gets too cold. Gelling starts at about 10° F.

glad hand: air hose connector from the tractor to the trailer [see 12. Glad hands and a pigtail].

gross weight: the weight of the truck plus its load, as opposed to tare weight, which is the truck's empty weight.

hazmat: abbreviation for hazardous material.

high-siding a curve: steering to the outside of a curve to prevent the trailer tires from going off the road because of off-tracking [see 4. Diagram of off-tracking].

HIT: heated in transit. Some materials that are hauled in tankers will solidify at normal air temperatures.

home time: time off; it can often be taken anywhere in the country.

hook: connect a tractor to a trailer, pick up, couple.

HOS regulations: Hours Of Service regulations as mandated by the federal government.

IdleAir: a service provided at some truck stops which gives in-cab services to truckers via centralized systems [see 1. Pictures of IdleAir].

independent truck stop: one not owned by any of the major truck stop companies.

intermodal (container): a container which can be used for multiple modes of transportation (e.g., rail, ship, and truck), without any handling of the freight itself when changing modes.

jackknife: to turn and form an angle of 90° or less with each other. Used esp. of tractor-trailer combinations.

kingpin: the metal pin on the underneath of a trailer, used to connect the trailer to the fifth wheel of a tractor.

live load/unload (as opposed to drop and hook): loading or unloading done while the driver waits.

load lock or bar: a metal bar with a ratchet, used to brace a load.

lumper/lumping service: a third company which loads or unloads a trailer for a fee, mediating between the carrier and the shipper or receiver. It is also used as a verb; to "lump" means to load or unload.

macro: a pre-existing form on a Qualcomm.

off-tracking: the tendency of the trailer tires to take a different path than the steer tires on a curve or turn [see 4. Diagram of off-tracking].

OS&D: Overage, Shortage and Damage.

out: trucker parlance for not at home, on the road.

out of route: deviation from the shortest practical route.

owner operators: drivers who own and operate their own trucks, hence who are responsible for fueling, repairs and maintenance.

pick up: 1) connect to a trailer or 2) get a load.

pickup window: the time slot during which a shipper allows drivers to pick up loads.

pigtail: the electrical connector between a vehicle and the trailer it tows.

power downshift: shifting down a gear when the tractor is "under power," pulling a load up a hill or mountain.

product: whatever is loaded in the trailer.

Qualcomm: the satellite communication device with which most semis are equipped.

receiver: the company receiving a load, as opposed to "shipper."

reefer: a trailer equipped with a refrigeration unit. They can hold a load at any temperature from about -20° to +80° F.

relay a load: Driver #1 picks up a load and drives it part of the way to the receiver. Driver #2 swaps out with the first driver and takes the load the rest of the way to delivery.

running up the gears: the process of moving from a standstill to full speed, usually starting from second or third gear, shifting to fourth, then fifth ... all the way up to top gear.

running: trucker parlance for driving.

scale: weigh a load.

shipper: the company shipping a load, as opposed to "receiver."

slave pump: the off-side pump at a fuel stop, which works only if the main pump, also called the master pump, is turned on.

sliding tandems: moving the tandem axle suspension back and forth at the rear of a semitrailer, for the purpose of adjusting the distribution of weight between the drive axles and tandems.

snub braking: one of several braking techniques used to control the speed of a tow vehicle and trailer when descending relatively long and/or steep grades. The snub braking technique aims to reduce brake fade through brief moments of heavy brake input followed by a brief moment of coasting.

spotter: a person employed to move trailers around within a yard (see yard dog).

spotted trailer or load: a preloaded trailer, parked usually in a drop lot until it's picked up.

swapping out: part of the relay process. Two drivers arrive at a place and switch trailers. Then Driver #1 drives off with trailer #2, while Driver #2 leaves with trailer #1.

tandem: a term for the axles on a trailer.

tanker yanker: old trucker parlance for someone who drives tankers.

trailer washout: the washing out of the inside of a reefer trailer with a hose.

under a load: in the state of having been assigned to a particular load and not yet having delivered it.

yard: a place where trailers can be parked, similar to a drop lot. Can be used to refer to company headquarters.

yard check: writing down numbers, status and reefer tank fuel level, if applicable, of all trailers belonging to a particular company at a shipper or receiver, or in a drop lot or yard.

yard dog: same as spotter, but not usually said to their faces.

LIST OF PHOTOS AND DIAGRAMS

APPENDIX

Pre-Trip Inspection Sheets

PRE-TRIP INSPECTION GUIDE
Tractor/Trailer

to be memorized

A *pre-trip inspection* must be preformed before each trip to identify any potential problems that may
cause either a breakdown or an accident.

* *The keys should be in your possession before starting your pre-trip inspection.*

Approaching The Vehicle:
Check vehicle for leaning [broken spring, flat tire, loaded on one side, etc].
Check under vehicle [leaks of fresh oil, coolant or grease].
Check wind breaker [damage or loose fastners].
Check *windshield* [cracks, nicks or dirty].
Check *lights and reflectors* [clean, proper color & not broken].
Check *windshield wipers* [blade rubber in good condition & proper spring tension].

Engine Compartment: Hood Open/Right Side.
Check engine *oil level* [within operating range].
Check *coolant level* [overflow tank, sight glass or radiator cap] caution if hot!
Check *water pump* [coolant leaks].
Check water and heater hoses [condition, coolant leaks, & loose or broken clamps].
Check *alternator* [condition of mounting bolts and brackets & wiring].
Check alternator belt [condition and tension (3/4 inch or less)].
Check for *leaks* on side of engine [oil, coolant and etc].

Engine Compartment: Hood Open/Left Side.
Check *power steering oil level* [within operating range].
Check power *steering box* and reservior [securely mounted & no leaks].
Check *steering linkage* [bent, loose, broken or missing parts].
Check all other belts [condition and tension (3/4 inch or less)].
Check electrical wiring [insulation cracked or worn, wires broken or loose].
Check air conditioner compressor [securely mounted, leaks & condition].
Check *air compressor* [securely mounted, leaks and condition].

Front Suspension: Left Side.
Check *frame* rail [cracked, broken, loose or missing bolts].
Check *spring* [leaves cracked, broken, shifted or missing].
Check *spring mounts* [cracked, broken or worn excessively].
Check u-bolts [cracked, loose or broken].
Check *shock absorber* [securely mounted or leaking].

Front Brakes: Left Side.
Check brake *air line* [cracked, frayed or leaking].
Check brake *air chamber* [dented, cracked or leakng].
Check *slack adjuster* [missing or broken parts & not more than 1 inch play].
Check *brake drum* [cracked or broken].

271

metal valve stem caps

6. <u>Front Tire And Wheel</u>: Left Side.
Check *tire* [cuts, abrasions, bulges and at least 4/32 tread].
Check *rim*/wheel [cracks, welds or bent].
Check *lug nuts* [missing, rust streaks or loose].
Check *hub oil seal* [leaks, oil level and damage].

7. <u>Fuel Area</u>: Left Side.
Check *mirrors* [broken, cracked, dirty or loose].
Check mirror mounts [loose or broken].
Check *door*, latch and seal [open and shut properly & rubber seal intact].
Check *steps* [damage, loose or missing parts].
Check *battery box* cover [condition & secure].
Check grab handles [loose or damaged].
Check *fuel tank* [cap, damage, *leaks*, loose or broken straps or mounts].

<u>Cab</u>: Rear.
Check *air lines & electrical cord* [secure connections, breaks or cracks].
Check *catwalk* [securely fastened].
Check *frame* rail [cracked, broken, loose or missing bolts].
Check *drive shaft* [bent, cracked or loose u-joints].
Check *exhaust system* [muffler and pipes secure & no leaks].

air dryer

<u>Rear Suspension</u>: Left Side.(If two axles, check both).   *8 airbag*
Check *frame* rail [cracked, broken, loose or missing bolts].
Check *spring* [leaves cracked, broken, shifted or missing].
Check u-bolts [cracked, loose or broken].
Check *spring mounts* [cracked, broken or worn].
Check *torsion bar* [broken, bent or loose].
Check *shock absorber* [securely mounted or leaking].

<u>Rear Brakes</u>: Left Side.(If two axles check both).
Check brake *air line* [cracked, frayed or leaking].
Check brake *air chamber* [dented, cracked or leaking].
Check *slack adjuster* [missing or broken parts & not more than 1 inch play].
Check *brake drum* [cracked or broken].

<u>Rear Tires And Wheels</u>: Left Side.(If two axles, check all).
Check *tires* [cuts, abrasions, bulges and at least 2/32 inch tread].
Check dual tires [matched size, tread & ply (radial or bias).
Check *spacer* [bent or cracked & nothing between dual tires].
Check *rims*/wheels [cracked, welds or bent].
Check *lug nuts* [missing, rust streaks or loose].
Check *axle seal* [leaks].

Fifth Wheel Area:
Check *sliding 5th wheel* [securely mounted, broken air line or loose parts].
Check sliding 5th wheel *locking pins* [locked securely].
Check *mounting bolts* [missing, broken or loose].
Check 5th wheel *release arm* [in locked position & not bent].
Check release arm *safety latch* [locked over release arm].
Check 5th wheel *platform* [cracks, loose or missing parts]
Check *coupling system* [5th wheel locked on king pin].

Rear Of Tractor:
Check *lights & reflectors* [clean, proper color & not broken].
Check *signal & brake lights* [clean, proper color & not broken].
Check mud flaps/*splash guards* [securely fastened & not torn].

Pre Trip Amendment
Address To Doubles and Triples
Ball Pintle Hitch
Safety Latch / Safety Chain Latch

Trailer: Left Side/Front.
Check *air lines & electrical cord* [secure connections, breaks or cracks].
Check *kingpin/apron* [damaged or bent].
Check *header board* [damaged, dents or holes].
Check *lights & reflectors* [clean, proper color & not broken].

Trailer: Left Side.
Check *lights & reflectors* [clean, proper color & not broken].
Check *landing gear* [secure, no broken, bent or loose braces & raised].
Check *frame* & cross members [broken, bent or damaged].
Check side & top edge [damage & holes].
Check *door ties* [securely mounted].

Trailer Suspension: Left side. (If two axles, check both).
Check spring [leaves cracked, broken, shifted or missing].
Check spring mounts [cracked, broken or worn].
Check torsion bar [broken, bent or loose].

Trailer Brakes: Left Side. (If two axles, check both).
Check brake *air line* [cracked, frayed or leaking].
Check brake *air chamber* [dented, cracked or leaking].
Check *slack adjuster* [missing or broken parts & not more than 1 inch play].
Check *brake drum* [cracked or broken].

Trailer Tires & Wheels: Left Side. (If two axles, check all).
Check *tires* [cuts, abrasions, bulges & at least 2/32 inch tread],
Check dual tires [matched size, tread & ply (radial or bias).
Check *spacer* [bent or cracked & nothing between dual tires].
Check *rims*/wheels[cracked, welds or bent].
Check *lug nuts* [missing, rust streaks or loose].
Check *hub oil seal* [leaks, oil level & damage].

9. Trailer Rear:
Check *doors* [condition of hinges & latches or cables, seals & ties].
Check *lights & reflectors* [clean, proper color & not broken].
Check D.O.T. bumper [damaged, bent, loose & securely fastened].
Check mud flaps/*splash guards* [securely fastened & not torn].

0. Trailer: Right Side. [Same as left] Exceptions:
Check spare tire rack [securely mounted & tire chained & locked].
Check curb side doors [condition of hinges & latches, seals & ties].

1. Tractor: Inside Cab.
Check *emergency equipment*:
*3 red reflective triangles.
*Fire extinguisher.
*Spare electrical fuses.
Check *Clutch* [at least 1 inch free travel].
Check *steering play* [not more than 2 inches in a 20 inch wheel].
Check *gearshift* [excessive play].
Check *parking brake* [working properly].
Check *oil psi, air psi, & amp gauge* [working properly].
Check *lighting indicators* [working properly].
Check *air & city horn* [working properly].
Check *heater/defroster* [working properly[.
Check w/shield wipers [working properly].

2. Air Brake Check:
Run engine to build air pressure to 120 psi. Shut off engine. Release the parking brakes. Air loss should be less than 3 psi in one minute. Apply the foot brake firmly.
Air loss should be less than 4 psi in one minute.
Turn the ignition switch on. Step on and off the foot brake to reduce tank pressure. The low air warning light/buzzer must come on before air pressure drops below 60 psi.
Turn the ignition switch off. Step on and off the foot brake to reduce tank pressure. The parking brake knob should pop out between 20 & 40 psi.
Start engine and run at operating RPM. Air pressure should build from 85 to 100 psi within 45 seconds.

ABOUT THE AUTHOR

Annette F. Wilcox, MA, is a mother of four and grandmother of five. She has been a translator, librarian, ESL instructor and has taught school in three countries, the last being as a lay missionary with the Holy Spirit Fathers in Moshi, Tanzania, East Africa. A family friend once remarked that he admired the way she kept "recycling" herself. The most recent recycle is twelve years in the trucking world where she has driven 1.1 million miles in a semi, hauling heavy loads of all sorts of things on the roads of all forty-eight contiguous United States and six of the provinces of Canada.

Made in the USA
Middletown, DE
20 October 2020